E-BUSINESS INNOVATION

Cases and Online Readings

Dianne Cyr
Technical University of British Columbia

Jasbir Dhaliwal
Norwegian School of Management

Ajax Persaud
University of Ottawa

Toronto

National Library of Canada Cataloguing in Publication Data

Cyr, Dianne J. (Dianne Jane), 1952-
E-business innovation: cases and online readings

Includes index.
ISBN 0-13-093414-3

1. Electronic commerce–Management. I. Dhaliwal, Jasbir Singh, 1958-
II. Persaud, Ajax, 1959- III. Title.

HF5548.32.C79 2002 658'.05 C2001-902174-7

ISBN 0-13-093414-3

Vice President, Editorial Director: Michael Young
Executive Marketing Manager: Cas Shields
Developmental Editor: Toni Chahley
Production Editor: Julia Hubble
Copy Editor: Rodney Rawlings
Production Coordinator: Janette Lush
Page Layout: Carol Magee
Art Director: Mary Opper
Interior and Cover Design: Sarah Battersby
Cover Image: PhotoDisc

1 2 3 4 5 06 05 04 03 02

Printed and bound in Canada

Contents

Foreword

I meet many executives who think that the dot-com stock market collapse that began in the spring of 2000 was a major setback for Internet-based businesses, and that the e-business turmoil has slackened. After all, most dot-com startups crashed and burned, and the Amazons of the world had their market capitalizations slashed. So while these executives agree the impact of the Internet will be substantial, they feel much of the uncertainty is gone. We know what the Net looks like and what forms of commerce it will sustain.

Such complacency is misguided. The jaw-dropping turmoil unleashed by the Net—the stock market gyrations, the soaring market capitalization of startups, so-called Old Economy companies embracing revolutionary business models, escalating productivity gains—will pale in comparison to what will happen in the near future.

Pundits misread what lies ahead for two basic reasons. First, they misunderstand where the technology of the Internet is headed. Second, they don't appreciate what changes to business behaviour the Internet has already brought, and how these changes will accelerate.

On the first issue, most assume that the Internet we see today is the same Internet we will see tomorrow—that is, a network that connects desktop computers. So just as radio and television technologies have remained much the same since their birth, so too will the Internet.

This is nonsense. The Net continues to soar in ubiquity, bandwidth, and function. It is the means not only by which computers will connect, but the mechanism by which individuals and organizations will collaborate, exchange money, conduct transactions, and communicate facts, knowledge, insight, and opinion. Mobile computing devices, broadband access, wireless networks, and computing power embedded in everything from refrigerators to automobiles are converging into a global network.

The Internet of tomorrow will be as dramatic a change from the Internet of today as today's Internet is from the primitive, unconnected, proprietary computing networks of yesterday.

Ray Kurzweil, the brilliant U.S. inventor and author, coined the expression that we are on "the second half of the chessboard." It stems from a tale about the Emperor of China and the inventor of chess. The Emperor was so delighted by the game that he offered the inventor anything he wanted in the kingdom. The inventor surprised the Emperor by asking only for rice.

"I would like one grain of rice on the first square of the chessboard, two grains of rice on the second square, four grains of rice on the third square," and so on. Thinking this would amount to little, the Emperor readily agreed.

Of course, fulfilling the inventor's request was impossible, because 2 to the 64th power (there being 64 squares on a chessboard) is 18 million billion grains of rice. At 10 grains of rice per square inch of rice fields, that would mean that the entire surface of the earth would have to be covered with rice fields two times over, oceans included. (I borrowed the

Don Tapscott is Chairman of Itemus, Inc. <www.itemus.com> and co-author of *Digital Capital: Harnessing the Power of Business Webs.*

math from George Gilder.) While the amounts of rice are minuscule in the beginning, by halfway through the chessboard they become substantial, about four billion grains. At this point each increment is massive in absolute terms.

Kurzweil originally made his comparison to computers in the early 1990s, and noted that processor power had already doubled 32 times since the first computers in the early 1940s. We are on the second half of the board.

The absolute magnitude of the gains systematically achieved in digital technologies grows more astounding by the week. And for many technologies there is no end to the gains in sight, at least not for a couple of decades. Transistors will continue to shrink, processor power will continue to double and redouble, chips will be embedded in every object, Internet bandwidth will continue to expand, and humans will create more and more Web-based solutions to the infinite challenges of life.

Technology-adoption rates are blindingly fast, because happy consumers use the Internet to tell friends and family around the world about the great new product or service they have discovered.

Netscape Navigator, Napster, and Japan's I-mode phone are some of the best examples, but there are many others. No business will be left untouched. We are entering a world where getting customers' attention will become even more difficult. Your mobile customers will pull goods, services, and information from the network whenever the impulse strikes, while blocking your attempts to push communications at them. Customers will be accustomed to full customization and immediate gratification. They won't want to be forced to settle for the model of car the dealer happens to have on the lot; they will want a new vehicle built to their specifications and delivered to their door within a few days.

So the Internet must be recognized for what it is. It is not, as some suggest, simply the next step in the evolution of information technology. It is a profound advancement in communication technology. The Net will be infused throughout the home, school, offices, factories, and hospitals. The behaviour of all these institutions will be fundamentally transformed. When an institution such as MIT says it will post its entire curriculum—including items such as lecture notes and course reading lists—on the Net, it is trying to shape the nature of pedagogy and learning around the world.

In the private sector, we can already see that the basic architecture of wealth creation is being redrawn. And I am not referring to the NASDAQ dot-com craze. Our grandchildren will look back on the era of insta-billionaires and IPO frenzy from 1998 to March 2000 and wonder how so many investors could have got it so wrong. We went from a mindset that "the Internet changes everything" (which is true), to "everything done on the Internet will be profitable" (which is nonsense). Fortunately that period is behind us.

But with the dot-com distractions removed, it is increasingly clear that a much more profound transformation is under way. The economic rationale for the vertically integrated industrial corporation is evaporating.

In 1937, economist Ronald Coase—who later won a Nobel Prize for his work—asked why corporations existed. After all, the marketplace was theoretically the best mechanism for equalizing supply and demand, establishing prices, and extracting the most from finite resources. So why weren't all individuals acting as individual buyers and sellers, rather than gathering in companies with tens of thousands of workers? The Ford Motor Co. was the quintessential example of this. At one point the company owned iron mines, a rubber plantation in Brazil, a steel mill, a glass factory, and virtually everything else needed to build an automobile. Henry Ford correctly concluded that the best capitalism required shielding his production processes from marketplace discipline.

Coase argued that there were good reasons for the seemingly contradictory behaviour of the vertically integrated corporation. The marketplace was fine in theory, but in day-to-day practice it was not practical to break down manufacturing into a series of separately negotiated transactions. Each transaction would incur costs that would outweigh whatever savings were achieved by the marketplace. First, there would be search costs, such as finding different suppliers and determining if their goods were appropriate. Second, there would be contracting costs, such as negotiating the price and contract conditions. Third, there would be the costs of coordinating the different products and processes. Most corporations concluded it made the most sense to perform as many functions as possible in-house.

But that was then, and the Internet is now. The Internet is a deep, rich, publicly available information infrastructure that is relentlessly growing in capability and bandwidth. The result is that Coase's notion of separately negotiated transactions no longer seems impractical. We can increase wealth by adding knowledge to a product or service—through innovation, enhancement, cost reduction, or customization—at each step in its life cycle.

The upshot is that a new business architecture has risen to challenge the industrial-age corporation as the basis for competitive strategy. I call it the business Web, or b-Web, and I define it as any system—of suppliers, distributors, service providers, infrastructure providers, and customers—that uses the Internet as the basis for business communications and transactions. The Internet makes collaboration and transactions available anytime and anywhere—at essentially no cost. In the most successful business Webs, each constituent focuses on its core competency. Together, in industry after industry, these new vehicles of value creation are proving more supple, cost-efficient, and innovative than their traditional competitors.

Established businesses such as Enron, Citibank, Herman Miller, Dow Chemical, American Airlines, Nortel, Schwab, and many product divisions of GE are now transforming themselves by partnering in areas that were previously unthinkable. The CEO of Boeing calls his company a systems integrator, not an aircraft manufacturer. IBM is a computer company that doesn't make its computers—its partner network does. Newer companies based on the Internet, like eBay, Travelocity, Etrade, and Amazon are growing dramatically and competing well despite volatility in their stock prices. Despite chaos in many B2B exchanges, successes like Transora foreshadow upheaval in the value chains in entire industries.

The key to competing in the digital economy is business-model innovation that exploits business-Web power. Smart companies are using the Web to achieve goals toward which they have been striving for the past 25 years: focusing on core competencies, reducing transaction costs, innovating more effectively, and finding new ways to achieve deep customer relationships.

Internet skeptics dream up all sorts of reasons to dismiss the early indicators of the turbulence ahead. For example, the Net is beginning to enable self-organizing systems that create value without central orchestration or even ownership. Look at Linux. IBM spent more than US$1 billion developing an excellent operating system called OS/2 that failed miserably against Microsoft Windows. Then came Linux, cobbled together by thousands of Digital Rotarians voluntarily collaborating on the Net. They weren't motivated by profit, didn't have a stock option plan, R&D or HR department, ad agency, or any of the other trappings of a modern corporation. Instead, their motivation was simply to create an operating system that would make their jobs as computer technicians easier.

Linux is making inroads everywhere. Computer makers are scrambling to look Linux-savvy. The "rebel code" has a virtual hammerlock on supercomputing and its large share of the Internet server market continues to expand. Bear in mind all this was done while the Net was still in its infancy. The Linux folks had to rely on email and file transfers.

Isolated incident? Not at all. Napster has caused chaos in the music industry and has forced every company to rethink their value proposition. And the Open Source Schoolbook intends to create all texts using the Linux "open source" model. If it succeeds, it will wipe out the entire textbook industry and challenge the education system. For example, a new b-Web called The Vines is a self-organizing alliance for the creation and distribution of content; authors write for the site and their work is rated by readers, not unlike eBay's feedback forum.

The lesson of the recent carnage is that the Internet is not about dot-coms. But this should not be construed to mean that we aren't engaged in a profound transformation in the way societies create wealth. We've only just begun.

Don Tapscott

Introduction

In the New Economy business transacted on the Internet is causing a major restructuring of our assumptions about the firm. Business in this context, or e-business, may well represent the biggest paradigm change since the Industrial Revolution. This shift is altering the shape of competition, the speed of action, and the nature of leadership. Intensified competition and new e-business opportunities are pressing traditional companies to build business models that are flexible, fast-moving, and customer-focused. Small and medium-sized Internet startups are challenged to navigate the complex fusion of evolving business processes, enterprise applications, and organizational structures necessary to create a high-performance business. Despite the pervasiveness of e-business as a key industry driver, the strategies, processes, and implementation tactics for success are elusive and contradictory.

Within the expanding and increasingly strategic scope of e-business, this book focuses on contemporary and emerging issues. Cases and readings are selected to provide insights into the content and processes required for effective business consequences in the Internet age. Theoretical and practical perspectives are presented as they relate to both larger and smaller companies. Convention is blended with innovation and entrepreneurship. Traditional frameworks and nascent strategies are profiled to demonstrate new possibilities for leveraging of business opportunities on the Internet.

HISTORY AS EVOLUTION

To understand e-business innovation, it is important to appreciate the historical developments that have taken place over the past decade, and to understand the ways in which the Internet is changing business and management. The historical evolution of the Internet, and its use for the purposes of e-business, can be described in the following overlapping phases.

Phase 1: Evolution of the Technologies

Ever since the early days of the use of computers for business operations, users have been clamouring for hardware and software that was "inter-operable"—that is, able to be run on multiple technical platforms, and in multiple operating system contexts. For nearly two-and-a-half decades these forms of technology remained untenable, and it was not in the interest of any vendor to be the "first mover" to make hardware or software platforms an open system. With the advent of systems like Linux, or the recent decision of MIT to make its teaching material free over the Internet, the culture and "possessiveness" of content and processes on the Web is changing. An open-system orientation represents both a threat and an opportunity for e-business. There exists the opportunity for use of freeware to facilitate the exchange of data; however, with this comes the risk of faulty systems, or lost revenues to organizations in competition with those providing freeware.

Phase 2: Consumer Acceptance of the Opportunity

New technologies generally require time for adoption by a large enough segment of the population to be sustainable as a viable component of business. This can be termed the "critical mass" issue, and it has been suggested by many that of all technologies in our history, the Internet has advanced most rapidly to the critical-mass point. For example, although it took radio 38 years to reach 50 million listeners and television 13 years to do the same, Internet usage reached 50 million people in a mere 5 years. Acceptance of Internet usage and e-business was further stimulated by the rapid decline in computer and access costs. The Internet quickly became an affordable reality. For e-business this provided the medium through which new forms of business could be conducted.

Phase 3: Establishing Customer Loyalty

Consumers experimented with business on the Internet, but customer loyalty appeared hard to win. While online sales increased significantly in the time frame around 1999, the industry was dominated by stories of poor customer service and operational failures. Many would argue the physical side of operations and supply chain management had failed to keep up with new requirements of e-business. Further, the reality was quickly setting in that customer acquisition costs were significant, and customer loyalty was lower in e-business than traditional "bricks and mortar" venues. Companies realized pre-transaction (marketing and pre-sales) and post-transaction (customer service) activities could be usefully handled by the Internet—but must be done well for the attraction and retention of customers.

Phase 4: Dot-com Mania

In the euphoria that followed the first wave of using the Internet as a new channel for e-business, many executives, entrepreneurs, and even pundits thought the Internet would eventually create a new breed of businesses—the so-called "pure Internet plays" or dot-coms. Huge amounts of investment capital were poured into companies that often lacked even a basic business plan. In the past couple of years, thousands of dot-coms have disintegrated, sending a signal to the business community that sound business principles are not dead. As Michael Porter recently admonished in the *Harvard Business Review* (2001),[1]

> First, many businesses active on the Internet are artificial businesses competing by artificial means and propped up by capital that until recently had been readily available. Second, in periods of transition such as the one we have been going through, it often appears as if there are new rules of competition. But as market forces play out, as they are now, the old rules regain their currency. The creation of true economic value once again becomes the final arbiter of business success.

Phase 5: Stability and Integration

There is growing recognition that the ubiquitous nature of the Internet is integrated into business without hype or fear. Over time, e-business is becoming an integral component of business practice, rather than an add-on novelty. E-business is no longer viewed as a separate entity, technology, or application area. For example, having the URL published on business cards, advertisements, or product labels is standard business practice in diverse corners of the world. Indeed, for all-sized businesses, regardless of sector, e-business is generally no longer an option. This is not the end or the fading away of the "e" in e-business, but rather the beginning, as innovative applications and services on the Internet continue to develop and pervade.

E-BUSINESS INNOVATION

The historical phases noted above heralded fundamental changes in the way in which business is conducted. In part, this has resulted in changes in *content*; but it is important to realize how the *processes* involved in the transaction of business have also been fundamentally altered.

First, considering content, which overall has received far too little attention on the e-business moonscape, a driving question is whether the way in which products or services are presented map to consumer expectations. Large companies such as IBM or Dell typically contain 100 000 to one million pages of content and require as many as 250 daily changes. Maintaining currency of information is one issue. Another issue is adaptation of the content to international clients. Using a term coined by Barber and Badre,[2] "culturability" or the merging of culture and usability is an important step if e-business is to become a truly accepted global reality for communication, participation, and transaction. Another key issue related to content is how it might best be safeguarded. The adventures of Napster provide a case in point. After much borrowing freely from artists' works, Napster is now implementing sound fingerprinting to block the free exchange of copyright songs. According to a message on the Napster site in May, 2001,[3]

> As the technology available for the identification and tracking of music files has evolved extremely rapidly over the past few months, Napster has quickly embraced it in order to better protect copyright holders and improve our users' experience.

It might be expected that this is only the beginning of various movements to protect content rights of originators and of users on the Internet.

Concerning process, the alterations to traditional business practice caused by e-business are even more prevalent. Strategy and e-business models are under modification. Further, there is evidence the nature of the transaction itself has changed. Traditionally paper-driven tracking and exchanges have made way for applications of information technology. In e-business the Internet is used for processing data, information, and knowledge, and also changes the time and space definition of transactions. For example, if an item is for sale on the Internet, the quantity sold is theoretically only limited by the transaction servers and telecommunication lines. The sales can occur multiple times and in millisecond time frames. Greater bandwidth and new technologies have been the result. The speed and accessibility provided by the Internet has fundamentally changed the link to both customers and suppliers. Online connections to the storage shelf and real-time product processing have increased the complexity of supply chain management. Further, customers have opportunities to co-construct the firm's value proposition by providing immediate feedback, and by sharing information about product and service offerings through digital communities and other online media. The test of customer satisfaction is only a click away.

Within this fast-paced, often volatile environment, the question looms of how the Internet and e-business have altered what we have known as management. Operating within the context of a networked economy, the Internet has profoundly changed a critical assumption underlying modern scientific management—quantifying that which can be measured. However, in a new environment where physical and virtual operations are integrated, and value is derived from being part of a network, quantification of the business from the value derived from the network is difficult. Consequently, managers require strategies not only for enhancing their business proposition but also for increasing their value within the larger network. New organizational frameworks and logic are needed. Networks now entertain new perspectives on fluidity of information exchange, security, technology enhancement, or skills development. E-business and online communities will herald and command new forms of e-marketing and customer relationship management as key to business success. New business models and strategies will arise. Legal issues will be different. There is no turning back. The revolution has begun.

THEMES AND FOCUS OF THIS BOOK

With a backdrop of history and evolving business practice as outlined above, this book is focused on five themes that represent compelling and contemporary issues in e-business. The themes are chosen because they address fundamentals of sound business practice, and are essential regardless of the size or sector of the organization. They relate to the ongoing evolution of technology, the continuing development of quintessential service to customers, and the quest for suitable strategies, systems, and processes that serve to support business as conducted on the Internet.

Collectively the themes provide the understructure for success in an e-business environment. They are:

1. *E-business strategy and models.* E-business has given birth to newer conceptualizations of business models and has transformed traditional models. Business strategy has become more important in the face of increased competition. Although some might argue e-business has led to the demise of long-term strategic planning, many would argue the opposite. This book analyzes the impact of these strategic trends using the terminology of the New Economy. Topics include how industry is being shaped by new e-business developments, threats and opportunities in e-business, roles of leaders, structural transformation issues, flexible business designs, and alliances.
2. *Customer relationship and service management.* E-business has seen the move from a "one-to-many" approach in customer servicing to a "one-to-one" approach for building customer relationships. Determining customer preferences is an ongoing challenge, complicated by real-time data warehousing/mining and interactivity. In e-business, new challenges for managers relate to the measurement of service, customer relationship management, service guarantees, and Internet time (24/7). The case studies in this book address changes in customer service and customer expectations in a variety of contexts and environments. Topics include e-loyalty, integrated service solutions, customer relationship management, and selling-chain management.
3. *E-business operations and supply chain issues.* E-business has imposed new standards of performance on the optimization of business operations to meet customer needs.

The role of operations research and the automation of business processes have come to the fore in operations planning and management for the e-business sector. The evolution of logistics into supply chain management has paralleled the explosion of electronic commerce. Electronic business has made concepts such as efficient consumer response possible through the integration and synchronization of physical, financial, and information flows. This book will document these changes and attempt to highlight their impact. Related topics are enterprise resource planning, the e-supply chain, and e-procurement.

4. *Localization and e-business implementation.* E-business has enabled businesses to readily "go global." In various cases in this book, issues pertaining to global customers, internationalization versus localization factors, and cultural differences are highlighted. Changes in organizational structures and the technology infrastructure required for servicing the global customer base of e-business are discussed, as are the practical managerial challenges involved in implementing such changes. Strategies for success, and lessons learned from failure, are examined as they relate to e-business implementation. Topics include localization issues including relationship building in cross-cultural contexts, content issues in Web design, and translating e-business strategy into solutions.
5. *Future developments.* Due to the fluid nature of e-business, this final theme will address changing developments in the area of technology and legal issues. Trends in e-business technologies will consider new programs and platforms that support business online. Legal considerations involve changes in privacy or other laws to match evolving value propositions. Global harmonization of law as it impacts e-business will continue to be a pressing issue. Topics include technology trends and updates, e-risk and the law, and harmonization of international law.

HOW TO USE THIS BOOK

To match the digital age in which e-business exists, this book is a unique combination of print and digital media. The print portions of the book include a foreword, by Internet guru Don Tapscott, an introduction, Theme and Part openers to focus each section, and the cases. Digital readings, including the Future Developments section, are accessed online at **www.pearsoned.ca/cyr,** and reflect a requirement and commitment to modify material on a timely basis to match industry shifts and developments. Weblink icons located in the overview of each part direct the reader to our online readings and updates. Summarized below are the unique features of the book.

- *Managerial orientation.* The readings and cases challenge the reader to analyze and assess the tenets for success and failure of e-business. Numerous examples of real companies are presented in a format that makes comprehensive business sense. The orientation and content of the book is suitable for undergraduate and graduate learners, managers, and others with an interest in e-business innovation.
- *Theoretical and practical.* The readings include articles from leading business publications, and shorter articles gleaned from the Web on contemporary topics. There is a theoretical and practical articulation of the content and process of e-business. The

readings are accompanied by cases that provide a practical backdrop for the theoretical perspective, and lend substance to the issues as presented.

- *Original content.* The book includes sixteen unique cases that demonstrate key issues in e-business. Ten of the cases are original and written by the authors for the book. Both large companies and smaller dot-coms are profiled.
- *Print and digital format.* The book is a combination of print and digital materials. As noted above, e-business is changing rapidly. To keep pace with the field, readings appear on the Companion Website that accompanies this text and will be updated each semester by the authors. An online site map provides easy direction and accessibility to readings and other online components. Case updates will also appear in digital format. Online readings and updates to cases can be found at **www.pearsoned.ca/cyr.**
- *Currency.* All readings and cases are recent publications. Also included is a Future Developments section in which rapidly evolving topics in technology and legal issues are addressed. Digital content in that section is updated periodically by this book's authors or by other experts in the field.
- *Online instructor notes.* As a further online component, instructor's notes will be provided to aid in the presentation and analysis of each case. Focus questions and additional readings are included.

ACKNOWLEDGEMENTS

The authors would like to especially thank Toni Chahley, developmental editor at Pearson Education Canada, for her insights and support in the development and culmination of this project. In addition, the production and editing team at Pearson are to be commended for their invaluable contributions. Rodney Rawlings added superlative copyediting experise. Thomas Lee provided administrative support and assisted in case creation. Dan McGuire, Digital Licensing Specialist at TechBC, provided extraordinary help in securing permissions and digital rights for this project. Further, appreciation is sincerely extended to the companies that opened their doors to investigation for the cases, and the individuals in each company who made the process of case writing possible. We are grateful, finally, for financial support provided by the Technical University of British Columbia that contributed to the development of several of the cases written for this book.

NOTES

1. M. Porter, "Strategy and the Internet," *Harvard Business Review*, March 2001.
2. W. Barber and A. Badre, "Culturability: the merging of culture and usability," conference proceedings at <www.research.att.com/conf/hfweb/proceedings/barber/index.html>. Accessed April 24, 2001.
3. "Napster has fingerprinting software," *New York Times*, May 7, 2001.

About the Authors

Dr. Dianne Cyr has a Ph.D. from the University of British Columbia, a Master's degree from the University of New Brunswick, and a Bachelor's degree from the University of Victoria. She received the prestigious Chateaubriand research fellowship to conduct post-doctoral work at INSEAD in France. Dr. Cyr is currently an Associate Professor at the Technical University of British Columbia (TechBC), which is Canada's newest university and focused on programs for the high-technology industries. At TechBC she is a founding faculty member, the leader in development of the Management and Technology program, and Co-Director of the Center for E-Business. Dr. Cyr is the author of *Management: Leading People and Organizations in the 21st Century* (Prentice-Hall, 2001), *Scaling the Ivory Tower: Stories from Women in Business School Faculties* (Praeger, 1996), and *The Human Resource Challenge of International Joint Ventures* (Quorum, 1995). She is also the author of numerous papers published in journals such as the Academy of Management Executive, Management International Review, and Organization Studies. Current research interests are in the areas of localization, e-loyalty, and innovation in universities involved in the delivery of programs aided by technology. She is very proud of Jim, Andrea, Robert, and Ryan, who light up her life.

Dr. Jasbir Dhaliwal grew up in Petaling Jaya, Malaysia in a Punjabi immigrant family with Canadian roots in Vancouver. He holds the MBA and Ph.D. qualifications from the University of British Columbia and now lives in Oslo where he is Associate Professor at the Norwegian School of Management. Prior to this, he founded the Centre for Electronic Commerce at the Technical University of British Columbia and served as Deputy Director of the Centre for Management of Technology at the National University of Singapore. His research interests include intelligent interface design, supply chain reengineering, diffusion of new technologies, intrapreneurship, and electronic commerce business models. His research has appeared in scholarly journals such as *Information Systems Research, Journal of Organisational Computing & Electronic Commerce, Knowledge Acquisition, Education & Information Technologies, Information & Management* as well as in the proceedings of numerous international technology conferences. He is also active as an executive trainer and technology management advisor and has completed e-business projects for large, small, and new companies all over the world. His other interests focus primarily on his three young sons, canoeing, Canadian immigrant stories, and angel investment in new technology ventures.

Dr. Ajax Persaud is an immigrant from Enmore, a small, remote village on the east coast of Demerara, Guyana in the Caribbean. He holds a Bachelor's in Economics from the University of Guyana, a Master's in Banking and Finance from the University of Wales, and a Master's and Ph.D. in Management from Carleton University. Ajax has won several awards, including the prestigious Chancellor's Medal for the second-best graduating student from the University of Guyana. His research interests are in technology and innovation management, high-tech marketing, technology entrepreneurship, e-business innovations, and new venture development. His research has appeared in several scholarly journals and academic conferences. He has provided consulting advice to numerous small businesses, e-commerce ventures, and communities in both Canada and Guyana. He is a family man who enjoys comedy.

theme one overview

E-Business Strategy and Models

The Internet as a new technology has revolutionized the business landscape within a very short time horizon. Old business processes and practices, organizational forms, business models, and strategies have been changed in profound ways, and new ones have emerged. A new class of business—electronic business or "e-business"—has evolved, and it is based on the promise and potential of a digital, networked economy. Even a new language set associated with characteristics of the Internet economy is emerging.

Distinctive characteristics of electronic business and electronic marketplaces facilitated through the Internet have been articulated in terms of the five C's of e-commerce—content, commerce, connectivity, communities, and convergence. The underlying logic is that the Internet is a content-rich medium, where people can explore, and in some instances exploit, information asymmetry, products, and services for profit anytime and anywhere.

Connections between buyers and sellers are made at any moment, and almost in real time. Consequently, the Internet has resulted in a convergence of time, geography, and culture that in effect has levelled the playing field across e-markets. Corporate size, location, history, culture, time zones, and other details can be easily masked from the Internet viewer. Interestingly, digital communities (groups of people with similar interests who exchange ideas and share information over the Internet) have exerted substantial influence on corporate behaviour, since their feedback—negative or positive—is immediate and disseminated quickly to a large audience.

In the euphoria following the introduction of the Internet, many executives, entrepreneurs, observers, and even pundits and academics have flirted with the idea that the realities of the Internet as articulated in the five C's have rendered strategy obsolete. Some overzealous observers even went so far as to suggest that the advent of the Internet marks the "beginning of the end" of traditional bricks-and-mortar operations, along with their attendant strategies. Hindsight suggests that, in reality, strategy is not obsolete but in fact needed more than ever. Strategy will likely be the battleground where competitive advantage is won or lost.

The dot-com crash and burn of 2000 is evidence of the detrimental consequences and misguided beliefs about the Internet and its inappropriate use. Indeed, the Internet has changed the nature of competition, industry structure, profitability, and even the definition of the firm. It would appear the real winners in the New Economy will be those who view the Internet as a complement to, rather than a replacement for, traditional strategies for competing effectively.

The cases and readings in this Theme explore the relevance, application, and consequences of strategy in the Internet age. The readings provide both a theoretical and a practical articulation of the relevance of traditional strategic frameworks and emerging strategies. The cases offer thorough descriptions of the strategies some companies use to harness and leverage business opportunities resulting from the Internet. Also, hidden in the cases are keen insights into some of the emerging strategies companies are using against which more traditional strategies and approaches might be benchmarked.

part one overview

E-Business Strategy

The cases in this section offer material for serious discussion and analysis related to the relevance, utility, strengths, and weaknesses of some of the conceptual arguments highlighted in the articles. The MP3 case can be described as "pure Internet play," since there is no history of operating in the physical world, and the company was created specifically to explore business opportunities resulting from the Internet.

The story of *epost* is an excellent example of Internet business strategy based on a network of organizations and people. In the case are identified some of the issues, challenges, and strategic choices made by the company's senior management in order to create a viable business. This case also serves as a backdrop for discussing issues raised in the readings with respect to value chain analysis, value in a networked economy, strategic alliances in online environments, the complementary nature of Internet businesses with traditional business, and the concept of what constitutes the firm in the digital and networked economy.

The stories unfolding in each company provide an interesting context for discussing how larger companies have transitioned to the Internet, as well as the challenges faced by small "pure plays."

The readings in this section probe the nature of the Internet and its strategic implications for businesses. The readings and the cases address issues such as how the Internet as an enabling technology can be used wisely or unwisely, in almost any industry and as part of any strategy. Other issues considered are how the Internet has affected the structure of industries and competition, the notion of first-mover advantage, profitability, and the future of competition. The readings debunk some of the myths about the Internet and profitability, and outline several key principles of strategic positioning.

Various online business strategies are presented, along with the preconditions for their effectiveness. The importance of clear vision, commitment, and allocation of appropriate resources and authority for the success of online businesses is emphasized.

case one

MP3.com: Keep On Rocking in the Free World?

Paramesh Anantharaman
Colin Gillis
Anne-Sophie Montillot
Gonzalo Nieto
Tanaz Parmar

As Michael Robertson flew across the country from California to New York, he wondered if 13 would be his lucky number. On November 13, 2000 he would appear in Manhattan federal court for proceedings to determine the damages that Universal Music Group was due for copyright infringement by the My.MP3.com Beam-it service. If U.S. District Judge Jed S. Rakoff continued his trend of harsh findings against MP3.com, the damage award could be as high as $250 million, an amount that could drive Robertson's company into bankruptcy. After weeks of uncertainty, Michael Robertson's wild ride could come to a screeching halt.

SEARCHING THROUGH THE LOGS

In the summer of 1997, Michael Robertson was best known as the founder of the Filez.com search engine. Michael found he could spot trends by reviewing the aggregate totals of searched terms from his site. Recalling the period he said: "I like to look at the bottom, and from the bottom of those charts, I started seeing some sites that had MP3 in the name. I was curious about what exactly MP3 was. And that's exactly how we stumbled onto it."[1] Shortly afterwards in November of 1997, Robertson founded

MBA candidates Paramesh Anantharaman, Colin Gillis, Anne-Sophie Montillot, Gonzalo Nieto, and Tanaz Parmar prepared this case under the supervision of Professor Christopher L. Tucci.

MP3.com, a portal for music news and an aggregation of links to MP3 files. Robertson had no involvement in the creation of the popular music file format MP3; he just saw the rising wave of interest.

In early 1998, Robertson announced that MP3.com had formed a record label called Digital Automatic Music (DAM) that charged no fees to list artists online. The label also announced that gross revenue from the sale of DAM CDs on MP3.com would be split 50-50 with the artist, terms that were significantly more favourable to the artists than offerings from the traditional record labels. The battle against the old-economy music giants had begun.

MONEY POURS IN

In January of 1999, MP3.com had just finished a year of hockey-stick growth. Registered artists climbed to over 4000, and 3 000 000 unique visitors per month were visiting the site. The money was about to pour in. On January 20, 1999 MP3.com announced it had received financing from two big venture capital firms. Sequoia Capital and Idealab! invested respectively $10M and $1M in MP3.com.[2] As part of the deal, Robin Richards, COO of Tickets.com, was named President of MP3.com, while Robertson retained the CEO title. The support from Sequoia Capital proved important, not only in purely economic terms but also from a marketing and public-relevance perspective. Sequoia Capital had a history of big wins with investments in such firms as Yahoo!, Apple, and Oracle. The news of MP3.com was starting to hit the mainstream media. Thus the Chicago *Sun-Times* after the funding was announced:

> Michael Robertson has just been handed $11 million. What he does with it could determine the record industry's future. The 31-year-old San Diego resident is the digital music guru behind MP3.com (www.mp3.com). The Internet site is the main hub for MPEG 1 Layer 3, the sound-compression format that has taken music fans by storm.[3]

Commenting on the deal, Robertson explained very clearly what MP3.com was aiming at: "When you look at our editorial area, which has become an influential vehicle, and how we've galvanized 4,000 artists and literally millions of customers into one big movement, we are really leading a revolution."[4]

MANIA BUILDS: HEADING TO AN IPO

In May 1999, MP3.com announced for the first time its intention to hold an initial public offering (IPO) that was expected to raise $115 million in capital.[5] This started a cycle that would increase the value of the company more than tenfold in a mere three months. On June 9 it was announced that Cox Interactive Media had acquired a 10% stake in MP3.com for $45 million.[6] This number valued the whole company at $450 million, a substantial boost from one month earlier.

July 1999 brought further boosts to the company valuation. By the end of the month MP3.com was hosting a catalogue of 22 000 artists representing 122 000 songs.[7] Site metrics had grown dramatically, with MP3.com serving 349 000 unique visitors a day,[8] representing a total of 72 million page views per month. Daniel H. Rimer, equity analyst for Hambrecht & Quist, reported, "MP3 is now one of the most searched terms on the Internet today, in many cases outpacing both hotmail and sex."[9] On the back of the excellent market response to the IPO of Liquid Audio, an industry peer, the terms of the MP3.com offering were raised. On July 13 MP3.com increased both the number of shares it intended to offer, from 9 to 12.3 million, and the price range, from \$9–11 to \$16–18, more than doubling the initial price talk.[10] On July 20, 1999 the company announced the first-quarter results.[11] While it reported a loss of 5 cents a share, worse than the 0.3 cents per share of the previous year, the site was gaining mass momentum, adding 125 artists and 660 new songs every day. The prospects for the major shareholders, Robertson with 39% of the company, Sequoia with 14.2%, and David Easterly with 9.5%, looked glamorous. Proceeds from the offering would be used to introduce new services, including concert and tour sponsorships. Additional funds would be used to expand marketing and promotional programs.

WHO WANTS TO BE A MILLIONAIRE?

On July 20, 1999, Credit Suisse First Boston, lead manager of the IPO, announced the IPO final price of \$28 per share, raising \$344.4 million for the company and valuing the firm at \$1.68 billion.[12] The magnitude of this valuation is best understood in the context of the following three points:

1. The entire online music distribution market was valued at just \$50 000 one year earlier.
2. Most MP3.com music was free.
3. MP3.com revenues from the first half of 1999 were less than \$3 million. July 21, 1999 represented the first day of trading for MP3.com. It was a wild success: the shares peaked at \$105 before closing at \$63.31, representing a 126% revalorization over the IPO price.[13] At these prices the company was worth roughly two-thirds of EMI, the world's third-biggest publicly traded music company (see Exhibit 1).

Despite the media buzz and the sensational IPO, a few critics started to raise their voices. Mark Hardie, senior analyst at Cambridge, Massachusetts–based Forrester Research, said of MP3.com's high stock offering, "It's bizarre," and Kevin Hause, while seeing the company as a potential acquisition target, questioned the long-term viability of MP3.com's business model.[14] It was true that the success would prove fleeting.

THE TECHNOLOGY

"MP3" stands for "Motion Picture Experts Group, audio layer 3." It is a file format that lets users compress music at near-CD-quality sound. The key point is that the resulting file is much smaller than competing formats of the same quality. This characteristic makes it very convenient for users to download music off the Internet. Even in this compressed format, however, a typical three-minute song takes 3 MB of storage and can take ten minutes to download over a conventional 56 kB/s modem.[15] Thus, downloading MP3 files depends on the advent of broadband (see Exhibit 2).

The nonproprietary aspect of the MP3 format allowed a variety of software players to sprout up on freeware and shareware Web sites—for example, the WinAmp player. A recent search for MP3 players on Tucows, the popular software library site <www.tucows.com> produced 590 matches, indicating the grassroots support for the standard. Considering the advantages of the format, the increased use and speed of Internet

EXHIBIT 1 MPPP Stock Price—Complete History

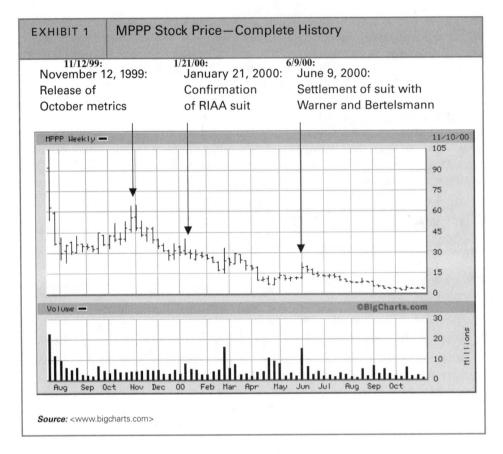

11/12/99: November 12, 1999: Release of October metrics

1/21/00: January 21, 2000: Confirmation of RIAA suit

6/9/00: June 9, 2000: Settlement of suit with Warner and Bertelsmann

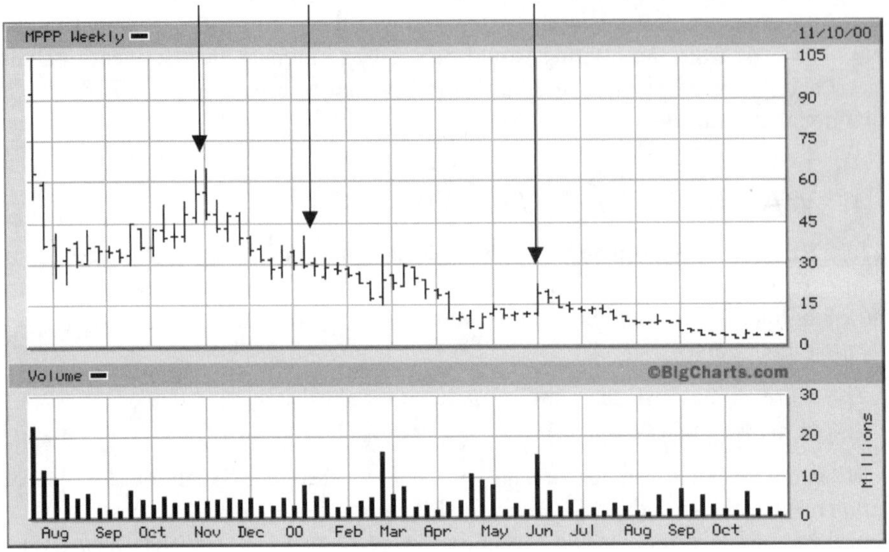

MPPP Weekly 11/10/00

Volume ©BigCharts.com

Aug Sep Oct Nov Dec 00 Feb Mar Apr May Jun Jul Aug Sep Oct

Millions

Source: <www.bigcharts.com>

connections, larger PC storage, and faster PC processing power, it is easy to see why the MP3 format caught on so dramatically. Visitors to MP3.com have the option of listening to songs played in a streaming format or of downloading songs to their local hard drive. Downloaded songs can be either played from a computer using any of the available free-ware/shareware applications or transferred onto a portable player. Portable players, such as the Diamond Rio, make use of flash-memory storage to hold roughly 30 to 60 minutes of music in a compact player that never skips. This adds to the appeal of the format for young users who are active and open to new music genres. The MP3.com Web site has no affiliation with the standards committee, and makes no revenue from the sales of players. Michael Robertson merely had the foresight to reserve an excellent domain name. By cleverly naming the company after the format, users looking for MP3 files would instinctively request the company's site or find it through a search engine.

THE ROTATING BUSINESS MODEL

Michael Robertson started MP3.com as a portal for music news and links to MP3 files. This quickly morphed into a record label, Digital Automated Music (DAM), to facilitate public access to new artists. While allowing artists and visitors free access to the online catalogue produced no revenue, MP3.com believed that customers who enjoyed the new

EXHIBIT 2 Broadband Penetration in the United States

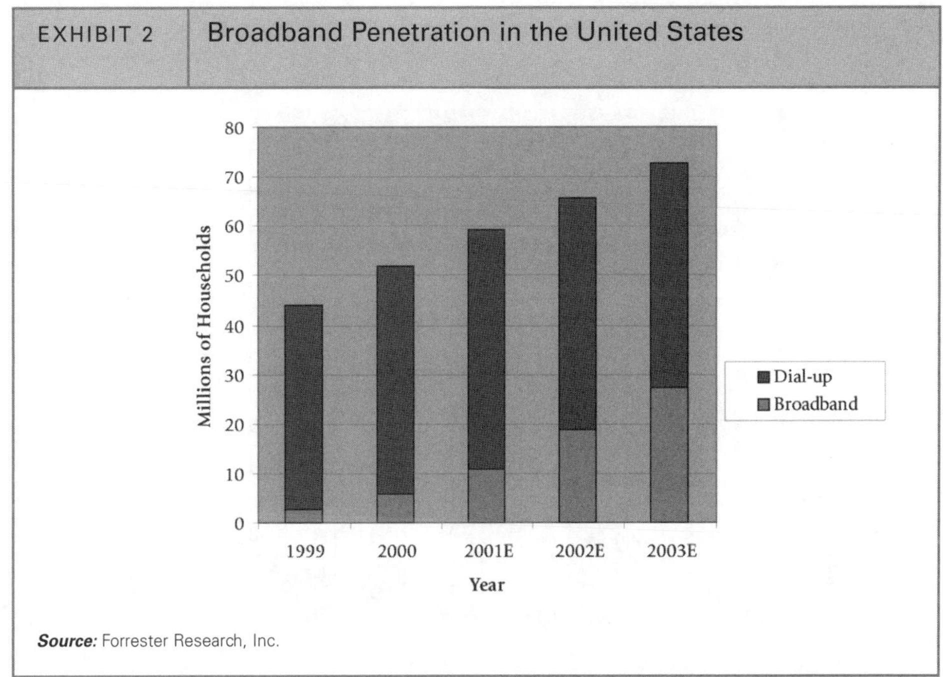

Source: Forrester Research, Inc.

artists would be willing to buy a CD. Each sale would generate revenue that would be split 50-50 with the artist.[16] This revenue sharing agreement contrasted sharply with the traditional deal between new bands and music companies whereby artists would receive a small payment up front and benefit very slightly from future sales. MP3.com introduced the following challenges to the industry:

1. Offering immediate distribution over the Internet of the artists' music
2. Sharing the revenues with the artists evenly, 50% for MP3.com, 50% for the artists

The problem was that very few CDs were sold online (see Exhibit 3). MP3.com had spent heavily in advertising with disappointing results. Sales of 18 300 CDs in October 1999 earned MP3.com fourth place in the e-music market with a 16% share.[17] More disturbing was how MP3.com trailed other e-music sites in consumer satisfaction, ranking tenth with 28% satisfied customers.[18] While the number of DAM CDs had been steadily increasing, it was clear that sales from DAM CDs would not sustain the market's expectation for revenue growth. It was time to find a new revenue driver. The solution? Advertising revenue.

The extent to which the MP3.com business model quickly became dependent on advertising revenues can be clearly seen from financial filings. During the first quarter of 2000, revenue from advertising accounted for 96.2% of net revenue, with a massive dependency on a small group of customers. Ten customers accounted for 79.6% of net revenue, and 56.7% came from only two customers, Groupe Arnault and Visitalk.[19] In fact, MP3.com had become dependent on advertising revenue during the spring of 1999.

Robertson knew he had to reinvent MP3.com to jumpstart page viewers, which had stagnated in the fall of 1999 (see Exhibit 6), while the number of artists listed continued to rise (see Exhibit 7). The bomb was about to drop.

EXHIBIT 3 United States Music Market—Online Versus Offline (in Billions)

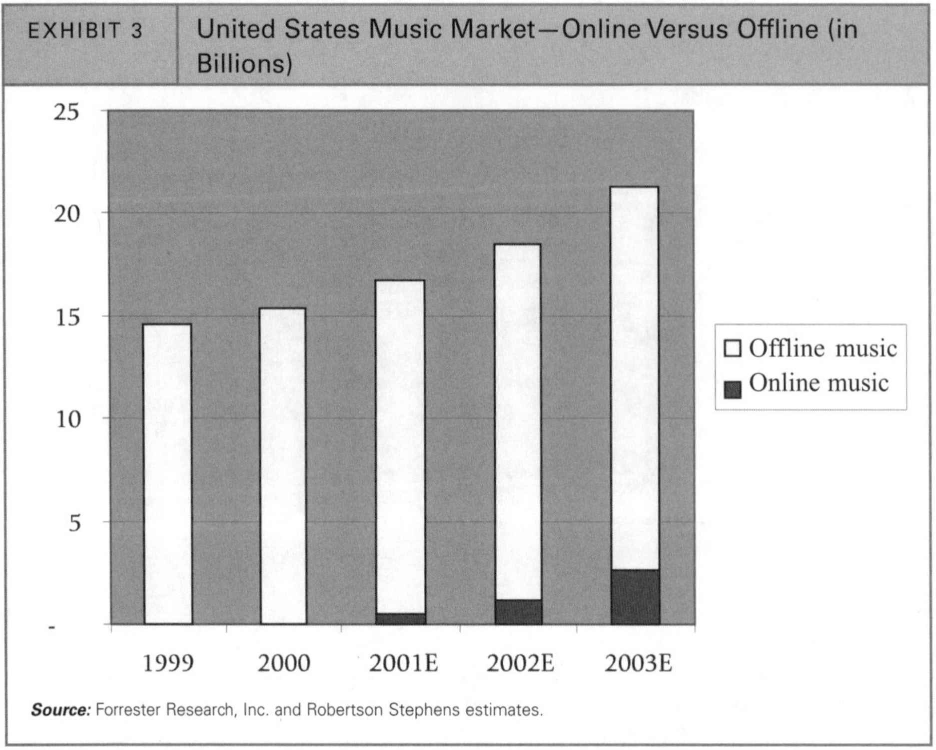

Source: Forrester Research, Inc. and Robertson Stephens estimates.

A GREAT IDEA BRINGS DEATH BY LAWYERS

On January 12, 2000 Robertson announced the launch of a new service in the My.MP3.com site. The Beam-it service (see Exhibits 8 and 9) allowed registered users to access copyrighted music from any Web browser through My.MP3.com. MP3.com would store the digitized versions of over 80 000 compact discs, allowing users to access music from anywhere in the world. MP3.com required that customers show they already owned

EXHIBIT 4 Distribution Chain for Digital Music

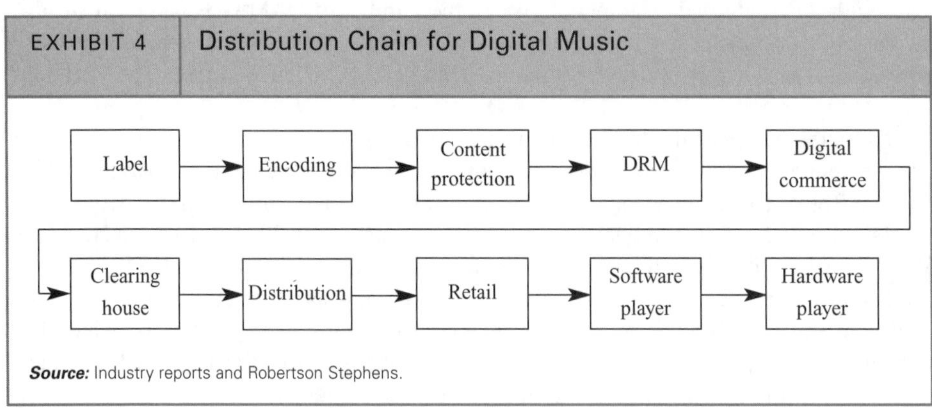

Source: Industry reports and Robertson Stephens.

EXHIBIT 5 Industry Participants and Capabilities

	Label	Encoding	Content Protection	DRM	Digital Commerce	Clearing House	Distribution	Retail	Software Player	Hardware Player
Universal	✔									
BMG	✔									
Sony	✔	✔								✔
Time-Warner/EMI	✔									
AT&T A2b		✔	✔							
Lucent (ePAC)		✔	✔							
IBM (EMMS)		✔	✔							
InterTrust			✔	✔						
Preview Systems			✔	✔						
Reciprocal				✔	✔	✔	✔			
Liquid Audio		✔	✔	✔	✔	✔	✔		✔	
Microsoft		✔	✔	✔	✔				✔	
Audiosoft/AOL			✔	✔	✔	✔			✔	
SuperTracks		✔		✔	✔	✔	✔			
Loudeye		✔	✔		✔		✔			
RealNetworks		✔	✔		✔			✔	✔	
Napster							✔			
Amazon								✔		
CDnow								✔		
eMusic								✔		
MP3.com								✔		
MusicMaker								✔		
Tunes.com								✔		
Yahoo Digital								✔		
Launch.com								✔		
Riffage.com								✔		
MusicMatch.com									✔	
WinAmp/AOL								✔	✔	
Diamond Multimedia										✔
Sanyo										✔
Samsung										✔

Source: Robertson Stephens.

EXHIBIT 6 Average Daily Unique Visitors per Day to MP3.com

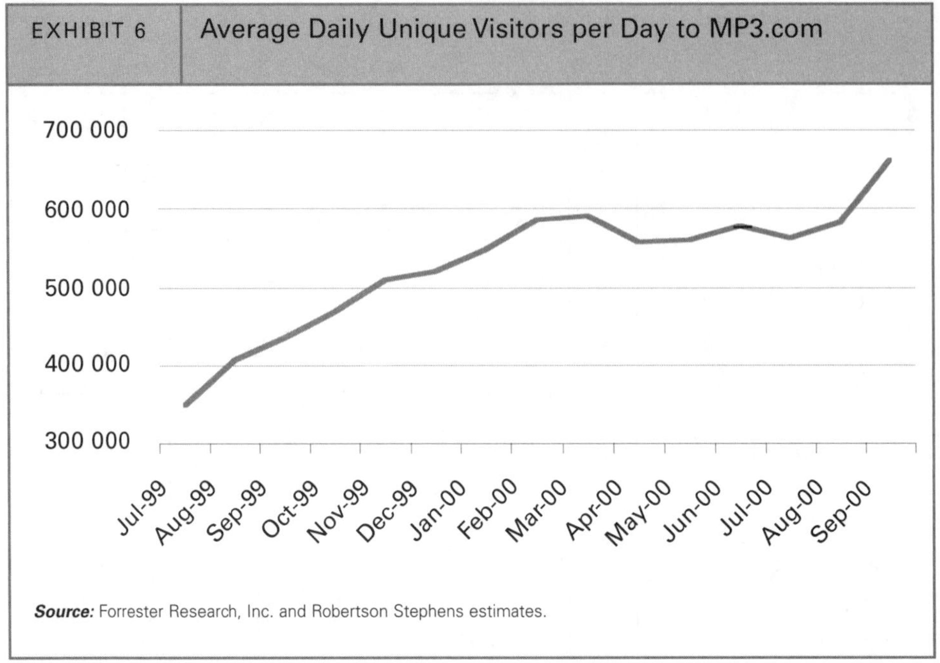

Source: Forrester Research, Inc. and Robertson Stephens estimates.

a particular CD. Subscribers verified they owned a CD by putting it into a computer and allowing MP3.com to scan it, or by buying the CD through an affiliated online retailer. The service was expected to become economically viable, since MP3.com could leverage detailed knowledge of users' musical tastes to attract premium advertising driven by strong targeting capability. Additionally, by partnering with e-music retailers, MP3.com earned revenue sharing from sales while providing customers with immediate access to the music purchased. The customer still waited for the physical CD to arrive in the mail, but could enjoy listening to the music via MP3.com immediately. This was seen as a clever and effective way to compete with the traditional sales channel.

It didn't take long for the old economy to fight back. On January 21, 2000 the recording industry, represented by the five major labels, EMI, Universal Music Group, Warner Music Group, Sony Music, and BMG Entertainment, filed a copyright lawsuit against MP3.com on the basis that the company was distributing music without paying royalties. MP3.com's stock dropped 16% when the suit hit the news. The first judicial decision came out on April 28, 2000. U.S. federal judge Jed Rakoff ruled that MP3.com had infringed on copyrights of record labels by transmitting for free tens of thousands of songs to computer users who signed up for My.MP3.com service.[20] MP3.com is "replaying for the subscribers converted versions of the recordings it copied, without authorization, from Plaintiff's copyrighted CDs," the Judge wrote.[21] Making things worse for MP3.com, he added: "The complex marvels of cyberspatial communication may create difficult legal issues; but not in this case."[22] He set an August 28 trial date to resolve any remaining issues in the case, including damages. But he gave the parties until May 25 to continue settlement discussions.

EXHIBIT 7 Total Number of Artists Listed at MP3.com

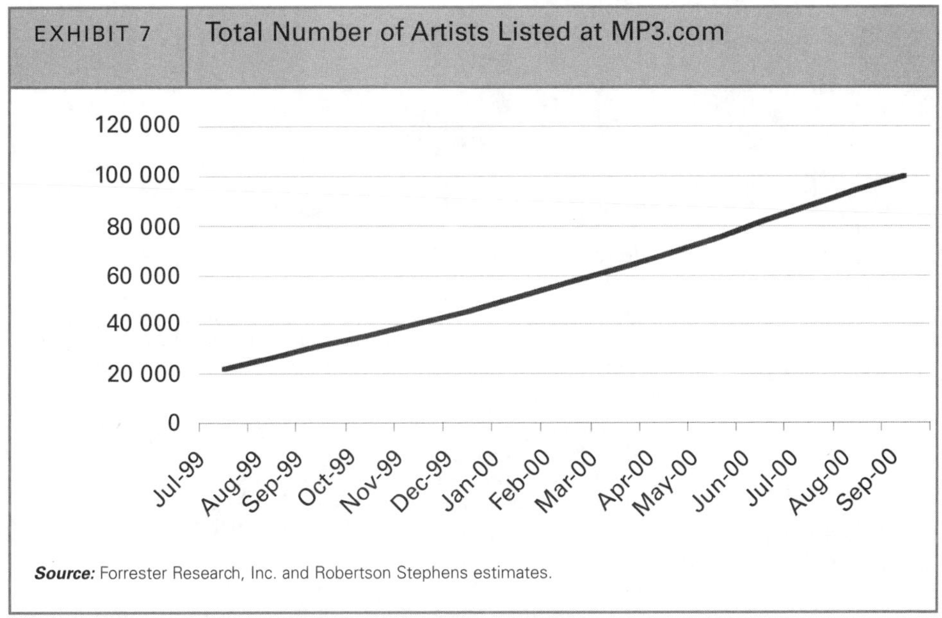

Source: Forrester Research, Inc. and Robertson Stephens estimates.

Although MP3.com's stock reacted positively in the days following the verdict in anticipation of an out-of-court settlement, it had plummeted from $30 to $8 in three months, the period between the filing of the suit and the verdict (see Exhibit 1). Death by lawyers now looked possible.

LET'S MAKE NICE

Compared to the carnage caused in the industry by Napster in the early summer of 2000, the problems with MP3.com looked diminutive and hopes for out-of-court settlements increased. On June 9, 2000 MP3.com announced that it had reached agreements with BMG and Warner that called for an undisclosed royalty payment.[23] At the same time, MP3.com and Warner announced a licensing agreement that allowed MP3 to access the Warner catalogue. The Warner Music Group Executive VP Paul Vidich stated, "The settlement agreement clearly affirms the right of copyright owners to be compensated for the use of their works on the Internet."[24] MP3.com's stock rose slightly, to close at $17.25. Settlements with EMI and Sony Music followed on July 28 and August 21.[25] While the summer of 2000 was far less glorious for Robertson and company than the star-sprinkled ride of 1999, the settlements were positive. While financial details were not disclosed, several reports cited $20 million as the average payment for both reparations and licensing fees made in each settlement.[24,26,27] The company took a one-time charge of $150 million in the second quarter to cover the legal and licensing expenses related to the lawsuits.

By the end of August 2000, MP3.com had settled with four of the five major record labels. The holdout was Universal Music Studios. Then another legal bomb dropped. On September 6, 2000 Judge Rakoff ruled against MP3.com, opining that MP3.com had

EXHIBIT 8 A Page from the MP3 Web Site

About MP#.com

MP3.com Info

Press Releases

Investor Relations

Contact MP3.com

Customer Service

Advertise

MP3 Summit

Link to MP3.com

Email Press Releases

Jobs

Home > About MP3.com
English—Français—Deutsch —Español

To receive MP3.com Press Release via email, subscribe to the Email Press Release list.

MP3.com is the premier Music Service Provider (MSP) allowing consumers to instantly discover, purchase, listen to, store and organize their music collection from anywhere, at any time, using any Internet device.

My.MP3.com:
MP3.com's flagship service lets you instantly add, organize and listen to your music collection online, wherever you can access a web-connected computer. Or add any free song on MP3.com to your My.MP3.com account with the click of a button.

Beam-it (TM):
MP3.com's free new software allows you to centralize your music collection so you can play it anywhere. Just place a CD in your CD-ROM drive once; Beam-it instantly recognizes the CD and adds it to your My.MP3.com account.

Instant Listening (TM):
Start listening immediately to the CDs you buy online from our Instant Listening retail partners or directly from MP3.com—before the album arrives in the mail!

Getting Started:
More than a million people visit our site daily to listen to and download MP3 songs. If you're new to MP3, our Getting Started page is designed to help you navigate the site quickly so you can start enjoying your music right away from our selection of 250,000-plus songs in diverse musical genres.

FREE Music:
MP3.com offers more than a quarter-million high-quality songs from 50,000-plus artists available for FREE downloading over the Internet. At various times we've featured special music from top artists such as Alanis Morissette, Tori Amos, Beastie Boys, Billy Idol, Tina Turner, Peter Townshend, Dionne Warwick, George Clinton and Master P. We also have the leading music archive of independent artists on the Internet.

Music Classics:
Through a partnership with Classic World Productions, one of the world's top labels for back-catalog music, you also can download at least one free MP3 track per album before deciding to purchase CDs by legendary pop musicians such as Bill Haley and the Comets, the Platters, Anne Murray, Petula Clark and George Benson.

Source: "About us," MP3.com Web site, accessed July 29, 2001 <www.mp3.com/aboutus.html>.

EXHIBIT 9	The Beam-it Service at the My.MP3.com Web Site

My.MP3.com Help

Using Beam-it™

Beam-it is a software program for you to use in conjunction with My.MP3.com. With Beam-it, you'll never need to lug your CDs from your house, car and work again! Beam-it identifies the CDs you own and instantly adds them to My.MP3.com, your personal online jukebox. This means you just put a CD in your computer's CD-ROM drive once, "beam" it to My.MP3.com, and you can listen to it online wherever and whenever you want. (Learn more about My.MP3.com in our quick Tour of Features.)

It's easy to add your CDs to the My.MP3.com jukebox:

1. Download and Install Free Beam-it Software
2. Launch Beam-it to Start Adding Your CDs
3. Go to My.MP3.com to Play CDs

Download and Install Free Beam-it Software

Step 1. Download the free software.

Just choose your platform to begin the downloading.

Windows (1.7 MB)

Macintosh (477 kB)

Linux users, we've got a whole separate page for you.

Step 2. Save to a folder.
As soon as you click one of the download icons above, you will be prompted to save the Beam-it file to a folder. Make sure you save Beam-it in an easy-to-find location on your hard drive—your desktop is a good example.

***Tip:** Bookmark this page so you can pick up where you left off when you reboot your computer.

Step 3. Install Beam-it.
After downloading Beam-it, find and open the newly downloaded file to begin the installation process and setup. Then follow the instructions on your screen. If you are updating an older version of Beam-it, the installer will automatically detect the older version on your computer and ask you to upgrade to the most current version.

Step 4. Reboot your computer and look for the Beam-it icon.
At the end of the installation, you will be prompted to reboot or restart your computer. Once you have done this, you should see the yellow Beam-it icon in your program tray or Windows Start Menu (or Control Panels folder with Macintosh).

Next, **Launch Beam-it** to Start Adding Your CDs

Source: "Add your CDs with Beam-it," MP3.com Web site, accessed July 29, 2001 <help.mp3.com/help/mymp3/tutorial/beamit.html>.

"wilfully infringed upon Universal Music's copyrights," and determined that MP3.com would have to pay $25 000 per infringed CD.[28] A hearing was scheduled for November 13 to determine how many of Universal's CDs were infringed. The aggregate damages would be anywhere in the range of $118–$250 million, depending on whether the number used is 4700 CDs (MP3's claim) or 10 000 CDs (Universal's claim).[29] MP3.com's cash position of $315 million at the end of June was dwindling fast. On October 11, 2000 the stock hit an all-time low of $2.50, fifteen months after it had reached $105. The wild slide of the stock price prompted the law firm Cauley & Geller to announce on September 20 the first of a series of class-action suits against the company on behalf of the equity shareholders.[30]

MORE ROTATING BUSINESS MODELS

Faced with legal battles over the My.MP3.com service, Robertson announced important moves in the development of its business plan. In May 2000, it launched the first-ever on-demand music subscription channel found on the Internet. The Classical Music Channel offered over 3400 tracks' worth of music for a $9.99 monthly fee.[31] The service offered unlimited access to streaming and over 300 free downloads. On October 6, 2000 MP3 changed the conditions of the subscription, offering a yearly subscription for the Classical Music Channel at a 75% discount from the monthly rate.[32] For a $29.99 charge, users could access more than 4000 classical tracks for a full year. Also, while the MP3.com site was receiving more hits, it was dependent on users' actually logging on. To access the larger audience that uses email, the company announced a Music Messenger Service[33]—a free song delivery service that enables fans to regularly receive music via email. The service emails songs directly to fans, reducing search time. Daily, weekly, and monthly frequency options are selectable.

Finally, in a move characterized by some investors as bizarre (or desperate), MP3.com announced that it would expand its business by opening physical stores similar to those of Sony or EMI.[34] Was the company returning to a focus on selling CDs?

DWINDLING FIRST-MOVER ADVANTAGE

As MP3.com wasted time and effort straightening out its legal woes, the company's important first-mover advantage was quickly dwindling. Musicbank struck two different deals to provide a service identical to that of My.MP3.com, with Warner Music[35] on October 23 and with Sony Music[36] on October 30. Also, the agreement reached on October 30 between Bertelsmann, the parent of BMG, and Napster presented unknown threats to MP3.com.[37] Bertelsmann Records and Napster would provide a subscription-based version of the original Napster service.

WHAT TO DO?

As Michael Robertson waited for the trial to begin on Monday November 13, he contemplated the actions he had undertaken to help his company in recent days. MP3.com had just announced the appointment of Justice Howard B. Wiener (Ret.), a former Justice of the California Court of Appeal, to its board of directors.[38] Additionally, the firm beefed up its legal defence team with the addition of the noted law firm Skadden, Arps, Slate, Meagher

& Flom LLP.[39] With cash dwindling and lawsuits mounting, Robertson wondered if the company could survive the upcoming week.

NOTES

1. "Net may change record industry; MP3: music for the masses," *Chicago Sun-Times*, February 4, 1999, p. 12.
2. "Sequoia Capital and Idealab! invest 10 and 1M US$ respectively in MP3.com," *MP3.com (PR Newswire)*, January 20, 1999.
3. "Net may change record industry; MP3: music for the masses," *Chicago Sun-Times*, February 4, 1999, p. 12.
4. See note 3.
5. "MP3.com announces its IPO expected to raise $115M," *The San Diego Union-Tribune*, May 15, 1999, p. C-1.
6. "Web site's technology to revolutionize the music industry," *The Atlanta Journal and Constitution*, June 9, 1999.
7. "MP3.com reports key metrics," *MP3.com (PR Newswire)*, September 14, 1999.
8. See note 7.
9. "MP3 stars in a music revolution," *The San Diego Union-Tribune*, September 5, 1999, p. C-1.
10. "MP3.com ups size, price of its IPO," *The San Diego Union-Tribune*, July 13, 1999.
11. "Will MP3.com soar to No. 1 with a bullet, or languish in the Wall St. cut-out bins?," *The New York Times,* July 20, 1999, p. C-11, column 4.
12. "MP3.com announces initial public offering of 12,300,000 shares of common stock," *Business Wire*, July 20, 1999.
13. "MP3.com soars on first trading day; Wall Street: music-download firm is briefly valued at $6.9 billion as the shares explode. Price settles at $63.31," *Los Angeles Times*, July 22, 1999, p. 1.
14. See note 12.
15. "MP3.com 10-Q quarterly report," *Freedgar.com*, April 24, 2000, p. 28.
16. "Music distributor in San Diego becomes an online maestro," *The San Diego Union-Tribune*, February 2, 1999, p. C-3.
17. "Amazon.com is more than twice as popular as MP3.com with online music shoppers; Greenfield Online study separates the superstar sites from those in the chorus," *Greenfield Online, Inc. (PR Newswire)*, October 21, 1999.
18. "Online music customers rate Amazon.com tops for service; MP3.com trails other e-music sites in customer satisfaction," *Greenfield Online, Inc. (PR Newswire)*, November 11, 1999.
19. "MP3.com 10-Q quarterly report," *Freedgar.com*, April 24, 2000, p. 26.
20. "MP3.com ruled in violation of copyrights," *The San Francisco Chronicle*, April 29, 2000, p. B-1.
21. "MP3.com arguments are called 'indefensible' by the judge," *Bloomberg Service News*, May 4, 2000.
22. "Thievery is thievery, judge in MP3 case says," *The Seattle Times*, May 5, 2000, p. C-3.
23. "Warner and BMG settle web rights dispute with MP3," *Financial Times*, June 10, 2000, p. 1.
24. "MP3.com settles with 2 record labels; deals part of expected $100 million agreement," *The San Francisco Chronicle*, June 10, 2000, p. B-1.
25. "MP3 and Sony reach copyright accord," *The New York Times*, August 22, 2000, p. C-8, column 5.

26. "MP3.com agrees $20m net deal to end EMI dispute," *The Times (London)*, July 29, 2000, Business Section.
27. "MP3 shares jump on word of possible settlement; major record labels may allow $100 million payoff," *The San Diego Union-Tribune*, June 8, 2000, p. C-1.
28. "The Networker: why it takes a law degree to make money from the net," *The Observer*, September 10, 2000, p. 8.
29. "MP3.com stock plummets in wake of adverse ruling," *The Philadelphia Inquirer*, September 8, 2000.
30. "Cauley & Geller, LLP announces class action lawsuit against MP3.com, Inc.; seeking damages on behalf of shareholders," *Business Wire*, September 20, 2000.
31. "MP3.com launches first-ever on-demand subscription channel; premiere music service provider goes for baroque," *MP3.com (PR Newswire)*, May 2, 2000.
32. "MP3.com launches first-ever on-demand subscription channel; premiere music service provider goes for baroque," *MP3.com (PR Newswire)*, October 6, 2000.
33. "MP3.com sends music directly to fans via e-mail; new, free music messenger service expands MP3.com's reach," *MP3.com (PR Newswire)*, April 5, 2000.
34. "MP3.com to make move into retail stores," *The San Diego Union-Tribune*, August 15, 2000, p. C-2.
35. "Musicbank and Warner Music Group sign licensing agreement; agreement precedes fall launch of Musicbank service," *Musicbank (PR Newswire)*, October 25, 2000.
36. "Online start-up Musicbank gets licensing rights to Sony Music catalog," *The Associated Press State & Local Wire*, October 30, 2000.
37. "Notorious Napster, a renegade Internet music provider targeted for destruction by the record industry, is making peace with one of its mortal enemies," *The San Diego Union-Tribune*, November 1, 2000, p. C-1.
38. "MP3.com appoints new board member; former California Court of Appeal Justice Howard B. Wiener joins board of directors," *MP3.com (PR Newswire)*, October 30, 2000.
39. "MP3.com faces Universal Monday in trial to assess damages," *Dow Jones Newswire*, November 10, 2000.

case two

epost: Moving the Mail Online

Ajax Persaud,
School of Management,
University of Ottawa

Jasbir Dhaliwal, Norwegian
School of Management

The Internet is here to stay. It will revolutionize corporate business models. It will change the way corporations do business with their customers. These were the thoughts that two of Canada's leading corporations—Canada Post Corporation and Cebra Inc., the e-commerce division of Bank of Montreal—were considering in the early-to-mid-1990s. Although the corporations' motivations were different, their dreams were remarkably similar: maximize the opportunities from this new channel to become the de facto leader of their industries in the new landscape created by the Internet. The pursuit of their dreams eventually led to the creation of *epost*, the world's first electronic post office, and a flagship achievement for the world's most connected nation.

Research undertaken by both Canada Post, a Crown corporation of the Government of Canada, and Bank of Montreal, a major Canadian bank, on Internet connectivity and usage by Canadians concluded that the majority of Canadians had or would soon have Internet access, many were transacting online, and many were early adopters of new technology. The adoption of telephone banking and debit cards were leading indicators of this trend. The early adopters were using the Internet for a variety of reasons, including business transactions, and were very excited at the opportunity to use it as a channel for consolidated electronic mail delivery service (a one-stop shop) for all kinds of mail-related services.

This case, prepared with the assistance of Roger Couldrey and Sarah Gambrill, is presented for class discussion purposes rather than to illustrate either effective or ineffective handling of a business.

WHAT IS *EPOST*?

epost began as a joint venture between Canada Post and Cebra, and was officially launched in November 1999. In November 2000, TELUS Corporation, Canada's second-largest telecommunications company and largest wireless provider, invested C$30 million in *epost*, thereby acquiring 5% of the company. Canada Post and Cebra each retained 47.5% of *epost*.

epost is a revolutionary concept designed to transform the delivery of mail from physical to electronic modes. It delivers the mail online for Canada Post through a secure end-to-end electronic delivery channel. It is a Web-based service that delivers all types of mail—bills, catalogues, forms, advertisements, surveys, statements, and more—digitally. The uniqueness of *epost* is summarized by Roger Couldrey, *epost*'s vice-president of marketing: "We are the first postal service in the world to have taken what we do in the physical world, which took decades to develop, and put it on the Web in a matter of two to three years. We did this through a partnership of two federally regulated corporations that are in very different businesses, with different philosophies, histories, and cultures, and which are governed by different rules, regulations, and regulatory agencies." Commenting on *epost*'s first-to-market advantage, Killen & Associates, a leading market research firm, recommend that "other postal administrations study *epost* to learn how a mix of services can be successfully bundled for the 21st-century postal e-business."

DESIGNING *EPOST*

Early in the design of their concepts, executives at Canada Post and Bank of Montreal realized that they were essentially pursuing the same venture. Cebra Inc. was examining ways to accelerate consumer bill collection for Bank of Montreal's corporate clients, and Canada Post was looking for effective ways to deal with the threat of decline in its physical letter mail services. With these related strategic rationales, a joint venture was formed to explore how each company could benefit from a partnership. These discussions eventually led to the *epost* concept.

EPOST PRODUCT DESIGN

The central theme of the *epost* business strategy was to build a product that provided the postal component of e-commerce functionality and services for Canadian businesses and consumers. The *epost* service allows businesses and consumers to move their mail online to a central location <www.epost.ca>. Because electronic bill presentment and payment (EBPP) is forecast to drive adoption of online mail delivery services such as *epost*, it was critical for the company to first establish itself as the dominant player in the Canadian EBPP market (see Exhibit 1).

At the operational level, *epost*'s strategy is to leverage the expertise of Canada Post, Cebra, Bank of Montreal, TELUS, and all of its partners, contractors, and mailers to derive maximum synergy, thereby increasing the value of its investment and creating wealth for its shareholders and customers. For example, because of the very specialized technical knowledge required to integrate the technology, data, and business processes of different mailers with their own, *epost* has outsourced many of these activities to organizations (e.g., NETdelivery, Xenos, EDS) in order to ensure that a fully functional system is developed

EXHIBIT 1

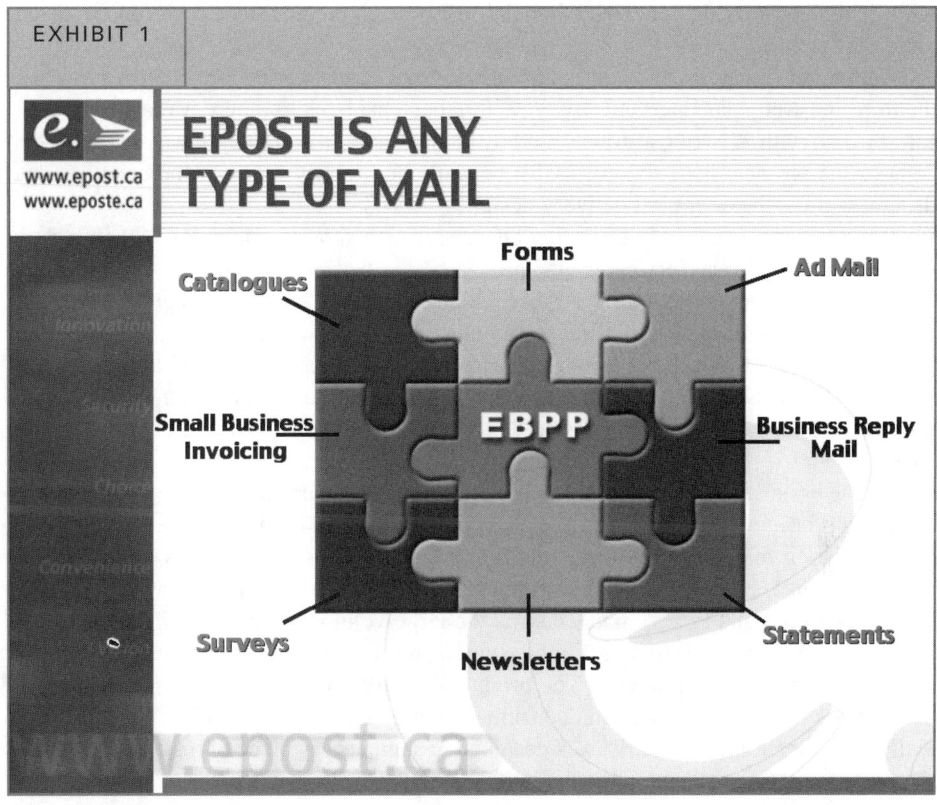

and implemented quickly. Similarly, when *epost* outsourced its call centre activities it partnered with a company that it believed could deliver, not only a cost-effective solution, but also an exceptionally high level of customer service.

Together, Canada Post and Cebra conducted extensive market research prior to the launch of *epost*. Cumulative research by PricewaterhouseCoopers, Ernst & Young, Angus Reid, and the Institute for the Future established some key trends with Canadian consumers:

- Consumers want choice.
- Consumers trust Canada Post for mail delivery.
- Consumers demand privacy and security.
- Interest was very high for a consolidated mail delivery service.
- Interest was in an anytime, anywhere, multimedia service.
- Canadians are early adopters of technology.

An Angus Reid survey conducted in 1999 revealed that consumers were interested in receiving a variety of documents electronically, including bills, statements, requested brochures, catalogues, and forms. In the same survey, consumers indicated they would like to receive this type of information from all of the types of companies they do business with, including utilities, retailers, financial institutions, credit cards, government, magazines, and airlines.

Additional research indicated that, behind email and research, personal banking was the third-most-popular Internet activity. Within personal banking, there was a strong interest in EBPP, with 12% of Canadians already paying their bills online. Since bills represent 23% of the physical mail stream, EBPP became the primary focus of the *epost* product design, within a broader mail delivery design.

Research conducted with Canadian businesses also showed a high level of interest in an online mail delivery service. Canadian businesses realized that their customers would demand e-billing and other online services. Many businesses already had plans under way to replace letter mail with electronic communication, cost reduction being the key driver behind this move. Like the consumer research, businesses also indicated a high level of trust with Canada Post, but they did not view the organization as an e-commerce leader. To mitigate this fact, businesses suggested that Canada Post partner with a technology leader such as Cebra.

On the basis of this market analysis, Canada Post and Cebra worked together on a product design for *epost*, one based on the concept of adding an online mail delivery channel to the existing mail delivery infrastructure in Canada. This channel was designed with security, choice, and access as the primary features. It addressed the needs of the key groups that send and receive mail, that is, the large-volume mailers, small and medium-sized enterprises, and consumers. For consumers, these needs included a range of payment options required for e-commerce. The product design also allowed for the delivery of all of the types of mail businesses and consumers expressed an interest in receiving electronically. An "Electronic Postmark" was designed to stamp every piece of mail when it enters the *epost* system to guarantee that the item has not been tampered with.

While the concept behind *epost* is relatively simple, the process of delivering mail online is complex, requiring sophisticated technologies that must be seamlessly integrated with that of both mailers and *epost*. According to Roger Couldrey, "We had to build a design to deal with hundreds of mailers, each having their own technologies, systems, and processes, built to execute against different strategies typically in a paper-based channel, to address the complexity of the implementation process." He adds that, once implemented, the transactional executions are straightforward. Also, the data, business systems, and processes of both mailers and *epost* must be synchronized for the service to work effectively. "We believe that building customized solutions for *epost* mailers is a key competitive advantage for *epost*," says Roger Couldrey.

Consumers complete a one-time registration process with *epost* by going to the *epost* Web site <www.epost.ca> and clicking "Register Now" to get their *epost box*. Once registered, they click "My Mailer Information" and choose the mailers they want to register for, then complete the enrollment form. A separate form must be completed for each mail item so that mailers can authenticate the customers. The same password and user ID chosen at the time of registration are used to access all *epost* mail anytime, anywhere, regardless of mailer, because all bills and mail are delivered to a single "*epost* box." Consumers can sign up for an email alert service that notifies them when they have new mail, and they can set up payment options for bills they choose to pay through *epost*.

Consumers can also register to access their online mail via *epost express*, a service that offers a direct window to *epost* mail from a financial institution's online banking Web site.

Currently "*epost* express" is available to consumers at BMO mbanx Direct, and it will be available at future online banking Web sites.

The *epost* pricing strategy offers mailers cost reduction benefits (electronic mail delivery is less expensive than paper mail), asset maximization, and opportunities for new revenue through enhanced customer relationship management online. Emphasizing the cost savings and efficiency value propositions of *epost*, Roger Couldrey states that "when mailers sign up with *epost* and their customers subscribe to our service, they can safely turn off the paper and the paper processing because *epost* is delivering mail on behalf of Canada Post in accordance with the Canada Post Act."

To establish a market leadership position, *epost*'s sales strategy is focused on offering a unique value proposition for mailers, and leveraging multiple channels to target potential business customers. *epost* started by aggressively targeting the largest national and regional Canadian billers, particularly in the retail and financial services sector, to get them to subscribe to its services. The second layer of its campaign strategy targets small and medium-sized enterprises, many of which are regional in nature. *epost* services are marketed through a direct sales force, the sales forces of Canada Post and Bank of Montreal, and the sales forces of major mail service providers.

MARKETING STRATEGY

epost has two primary target markets: mailers, particularly large-volume national and regional players, and consumers. Each audience is equally important, because while *epost* cannot deliver mail without the mailers, the mailers need to have their customers subscribed to *epost* in order to deliver online mail to them. In describing the approach taken by *epost*, Roger Couldrey noted that "the first priority has been to make the service relevant on a national scale, with national mailers, many of which are retailers." The secondary mailer focus is large regional mailers, such as utilities and telecommunications companies and organizations. With many of these mailers now in place, *epost* is focusing activity on the consumer audience.

The marketing strategy is presently focused on building the *epost* brand and attracting new consumers. To achieve these goals, *epost* has an aggressive marketing strategy in place; overall, it is designed to build a new category of online mail for Canadians, and to establish *epost* as the leader in this new market. The *epost* strategy leverages online and offline opportunities to reach target consumers, and employs a variety of tactics including brand advertising, direct mail, online advertising, and public relations. The *epost* acquisition strategy leverages key partners such as shareholders and new mailers, to attract new consumers to the *epost* service.

EPOST VALUE PROPOSITION

The services provided by *epost* benefit both the *mailers* and *consumers*. The mailers are large and small organizations, including businesses, government agencies, utilities, universities, and non-government organizations, that send bills, invoices, and statements. The consumers are the recipients of such pieces of mail.

For mailers, *epost* offers the following value proposition:

- It can deliver all types of mail digitally, for example, bills, catalogues, forms, advertising mail, surveys, statements, and newsletters.
- *epost* extends Canada Post's reputation for delivering the mail in a safe, secure, and confidential manner. *epost* guarantees this service with the *Electronic Postmark* (see Exhibit 2). This postmark appears on every piece of mail sent through the system to verify that the mail has not been tampered with. The Electronic Postmark is incorporated into the Canada Post Act, allowing businesses to turn off their paper mail stream with the assurance that the documents they send through *epost* are legitimately delivered.
- Mailers maintain their brand identity while enhancing their customer relationships online. *epost* does not interfere with the link between the mailers and their customers; it simply provides the secure delivery channel. *epost* acts as a conduit to drive traffic to a business' Web site, thereby promoting other e-commerce services that a business may offer.
- Mailers benefit from substantial cost savings and increased operational efficiency, which could have a positive impact on the companies' bottom line. For example, as of May 2001, *epost* will deliver a piece of mail for $0.39, in contrast to between $0.70 and $3 for paper-based mail. Greater operational efficiency results from substantially less paper mail to open, and with more customers paying online, there are fewer cheques to receive, open, and sort. There is also the potential for a significant reduction in telephone calls to customer service representatives since more information can be provided efficiently through online delivery. Companies may also benefit from improved cash flow through immediate online payments.

For consumers, *epost* offers the following value proposition:

- *Choice:* Consumers choose the mail that they receive through *epost*. For example, a consumer may want to receive all their bills through *epost* but not advertising mail or newsletters, or vice versa. Consumers can also choose to receive an email message alerting them that they have mail in their *epost box*.
- *Consolidation:* Consumers can get all of their mail sent to a single *epost box* requiring a single ID and password for access. This consolidation model replicates how paper mail is delivered in the physical world.
- *Security and privacy:* The *epost* system assures privacy, as no data is mined or shared by *epost*. The system is also secured through the latest 128-bit encryption SSL technology. The system is closed, so once you are inside the system, you are protected from intrusion by unwanted parties. The Electronic Postmark provides a guarantee that the system is secure and the mail has not been tampered with.
- *Convenience:* The *epost* service is Web-based, available anytime—"24/7/365"—anywhere, and is open to any consumer. The availability and accessibility of the service is a cornerstone of the *epost* concept.
- *Free of charge:* Customers do not pay for this service.
- *Environmental benefits:* Sending mail electronically means there is less paper and waste to deal with.

EXHIBIT 2

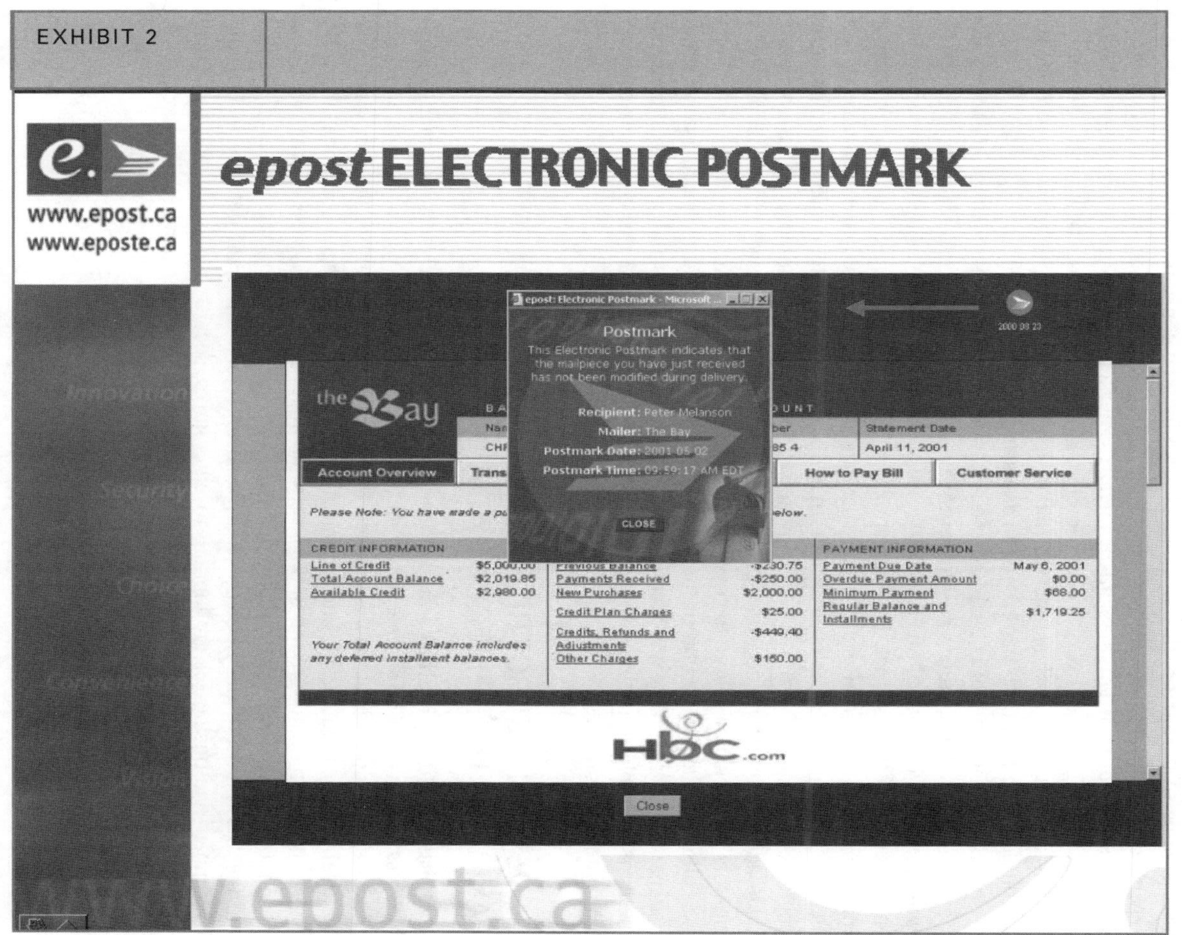
epost ELECTRONIC POSTMARK
www.epost.ca
www.eposte.ca
Postmark
This Electronic Postmark indicates that the mailpiece you have just received has not been modified during delivery.
Recipient: Peter Melanson
Mailer: The Bay
Postmark Date: 2001 05 02
Postmark Time: 09:59:17 AM EDT
CLOSE
the Bay
Statement Date
April 11, 2001
Account Overview
How to Pay Bill
Customer Service
CREDIT INFORMATION
Line of Credit $5,000.00
Total Account Balance $2,019.85
Available Credit $2,980.00
Your Total Account Balance includes any deferred installment balances.
Payments Received -$250.00
New Purchases $2,000.00
Credit Plan Charges $25.00
Credits, Refunds and Adjustments -$449.40
Other Charges $150.00
PAYMENT INFORMATION
Payment Due Date May 6, 2001
Overdue Payment Amount $0.00
Minimum Payment $68.00
Regular Balance and Installments $1,719.25
Hbc.com
Close
www.epost.ca

EPOST FINANCIAL PLAN

epost was conceived as a private-sector, profit-driven initiative. According to *epost* executives, the business model and financial forecasting are based on thorough research and analysis of all key factors in order to estimate volumes, revenues, costs, and profitability levels. Some of the factors that were considered include consumer adoption rates (which depend upon Internet penetration), electronic delivery penetration rates, the competitive landscape, actual mail volume statistics, *epost*'s marketing strategy, transaction volumes, sustainable pricing, delivery costs, implementation expenses, and scale dynamics. Traditional measures, such as internal rate of return (IRR), net present value (NPV), and discounted cash flows were employed in assessing the investment.

epost's revenue model is based on mailers, since it is a free service to consumers. By the foregoing analysis, *epost*'s current revenue model is founded on a per-transaction basis. *epost* charges a flat rate of \$0.39 to \$0.42 per piece of mail sent through *epost,* depending on the length of the contract. This rate applies to all mailers regardless of the size of mailers or the volume of mail sent; that is, the rate is the same whether a mailer sends 100 pieces of mail or 100 000 pieces of mail. In addition to the flat rate, mailers pay a one-time implementation cost, which is approximately C\$50 000, and mailers also have access to value-added implementation services available at incremental costs. There is, as well, a monthly maintenance charge to cover changes to presentment, etc.

Following the completion of the *epost* business strategies and financial assessment, a risk management strategy was identified to outline potential risks and strategies to address these risks. Table 1 outlines some of the risks identified, and the corresponding risk management strategies.

EPOST AND ELECTRONIC BILL PRESENTMENT AND PAYMENT (EBPP) IN CANADA

epost has established itself as a market leader in the consolidated electronic mail delivery business in Canada. The sample list of mailers listed on *epost*'s Web site gives an indication of *epost*'s dominance in this market. Its roster includes many of the major national, regional, and local businesses and organizations. According to Roger Couldrey, "the EBPP market is the first battleground in the electronic mail delivery business. We are well positioned to win the EBPP battle and to dominate the online mail market. However, EBPP is but the first phase of our strategy to drive secure electronic mail delivery in Canada." Consumers and businesses are looking for alternative, secure, accessible, and convenient ways of sending bills and receiving payments quickly. Internet banking is increasing in prominence, as a large number of consumers now transact a greater portion of their businesses, including paying bills, online. (Exhibit 3 shows *epost*'s EBPP model.)

COMPETITION IN CANADA

"The competition is alive and well," says Roger Couldrey. *epost*'s major Canadian competitor is the webdoxs service of e-route Inc., which is a consortium of Royal Bank of Canada, Canadian Imperial Bank of Commerce, TD Bank Financial Group, Scotiabank, National Bank of Canada, and Mouvement des Caisses Desjardins, led by BCE Emergis. e-route's

TABLE 1 *epost* Risk Management Strategies

Risk	Risk Management Strategy
Acceptance by mailers	• Ensure solid value proposition: multifaceted • Leverage existing relationship with Canada Post and Canada Post brand
Consumer adoption	• Offer free service, strong value proposition • Marketing strategy focused on early adopters and mailers' customers • Privacy and security guarantee
Competitive landscape	• Leverage Canada Post brand • Emphasize "all mail" and independence
Technology effectiveness and development control	• Due diligence on technology and technology vendors • Control rollout of service offerings • Stay on top of emerging technologies
Cost escalation	• Phased development • Strong project management

webdoxs, launched in March 2001, is primarily in the EBPP business, not the mail delivery business—they deliver and present bills to facilitate payment. This is because e-route's primary backers and customers are the banks who are in the consumer- and commercial-deposit-gathering business. Consumers connect to webdoxs through their online bank accounts, so only people who bank with one of its founding financial institutions can use the service to view and pay their bills. e-route's member banks are responsible for selling the product to their biller clients and for the presentment service.

e-route and *epost* are both aggressively pursuing the 10.7 million bank customers in Canada, about 25% of which either receive or pay their bills electronically. As of May 2001, *epost* had commitments from more than 90 mailers who intend to send mail through the *epost* service. Of the 90 mailers, over 25 were live. Over 150 000 consumers have registered with *epost*. e-route has 18 billers live and over 200 000 consumers registered with the webdoxs service.

Although there is no evidence that U.S. competitors are targeting Canada, the United States has over two dozen players in the EBPP space, who may be deemed potential competitors to *epost*. The main players in the U.S. market are Checkfree, Paytrust, Spectrum LLC, and CyberBills. Of these, CheckFree is the strongest U.S. competitor and by far the largest consolidator of bills in the world. CheckFree has a strong base in the physical world because of the uniqueness of their offering—a service where, for a monthly fee, a consumer could have all his or her bills collected by CheckFree, who would then pay the billers on his or her behalf. They have launched a Web-based service in the United States while continuing to offer it in the physical format.

Describing the competitive landscape in Canada, Roger Couldrey says, "basically you have two different strategies fighting it out in the same battleground." According to Peter Melanson, *epost*'s President and CEO, "it's going to be fierce, but competition always makes you stronger, and we are ready to take on the competition." Commenting on the EBPP developments in Canada and the United States, Avivah Litan, an analyst with Gartner Group Inc., says, "so far the main similarity in the Canadian and U.S. electronic billing markets appears to be the slowness of the bank consortia to get off the ground. It is always difficult to get different owners to agree on anything."

As the world's first electronic post office, *epost* is positioned to become a major player in the international area, thereby leveraging its "first mover" status. Peter Melanson, President and CEO of *epost*, observes that "postal administrations must act immediately to leverage their trusted brands and take advantage of new business opportunities that are emerging on the Internet." A Killen & Associates report concludes that *epost* is more advanced than any other postal authority in terms of exploiting these new opportunities. Not surprisingly, *epost* is negotiating with several international postal administrations to license *epost*'s technology and intellectual property. To effectively exploit both mail and non-mail opportunities with other national postal administrations, *epost* has created its *International Business and Technology Modules*, which offer the following:

- *Business Modeling Module.* The market research, reports, and analysis that help to build the business case for an *epost* service.

EXHIBIT 3

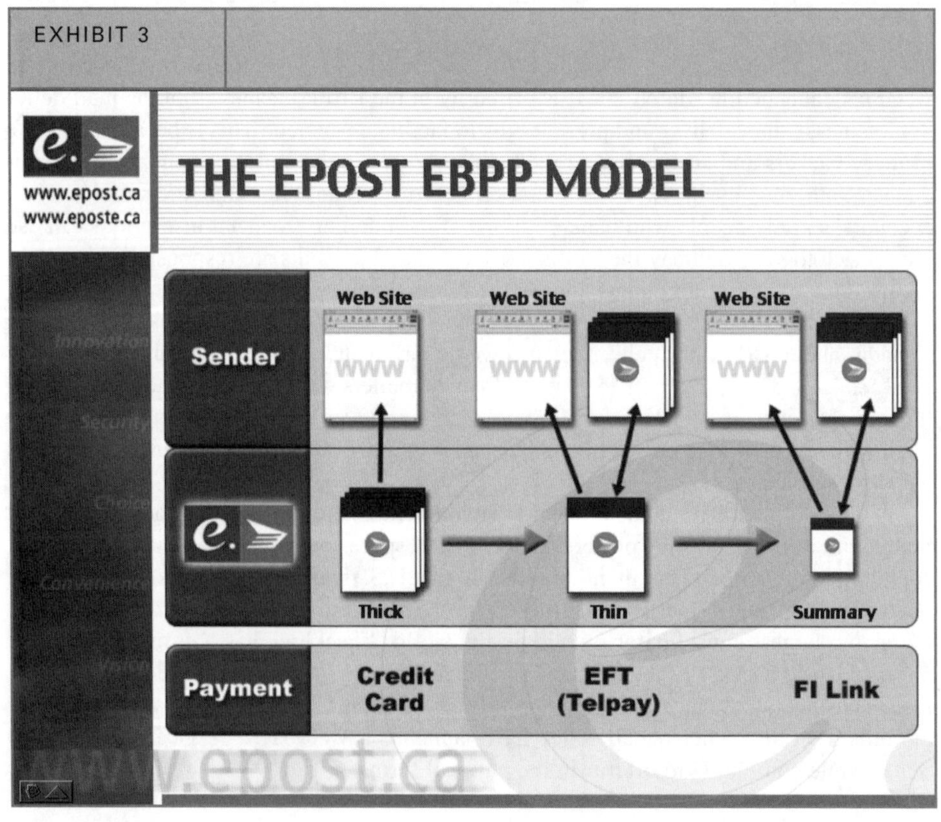

- *Electronic Delivery Management (EDM) Software Application Module.* Information about NETdelivery Corporation's EDM software that drives the *epost* solution, and the *epost* Electronic Postmark that authenticates all mail sent through the service.
- *Setup, Configuration, and Implementation Module.* Key learning and tools for planning, purchasing, and implementing decisions as they relate to infrastructure.
- *Sender Implementation and Client Care Services Module.* The solutions management, project management, technical analysis, and client care services and tools required to move mailers from the assessment phase through to postproduction implementation.
- *Sales, Marketing, and Product Management Strategies Modules.* The strategies and tools to increase the critical mass of mailers and maximize consumer adoption.
- *Human Resources, Organization, and Culture Module.* A proven understanding of the human capital, organization structure, and culture required to create *epost* service.
- epost express *Software Application Module.* The *epost express* application allows financial institutions to present *epost* documents directly at their online banking Web site—a critical element of the deployment strategy for *epost* services.

ACCOMPLISHMENTS TO DATE

Since launching in November 1999, *epost* has achieved a great deal, including the following:

- Launched world's first electronic post office
- Chosen as one of Canada's top 10 Internet companies
- TELUS invested $30 million for 5% interest in *epost*
- Selected for international licensing opportunity
- 150,000+ Canadians registered with *epost*
- 90+ Canadian companies commited to sending mail to *epost*; over 25 live, others in various stages of implementation
- Launched national marketing campaign with television, newspaper, radio, and online advertising

THE FUTURE

Although *epost* has pioneered the delivery of mail online and has become a dominant player in the Canadian marketplace, it faces several challenges as it tries to evolve and grow into a viable and profitable corporation. Some of the challenges *epost* must address include the following:

Consumer Perception and Adoption of EBPP

Says Avivah Litan, an analyst with Gartner Group Inc., "I don't think people view the postal service as a place to execute payments. It is the place to view mail, but not the place to manage accounts and execute payments." If this assessment is indeed widely shared among consumers, then *epost* may need to expand its consumer value proposition.

Researchers at Doculabs also found that "until the technology provides consumers significant value, adoption rates of electronic billing will remain disappointing." However, Canadians are early adopters of new technologies, and 70% of Canadians have access to the Internet.

Changing Technology

Researchers at Doculabs observed that a couple of years ago companies wishing to offer their customers EBPP "had very few viable options; however, today, there are dozens of products available with substantial functionality." Some of these products offer more than just bill payment capability; they include customer relationship management capabilities. It seems that technology providers are moving toward the concept of a totally integrated technology solution. These developments present significant challenges, because *epost* must continue to update its technology infrastructure—not only to stay ahead of the competition, but also to ensure that its technology is fully integrated with that of its mailers and consumers when they change or upgrade their technology. For example, *epost* must be able to deliver its services through a variety of wireless applications as more and more consumers adopt wireless technologies.

Market Maturity and Competition

Currently, *epost* and e-route are the two dominant players in Canada and there is no immediate threat from United States players; also, it seems that the battle is being fought in the business-to-consumer market. However, it is expected that over time the business-to-consumer EBPP market will grow and eventually attract more competitors. As the business-to-consumer market matures, the challenge for *epost* is to consolidate and grow its market share and move into other segments such as the business-to-business and international markets, which are currently underserved.

Growing Strategic Partnerships

As the markets, technology, and nature of competition continue to change at a rapid pace, *epost* will have to evolve its business model, particularly in the area of strategic partnerships, in order to respond effectively. Consequently, *epost* will have to develop the expertise, procedures, and policies to recruit and manage partners so as to maximize the value from each partnership.

Profitability

epost has adopted a revenue model that ensures that it generates revenues from its operations from the very beginning. Although *epost* is backed by three very financially strong corporations, it must become profitable in order to finance its growth and to continuously upgrade its technological infrastructure.

Are *epost*'s business model and strategies sustainable and capable of making it a viable entity in the long run? Is *epost* ready to take on the challenges and win?

part two overview

E-Business Models

The readings cases in this part provide a rigorous analysis of a variety of business models that have been used by Internet companies. Critical issues are examined surrounding the value creation potential of business models in the digital economy. Club, Inc. is a unique version of an online grocery model, in contrast to the traditional grocery business model. The case of WebHouse, with its unique "name-your-own-price" approach for groceries, illustrates how a novel bidding system operates, as customers bid for grocery items from a list of possible prices.

Another, equally captivating, example is found in MyCityMarket.com, whose customers within selected cities are provided the opportunity to shop on the Internet in a secure and convenient way. The underlying business model of this company reflects how to build a local marketplace with personalized service on the Web. Customers have the option of using the MyCityMarket site to window-shop or to purchase items online that can later be picked up in person. This feature set a new standard of integration, and created a novel model for business as a result.

The readings provide a thorough description of Internet business models based on conceptual considerations and empirical analysis. The meaning of "business model" is discussed and supported by several examples. The value creation potential of online business models and the factors that determine their likelihood of success are highlighted. Further, the impact on value creation of operating in a networked world, where everyone is connected, is discussed. Valuable practical insights are provided for how companies may effectively build business models and position themselves to compete in the digital economy.

case one

WebHouse Club, Inc.

Albert Fried

Merav Fried

Rainer Richter

Sebastian Ruta

David Saber

It was a cold, grey fall morning in New York. Jay Walker stared idly out the window of his limousine, barely seeing the city as it slid by. He was contemplating how he would tell his board of directors the bad news: WebHouse Club had again burned up all of its cash subsidizing consumer discounts while waiting for more manufacturers to partner with the service. With only $70 million left in its accounts, WebHouse would have to make a critical decision: shut down the service in an orderly fashion or seek more funding in a hostile market. If funds and partners didn't appear soon, they risked also bringing down their backer, Priceline.com. Either way, the ambitious young venture might soon be just another dot-com failure.

COMPANY BACKGROUND

Priceline.com was founded by Jay Walker in 1997 for the purpose of exploiting a unique consumer-oriented process innovation that had been developed in his earlier venture, Walker Digital, an intellectual property think tank. According to Priceline's demand collection system (DCS) business method, consumers log on to the company's

MBA candidates Albert Fried, Merav Fried, Rainer Richter, Sebastian Ruta, and David Saber prepared this case under the supervision of Professor Christopher L. Tucci.

Web site and name a price they would be willing to pay for a certain product. These offers are then conveyed to sellers, who decide whether or not they can meet the buyers' price. As the first company to develop and deploy a Web-based reverse auction, the company was able to obtain a patent on the method.

Priceline.com debuted its reverse auction process for purchases of leisure airline tickets in April 1998. The new arena for buying tickets online experienced tremendous growth in a short period of time: Priceline's Web site attracted more than one million visitors in its first week of operations.[1] Within the first 18 months of operations, Priceline.com expanded its product offering to include a travel service (offering airline tickets and hotel rooms), a personal finance service (offering home mortgages, refinancing and home equity loans), and an automotive rental service.[2] In 1999, groceries were added to the mix with the licensing of Priceline's reverse auction system to WebHouse Club, Inc.

THE TRADITIONAL GROCERY BUSINESS MODEL

In the traditional grocery value chain, product flows from the manufacturer either to a wholesale intermediary or to grocers directly, depending on the size of both the manufacturer and the grocer chain (see Figure A in Exhibit 1). Consumers purchase items directly from the grocery stores, which tend to be located in high-traffic areas, offering a wide variety of products. Delivery options vary, but they tend to be available after a consumer has made selections and purchased groceries in person. Grocers may promote certain items within their stores through couponing and in-store flyers. The manufacturer funds some of these promotions. Grocers usually also accept manufacturer's coupons, which they aggregate and are then reimbursed for. An overabundance of products vying for limited shelf space created an environment in which grocers could demand "slotting fees" from the product manufacturers—a legal kickback just to get a new product on the shelf or feature it more prominently.

THE ONLINE GROCERY INDUSTRY

While the U.S. market for food and related grocery products is large (approximately $460 billion), it grows at only 1 to 3% annually.[3] Few growth opportunities exist and competition is fierce. Although the market as a whole is expected to grow slowly, Jupiter Communications forecasts online grocery sales to rise from $0.2 billion in 1999 to $7.5 billion in 2003.[4]

Undisturbed by the fact that less than 1% of foods were delivered to the home by the late 1980s,[5] almost all online grocers base their business models on the central assumption that consumers have too little time for shopping, and that the convenience of home delivery constitutes a competitive advantage over storefront retailing. The observation was supported by some empirical evidence, such as a study in *American Demographics*, which found that over 60% of consumers dislike shopping for groceries.[6] In the late 1990s, online grocers, trying to exploit consumer dissatisfaction with the traditional retail offering, started recycling an idea popular in the pre-refrigerator and pre-supermarket era: home delivery of groceries. Figure B in Exhibit 1 shows the compression of the value chain used in most online grocery business models.

EXHIBIT 1 Grocery Business Models

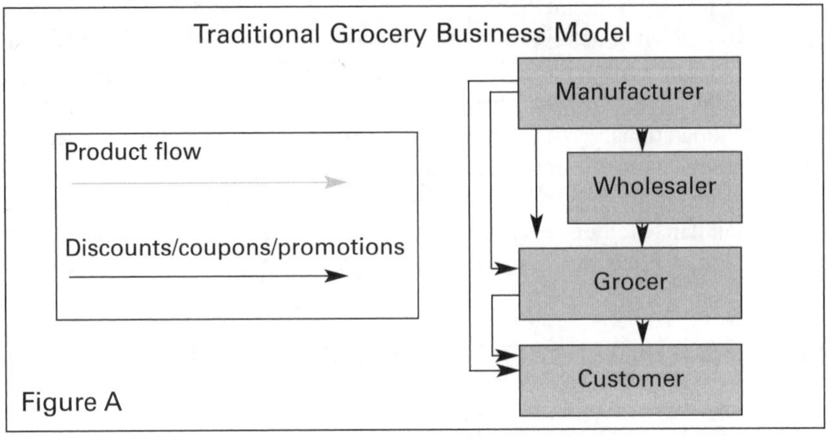

Traditional Grocery Business Model

Product flow

Discounts/coupons/promotions

Manufacturer

Wholesaler

Grocer

Customer

Figure A

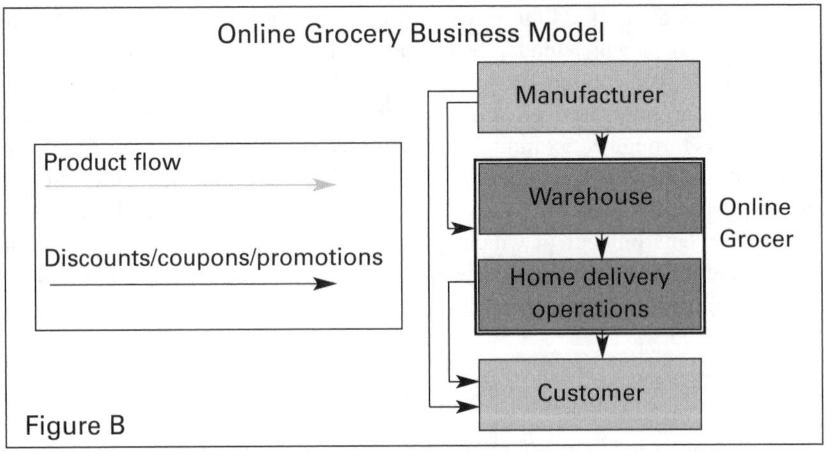

Online Grocery Business Model

Product flow

Discounts/coupons/promotions

Manufacturer

Warehouse

Home delivery operations

Online Grocer

Customer

Figure B

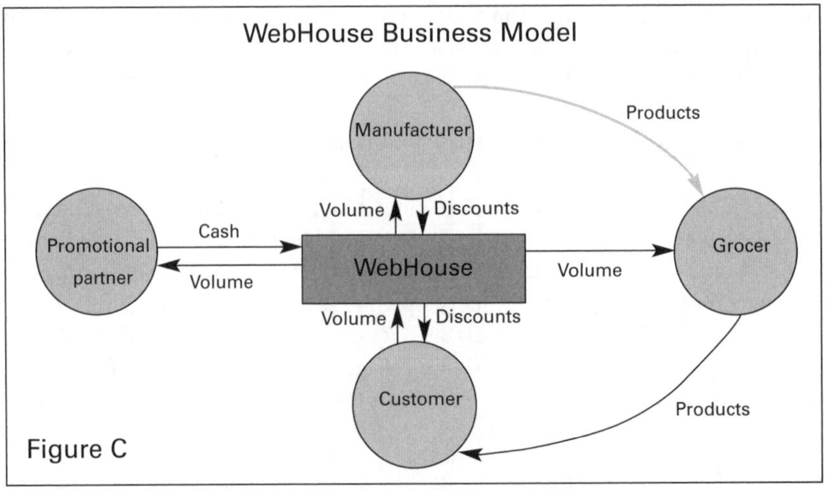

WebHouse Business Model

Manufacturer

Products

Promotional partner

Cash

Volume

Volume

Discounts

WebHouse

Volume

Grocer

Volume

Discounts

Customer

Products

Figure C

New ventures began to explore the potential of online grocery sales fairly early in the Internet's life cycle as a mass phenomenon. (See Exhibit 2.) The race was kicked off as early as 1989.

EXHIBIT 2 Comparison of Internet Grocers

	Peapod	Streamline	Netgrocer	Webvan[37]	WebHouse
Year Founded	1989	1993	1995	1999	1999
Locations Served	San Francisco, CT, DC, Chicago, MD, Boston, Long Island	Boston, New Jersey	Entire U.S.	San Francisco, Atlanta, Chicago, Portland, Seattle	NY, CT, CA
Membership Fee	Variable with location	$35–49/mo.	None	None	None for 90 days, $3/mo. thereafter
Delivery Fee	Variable with location: $4.95–$19.95	Included in membership fee	$5.99–$120	$4.95 for order under $75; otherwise none	None
Order Lead Time	1+ days	1 day	1–4 days	1 day	None
Delivery Window	120 minutes	1 day	1–4 days	30 minutes	N/A
Delivery Method	Unattended home delivery (select areas)	Unattended home delivery	FedEx	Attended home delivery	Customer pickup
Perishables	Yes	Yes	No	Yes	Yes
Public/Private	Public	Public	Private	Public	Private
Market Valuation	$37MM (11/00)	$3.5MM (11/00)	$136MM (3/00)[38]	$416MM (11/00)	$189MM (09/00)
Noteworthy Investors	Royal Ahold NV	Nordstrom	Parmalat	Louis Borders	Priceline.com
Number of SKUs	15 000	10 000+	9500	50 000	600
Number of Customers	90 000	Not available	Not available	520 000	1 500 000
Average Order Size	$117	$108	Not available	$90	Not available
Revenues	'99: $73MM	'99: $17.3MM	Not available	'00: $276 MM	Not available

Sources: Donaldson, Lufkin & Jenrette, Gomez Advisors, company reports, and Web sites and estimates.

Peapod was founded that year with the goal "to be the world's leading and preferred provider of interactive grocery shopping services."[7] Initially via telephone and fax, and later through custom software and their Web site, Peapod allowed consumers to place orders for home delivery of dry and fresh goods from local affiliated supermarkets, where items were hand-picked by Peapod employees. Peapod later moved to the more common warehouse distribution model and as of Fall 2000, was building out its own infrastructure.[8]

By the mid-1990s the World Wide Web had exploded, and the Internet grocery supply market began to attract other players.

Netgrocer, founded in 1995, ships dry packaged goods to consumers all across the United States via Federal Express. Unlike its competitors, it does not offer fresh meat or produce. Billed as a way to reduce the frequency and duration of trips to the supermarket and drugstore, Netgrocer offers subscription services to satisfy the "household replenishment" need.[9]

Streamline entered the fray in 1996, targeting the busy suburban family in the Boston and northern New Jersey areas (it had been founded in 1993 but only in a development phase). The company provides regular customers with a custom refrigerator and keypad entry system for their garages to enable regular unattended deliveries of fresh and dry goods. It also offers such value-added services as dry cleaning, UPS package shipping, film processing, and bottle redemption.[10]

Webvan used its deep pockets to commit to spending nearly $1 billion on a nationwide network of highly automated distribution centres. The company, founded by Louis Borders of Borders Books & Music fame, believes this infrastructure will reduce handling of product by as much as 50% and allow it to realize a greater net margin than its traditional retail grocery outlet brethren. By offering consumers a huge selection of foodstuffs and merchandise, delivered from custom vans within a half-hour window, Webvan appeals to the consumer with limited free time.[11]

As a group, online grocers enjoy certain cost advantages over traditional retailers. For instance, they do not require expensive real estate in desirable retail districts, have lower inventory levels, suffer less from spoilage, and require no sales and in-store stocking personnel.[12] On the other hand, home delivery is expensive and the costs are often borne almost entirely by the online grocer with some portion of the cost being passed on to convenience-loving consumers. Donaldson, Lufkin & Jenrette estimates total delivery cost for an average Webvan order of approximately $100 at $8.55.[13] Additional logistical complications exist; for instance, delivery is problematic when customers are not at home and storage of delivered goods in apartment buildings is a significant issue.

In 1999 and 2000, when a number of Web grocers moved into the spotlight, the capital markets fully agreed with their business rationale and online grocers became the "glamour category of the Web."[14] For example, Webvan's last financing round in July 2000 valued the firm at a staggering $4 billion.[15] Streamline went public the same month.

ENTER WEBHOUSE

On September 21, 1999, Priceline announced that WebHouse Club, Inc., a separate, closely held company, had licensed its reverse auction process and was planning to offer a "name your own price for groceries" service for consumers in New York, New Jersey, and Connecticut,[16] through Priceline.com. Priceline.com owned $189 million in warrants to

WebHouse Club's stock,[17] effectively controlling the new venture. By keeping it independent, Priceline.com did not have to assume the risk of adding the startup's potential losses to its own income statement.

The service launched on November 1, and consumers got their first chance to haggle over the prices of groceries—such as soda, frozen vegetables, and toilet paper—sold in neighbourhood supermarkets. First-round financing yielded $69 million from Goldman Sachs, Wit Capital, and Vulcan Ventures. In WebHouse's first week of operations, 15 000 consumers logged on to Priceline's Web site to check out the new service.[18]

Unlike other online grocery players, WebHouse had access to Priceline's patented reverse auction (DCS) method, the associated software solution, and Priceline's brand name, thanks to a licensing agreement. It was the first external party to obtain access to the proprietary business methods. WebHouse also paid Priceline royalties on each customer purchase. In order to create brand-awareness and attract customers to its site, WebHouse spent $25 million dollars on an advertising campaign featuring *Star Trek* actor William Shatner.[19]

LET'S GO SHOPPING

How does the WebHouse "name your own price for groceries" system work from the consumer's point of view? The following is a list of actions that a customer takes to use the system:

1. Obtain electronic WebHouse debit card from participating supermarkets or from newspaper ad inserts.
2. Log on to Priceline.com.
3. Click through to WebHouse.
4. Choose product category (e.g., Beverages), select subcategory (e.g., Sodas), identify two or more acceptable national brands from options within that category (e.g., Coca Cola, Pepsi Cola, and/or RC Cola) and quantity (e.g., 2 ×12-packs, any variety).
5. Select bid from a list of possible prices. Next to each price, the probability of each bid being accepted is presented. For example, if bidding on a 12-pack of soda, select from the following options: bid $2.29 with a 95% likelihood of being accepted, $1.99 with 80% likelihood, $1.72 with a 66% likelihood or $1.47 with a 50% likelihood.
6. Continue shopping until desired basket of goods is created.
7. Check out. Either enter previously registered username and password information, or create a user account.
8. If selected bid prices are accepted (processing may take up to one minute), the credit card on file is immediately charged for those items purchased.
9. Print out shopping list.
10. Pick up order at any participating supermarket within 90 days. At supermarket, pay for goods with electronic WebHouse debit card. Shoppers must separate non-WebHouse groceries from those on list and pay for them separately. Each WebHouse debit card is equipped with unique number and magnetic strip to identify WebHouse purchases.[20]

WEBHOUSE BUSINESS MODEL

While most Web grocers ask their customers to trade cost for convenience, Jay Walker developed a different business model. Translating the name-your-own-price technology to the online grocery, WebHouse customers trade convenience for discounts (see Figure C in Exhibit 1).

The model was designed to work as described above. First, the customer uses the Priceline.com Web site to bid on a basket of goods. The DCS algorithm searches for a match between the customer's bid and reduced price offers that manufacturers have submitted. If the system finds a match, the order is accepted and is charged immediately on his/her credit card (step 1 in Exhibit 3). Simultaneously, manufacturers grant WebHouse discounts for attracting new customers.

Next, the customer picks up the groceries at a participating local grocer and pays grocer full shelf price with WebHouse debit card (step 2 in Exhibit 3). Additional funds come from third-party promotional partners when customers purchase services, such as magazine subscriptions or long-distance phone service. WebHouse pockets the difference between these inflows and the discount offered to customer (step 3 in Exhibit 3).

GRAND OPENING

When WebHouse launched, the site offered 140 grocery items and worked with 600 supermarkets including A&P, Waldbaum's, Gristede's, and D'Agostino. The company's goal was to expand nationally and create a network of over 25 000 stores extending its retail reach into drugstores, toy stores, and gasoline stations.[21]

With its name-your-own-price approach to the online grocery market, WebHouse was clearly differentiated from the competition. For the first time, customers could bargain with manufacturers of Skippy, Uncle Ben's, and the like, pressing them to offer ongoing discounts on their products. WebHouse also aimed to benefit the manufacturers: initially, some big brand names believed that by joining WebHouse, they could get customers that would otherwise choose other brands to try their products because of the reduced prices.

"We wanted to gain as much market share as possible," says a spokesman for a large packaged-goods company that signed on. Companies that partnered initially included Nestlé, Heinz, Kellogg, and Hershey.[22] Other manufacturers weren't quite so sure of the benefits:

> Frankly, we don't understand how this system could ever make sense for manufacturers like us, or for our retail partners. For manufacturers, Priceline essentially amounts to a permanent promotion. ... Simply put, Priceline's approach will inevitably lower margins for both manufacturers and retailers.
>
> —Steve Reinemund, President, PepsiCo[23]

Moreover, some manufacturers were concerned with destroying the brand equity of their products. To this point, Jay Walker countered:

> When [a shopper comes] to Priceline, you can't be loyal to one brand. Loyal Tide customers can't shop with us, because you have to be willing to be flexible among a set of brands. So we get a lot of shoppers, but you want to know what we don't get? We don't get a lot of loyal shoppers. ... We can only give you non-loyal consumers. Do you want some of those? ... So as to the complaint that we're antibrand, it's absurd. It's not what we're about.[24]

EXHIBIT 3 WebHouse Club Business Model

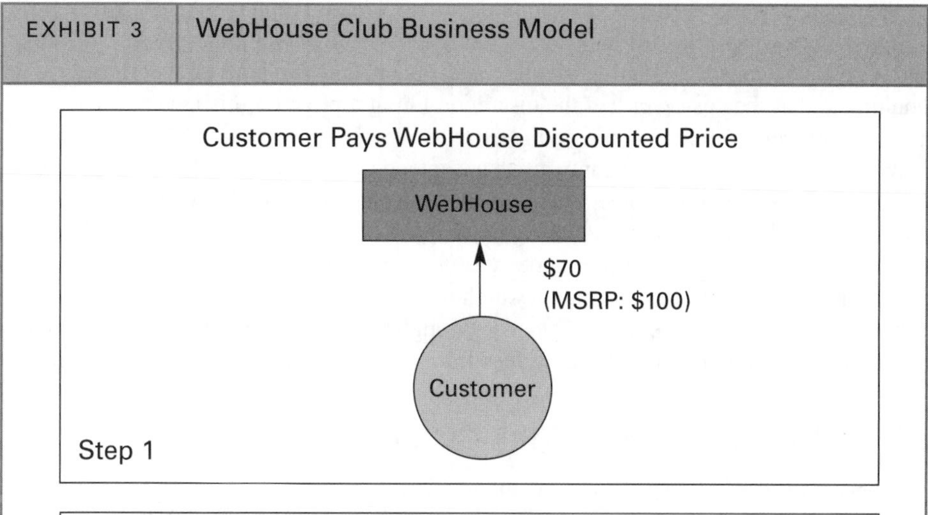

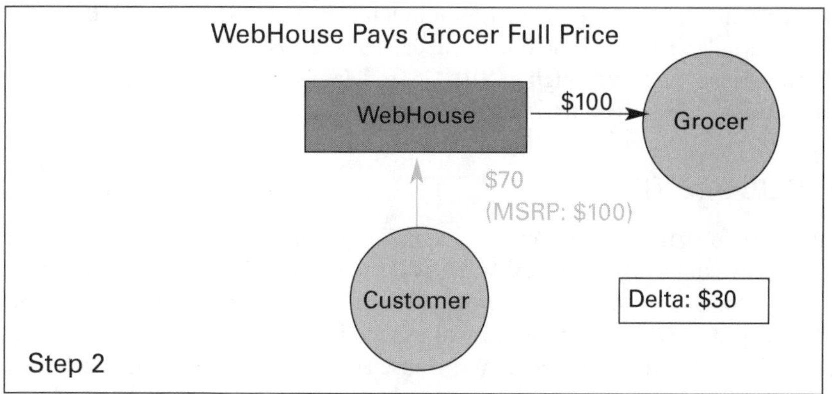

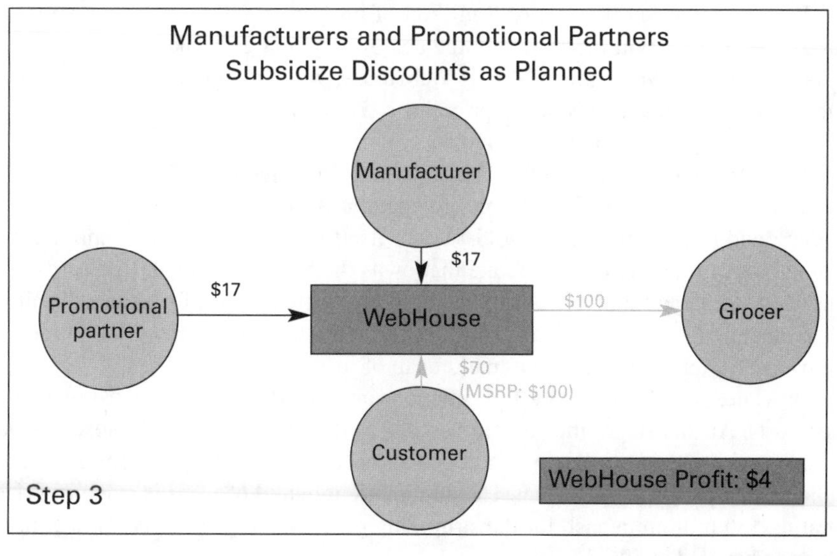

While other Web-based grocery shopping services were available, WebHouse was the only service in which the customer was responsible for the pickup of the order. Although this is an inconvenience to the customer (and thus a disadvantage to WebHouse), one should note that the customer had the discretion to put a price on this inconvenience and bid on the groceries after discounting the extra hassle of the pickup.[25]

WebHouse aimed to gain a competitive advantage over more typical Internet retailers, who delivered orders to customers, with a cost-savvy business model that eliminated the cost of buying delivery trucks and hiring personnel to pack and deliver orders.[26] In addition, since the company used supermarkets as its distributor, WebHouse also did not have to invest heavily in building distribution warehouses, as did other e-tailers such as Webvan. WebHouse expected to generate its revenues through transaction fees of 5 to 10% from the manufacturers and $3 monthly handing fees from its active customers.[27]

IF YOU BUILD IT, THEY WILL COME

The concept took off. By April 2000, six months after launching, WebHouse had signed up 500 000 customers,[28] which grew to 1.5 million members by September 2000—when the company was still signing up 100 000 members a week.[29] By March 2000, Priceline.com's stock price rose to a 52-week high of $104.25, reflecting to a large extent consumer adoption of WebHouse. However, troubled times were on the way.

THE BUBBLE BURSTS

An unfavourable market forced Netgrocer to pull its planned IPO in the spring of 2000 and it subsequently sold a 30% stake to Parmalat Finanziaria SpA, one of the world's leading international food companies. This increased Parmalat's distribution in North America and provided Netgrocer with the opportunity to expand into Europe and Latin America.[30]

Undaunted by market conditions, WebHouse added gasoline to its offerings in July of 2000. Investors were unconvinced, and drove the stock price down to $23.63. Hurting for cash, Walker announced the sale of 8 million of his personal Priceline shares in August. He used the $125 million income from the deal to buy a larger stake in WebHouse Club, Inc. As a result, he owned about 12% of WebHouse, while his majority stake in Priceline fell to 33%.[31] Priceline.com's stock price hit a 52-week low of $22.63. Priceline.com's stock price history is presented in Exhibit 5.

Other competitors also faced troubled times. In September 2000, Peapod bought Streamline's Washington, D.C. and Chicago operations for $12 million and the assumption of leases[32] and in the same month sold 51% of itself to Royal Ahold NV, an international consumer goods retailing conglomerate that owns the Stop & Shop and Edwards grocery chains.[33] In the same month, Webvan acquired Homegrocer.com for nearly $1 billion in stock, extending its geographic reach to the Pacific Northwest. By late 2000, its stock was down over 90% for the year, with a market cap of just over $400 million.[34]

Meanwhile, WebHouse cut 40 full-time jobs and 100 contract positions in an effort to reduce costs. At this stage, the service had 1.5 million members, with close to 100 000 members joining weekly.[35] Again, Walker announced his intent to sell more of his stake in Priceline to keep WebHouse afloat. He sold an additional 3.6% of his stake in Priceline, generating $50 million in cash for the struggling grocery and gas outfit.[36] Priceline.com's stock price hovered at $26.50.

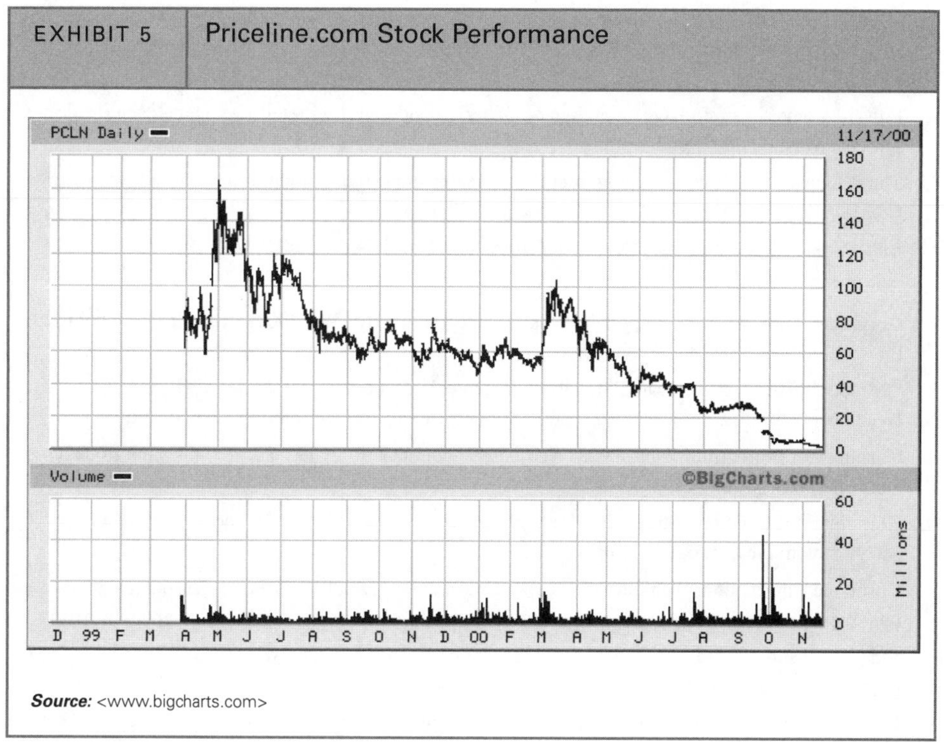

EXHIBIT 5 Priceline.com Stock Performance

Source: <www.bigcharts.com>

YOU'RE HERE, SIR

With diminishing reserves, no positive cash flow to support continued consumer discount subsidies, and declining hope that manufacturers would absorb the full costs of discounts, Walker's choices were limited. By the time his black stretch limousine eased to a stop, he had formulated a short list of strategic options:

- The company could try to initiate a third round of new financing, or he could personally sell more of his Priceline stock and use the cash to further invest in the company, buying more time.
- The company could change its business model in order to make it more attractive to manufacturers. But how, he wondered?
- Perhaps the grocery store partners would be willing to underwrite part of the discounts.

Or—he shuddered at the thought—they could close down operations.

NOTES

1. "Newcomer Priceline.com attracts more than one million visitors its first week," press release, April 15, 1998, accessed July 29, 2001 <www.corporate-ir.net/ireye/ir_site.zhtml?ticker=pcln&script=410&layout=-6&item_id=23933>.

2. "Budget Rent-a-Car to join Priceline.com network," press release, September 27, 1999, accessed July 29, 2001 <www.corporate-ir.net/ireye/ir_site.zhtml?ticker=pcln&script=410&layout=-6&item_id=53374>.
3. Edward Comeau, Jamie Kiggen, and Gary Balter, "Food and drug retailing," Donaldson, Lufkin & Jenrette, May 27, 2000, p. 2.
4. Marc Johnson, "Online shopping report: strategies for driving long-term profitability," *Jupiter Communications Online Intelligence*, January 2000, p. 39.
5. Barry Stouffer, "Peapod, Inc.," J.C. Bradford & Co., November 24, 1999, p. 4.
6. See note 5.
7. Corporate Information, Peapod Web site, accessed July 29, 2001 <www.peapod.com/fcgi-bin/fetch.fcg?msgid=1999>.
8. "Peapod opens first dedicated distribution center," corporate press release, Peapod Web site, December 3, 1998, accessed July 29, 2001 <www.peapod.com/fcgi-bin/fetch.fcg?msgid=5112>.
9. Corporate Information, Netgrocer Web site, accessed July 29, 2001 <www.netgrocer.com/CorpInfo/press/32100.cfm>.
10. Corporate Information, Streamline Web site, accessed June 26, 2001 [no longer in existence] <www.streamline.com/current/works.asp>.
11. Corporate Information, WebVan Web site, accessed June 26, 2001 [on July 9, 2001 Webvan ceased operations] <www000103.webvan.com/Marketing/zGlobal/Help/Aboutwebvan/companyinfo.asp>.
12. Sid Huff and David Beckow, "Homegrocer.com: a case study," *Ivey Business Journal*, 64(5)(May/June 2000): 90.
13. Edward Comeau, Jamie Kiggen and Gary Balter, "Food and drug retailing," Donaldson, Lufkin & Jenrette, p. 11.
14. "Online shopping report: strategies for driving long-term profitability," Jupiter Communications, January 2000, p. 55.
15. Drew Ianni, "Can Webvan save online grocery shopping?" Jupiter Communications, October 18, 1999, p. 1.
16. Anne Pollak, "WebHouse brings haggling to the supermarket," *Bloomberg News*, September 21, 1999. Available online, accessed August 19, 2001 <www.igec.umbc.edu/ectech/web/News/Sep_1999/index.shtml>.
17. Stephanie Stoughton, "Priceline dropping gasoline, groceries licensee's collapse ends part of Web site's name-a-price service," *Boston Globe*, October 6, 2000, p. C1.
18. Julia Angwin and Nick Wingfield, "Discounted out: how Jay Walker built WebHouse on a theory he couldn't prove," *Wall Street Journal*, October 16, 2000, p. A-1.
19. See note 16.
20. Nick Wingfield, "Online: new battle for Priceline is diapers, tuna," *Wall Street Journal*, September 22, 1999, p. B-1.
21. See note 16.
22. See note 20.
23. See note 20.
24. Al Urbanski, "In the chat room with Priceline's Jay Walker," *Supermarket Business*, vol. 55, no. 6 (June 15, 2000), p. 60.
25. Jay Walker, Priceline.com's vice-chairman, and Walker Digital's chairman in an interview with Anne Pollak from *Bloomberg News*, September 21, 1999.

26. See note 16.

27. See note 20.

28. Clay Shirky, "Haggling goes high-tech," *Wall Street Journal*, April 10, 2000, p. 1.

29. Associated Press, "Priceline.com's WebHouse Club is planning layoffs," *New York Times*, September 16, 2000, p. C-3.

30. "NetGrocer.Com signs memorandum of understanding with Parmalat SpA for $30 million in equity financing," press release, March 21, 2000, accessed July 29, 2001 <www.netgrocer.com/CorpInfo/press/32100.cfm>.

31. Julia Angwin, "Priceline.com founder plans to sell eight million shares to pair of investors," *Wall Street Journal*, August 2, 2000, p. B-6.

32. "Peapod acquires Streamline.com, Inc.'s operations in two key markets," press release, September 7, 2000, accessed July 29, 2001 <www.peapod.com/fcgi-bin/fetch.fcg?msgid=6023>.

33. "Ahold forms partnership with US Internet grocer Peapod," press release, April 14, 2000, accessed July 29, 2001 <www.peapod.com/fcgi-bin/fetch.fcg?msgid=5718>.

34. "Webvan completes merger with HomeGrocer.com," press release, September 5, 2000, *Business Wire* Web site, accessed July 29, 2001 <www.businesswire.com/webbox/bw.090500/202490777.htm>.

35. See note 29.

36. Julia Angwin, "Priceline.com founder will sell shares to Saudi prince, use cash for a startup," *Wall Street Journal*, September 12, 2000, p. B-6.

37. "Webvan Group, Inc.," Salomon Smith Barney Access, October 19, 2000 <www.salomonsmithbarney.com>.

38. Associated Press, "Netgrocer.com selling 22% stake to Parmalat," *New York Times*, March 21, 2000, p. C-4.

case two

MyCityMarket.com: Surviving on the Edge

Ajax Persaud, School of Management, University of Ottawa

Jasbir Dhaliwal, Norwegian School of Management

MyCityMarket.com (MCM) is the brainchild of 31-year-old president and founder, Sodi Hundal, a former director of retail for a technology company, and a trained certified general accountant. Sodi came up with the idea of taking high-quality products provided by local retailers and making them available online to local residents within major Canadian and American cities and their surrounding communities. MCM is the fruition of this idea. Consumers visiting the MCM Web site can browse the various product offerings provided by local merchants and make purchases with the click of a mouse. The company offers convenience, quality service, speed, and security at a reasonable cost. Products can be delivered to customers' doors within hours or a couple of days, as opposed to weeks. Also, customers can use the Web site to pre-shop or place an order with any retailer, which they can later pick up in person from the local bricks-and-mortar stores. For local merchants, this is another opportunity to sell their products through a more powerful channel, the Internet, which is dubbed the wave of the future in shopping. Local merchants could get a presence on the Internet at very competitive rates—something many felt was virtually impossible at that time.

This case was prepared with the assistance of Sodi Hundal, for purposes of classroom discussion rather than to illustrate either effective or ineffective handling of a business or administrative situation.

MCM's initial focus was to provide consumers within selected cities and their surrounding communities (e.g., Vancouver, Toronto, Calgary, Seattle, and Washington) with the opportunity to shop over the Internet from well-known local merchants in a convenient and secure manner. As the name suggests, MCM's primary goal was to build local marketplaces on the Internet and to provide personalized services to consumers. The personalization features offered by MCM were leading-edge at the time the Web site went live in 1999. It provided local merchants with cost-effective Internet access, and the marketing support needed to generate online sales. The company was the recipient of the Marshall McLuhan award as the "Best B2B [business-to-business] Website" in the first annual eWorld Awards ceremony on October 25, 2000.

MCM is a privately owned Vancouver-based company. Its founder, Sodi Hundal, has acknowledged that he "knew little about the Internet, [but] had prior experience as an entrepreneur" before starting this company. The genesis of MCM is attributed to his early realization that the Internet is a new technology with tremendous potential to change, in a very profound way, how we live and shop. This realization, combined with his own frustrations of trying to shop on the Internet, drove him to action. According to Sodi, "I was basically frustrated by the shipping charges, the duty, the delays, and the inconvenience of the whole experience." He started to think about the local retailers within Vancouver and asked himself, "Why I am buying something from the Internet at the other end of the country when I know what I'm looking for is available down the street?" His motivations for buying online had more to do with convenience than anything else. He thought, "There has to be a way to set up such an operation, but what would be the mechanism?" Before long, he began to draft his thoughts on paper. The result was MCM.

THE CONCEPT

The concept behind MCM was simple, but innovative. The goals were to aggregate well-known, established local retail merchants in all product categories into a virtual marketplace; then, local residents within the city and its immediate surroundings could shop online from these merchants, at their own convenience. Additionally, customers were given the option to use the MCM Web site to window-shop or to purchase an item online, which they could later pick up in person at the local store where the item was kept. This feature, the seamless integration of clicks-and-bricks operations, was previously unheard of in the industry (late 1998–early 2000). According to Sodi, "The general thinking at the time was that shopping online would replace bricks-and-mortar operations, and pure Internet plays were the wave of the future. So most online businesses were established as pure Internet plays, separate from the physical side of the business. Hindsight exposed the fallacy of this thinking and justified my hunch. I believed that we could offer our local retail merchants great value by fully integrating their physical stores with their online operations into a seamless brick-and-click business."

Exhibit 1 shows the relationship between the local retail merchants, MCM, and consumers. In this model, the local retail merchants' individual physical stores would be the "warehouse" for all the items advertised on the MCM Web site. The local merchants would provide MCM with a list of all the products they were offering, along with pricing and other information such as special offers, discounts, and limits. This information is then uploaded to the MCM Web site. Consumers could view and purchase the items they required through the Web site. All transaction processing is done by MCM. Order information obtained from consumers through the Web site is immediately forwarded via email to the respective merchants, who then process the orders. MCM has an exclusive arrangement with Canada Post Corporation, who provides the merchants with shipping at very competitive rates. The merchants receive a monthly statement of all transactions executed through the Web site, along with a check covering the sales, after deducting fees and commissions.

MCM makes use of the latest Microsoft technology to enable merchants to gather valuable marketing information from the activity on their Web pages for use in future marketing campaigns and to monitor sales trends. All transactions done on the Web site are secured using the Verisign system to ensure that credit card numbers are kept safe. All sales are preapproved by an external credit card processing service and processed through Royal Bank of Canada. A key technical feature of the site is customers' ability to make purchases from different merchants with only one sales transaction—similarly to shopping at a department store. As of June 2001, delivery of purchased items is done by courier, but an internal delivery system may be set up as volumes grow.

VALUE PROPOSITION

MCM provides local retail merchants with cost-effective turnkey solutions including Web site development and maintenance, hosting, content development, transaction processing, marketing, and offline education on Internet strategies, usage, and developments. While the Web site is the primary locus for these activities, MCM also collaborates with traffic aggregators and shipping portals, and incorporates traditional advertising and marketing techniques such as in-store point-of-purchase, direct mail, and mainstream media. MCM provides all the technology to ensure that local merchants' operations are fully integrated with the Web site, and to facilitate a convenient and pleasant shopping experience for

EXHIBIT 1 MyCityMarket as an Aggregator

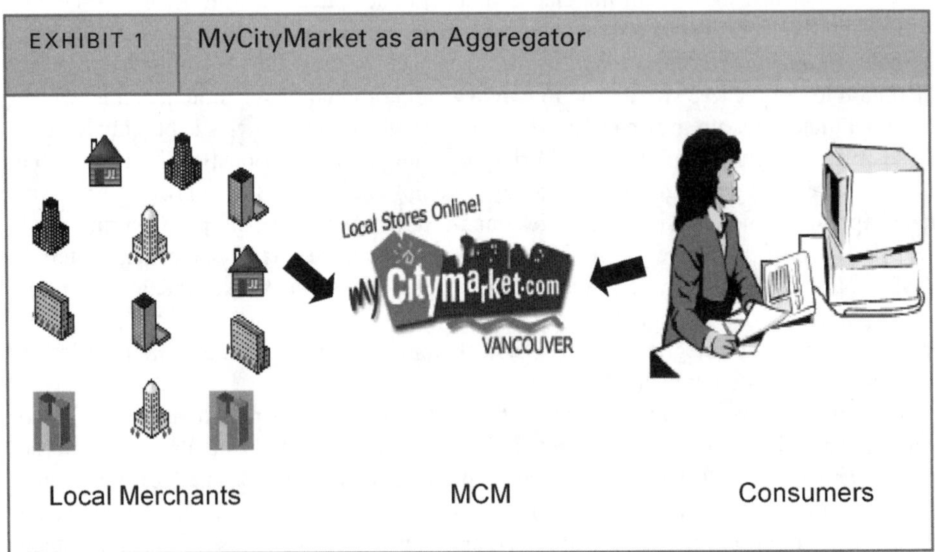

consumers. Ongoing maintenance of the technology, the Web site, and all accompanying databases are undertaken by MCM.

The company also provides the training the merchants require to understand, interact with, and use the site effectively with minimum frustration. Monthly seminars are sponsored by the company for all its retail clients, providing merchants with the opportunity to meet and discuss their experiences with other merchants, network with each other, get information about MCM's new products and services, discuss problems, and get general information about the state of online shopping on the Internet. The offline training, education, and discussion sessions "are highly valued by [MCM's] merchants, since many of them know very little about the Internet and the associated technologies required for establishing a successful online business," says Sodi.

As an aggregator, MCM provides its merchants with greater online exposure and lower transaction costs than if the merchants were to establish their own online stores, credit card fraud detection, cooperative marketing and advertising, customized consulting, Marketbucks Loyalty program, and exclusive shipping arrangements with Canada Post Corporation. The company provides merchants with the means to the market, and sells their products on the Internet with other merchants without conflicting product lines and danger of direct competition. Part of the exclusivity package that MCM provides merchants with is the tailoring of its e-commerce programs. For instance, the MCM Premium Program is an e-commerce solution for small and medium-sized businesses, and sells up to 1000 products. This package provides these merchants with a comprehensive Internet presence and thorough marketing and technical support. MCM generates awareness via portals/online ads, TV/radio, print ads, cross-channel marketing, directing mail, email, special events, and special incentives.

For local retail merchants, many of whom have less than ten employees, MCM's offer of an inexpensive and convenient way to establish an online store very quickly is unique. Several of the company's early clients admitted that although they were skeptical about the benefits of local e-commerce to their particular businesses, and they were not likely to have established a Web site on their own, they enlisted with MCM because they felt it was a unique, low-cost opportunity to learn more about this new technology and to experiment with it. Others who did not subscribe to the service felt that the Internet was just another passing fad. According to a 1999 study of Internet retailing by Ernst & Young, a large number of companies became increasingly concerned about the growing threat of e-tailers. They wanted to jump into the growing e-commerce market, but lacked the resources or the expertise to establish a presence for themselves on the Internet with secure capabilities.

PRODUCTS AND SERVICES

MCM makes it possible for consumers to shop online with confidence at the stores of well-known hometown merchants, as well as check on community activities and local discussions. The Web site provides consumers with a wide range of products at very competitive price points. MCM has over 500 different merchant subcategories, with plans to enlist merchants in each category, thereby offering the greatest range of goods over the Internet. While there are product overlaps, the marketing of each merchant is fairly specialized.

The Web site also has community features to attract consumers. The fast-growing community section features information on local arts, leisure, and special-interest organizations. As each organization is added, new potential customers are brought to the site. Discussion groups are another entertaining feature of the site that provide participants with a forum for many topics, including purchasing on the Web and community activities. There are also joint promotions by merchants for occasions such as Valentine's Day, in which lingerie, flowers, and chocolates can be conveniently offered to consumers at a special price. MCM "bucks," earned from making purchases on the site, are honoured by all of the merchants.

Although the company is still small and has not yet launched a full-blown marketing campaign, it has already registered over one million hits since going live in September 1999.

REVENUE MODEL

Merchants pay a setup fee prorated by the number of products and features that they want to present on their sites. In addition, MCM collects a commission on the merchandise sold on the site. Its revenue projections are based on an estimate that each of its subscribing retail merchants will have the equivalent of 1% of their existing physical store sales through the MCM Web site. An underlying assumption of MCM's business activities is based on data that indicates that 80% of the average person's Web expenditures are done at the local level (Estats, *EMarketer*, April 1999). Forecasts project that by the end of 2002, North American business-to-consumer e-commerce is expected to reach sales figures in the range of US$100 billion (*Business 2.0* magazine). MCM hopes to capitalize on this trend by taking advantage of the trust that consumers already have in local merchants and suppliers in generating e-commerce activity on its Web site. The objective of MCM is to become a significant player by providing local consumers with a network of established and widely known local businesses from which they can shop.

TARGET MARKET AND COMPETITORS

MCM targets established, well-known, local retail merchants in major Canadian and U.S. cities. Initially, three cities were targeted—Vancouver and Toronto in Canada, and Seattle in the United States—with a goal to target 60 major cities in Canada and the United States over the next five years. There are no restrictions as to the type of retailers or products, since MCM has the capability to offer over 500 subcategories of merchandise through its Web site in each city or region. A key requirement for becoming an MCM subscriber is that the local retail merchant must perceive a benefit from being on the Internet very quickly and cost-effectively. MCM's training and education program is also a key feature that current merchants can use to help them improve their knowledge and experience with the Internet in general, and online shopping in particular.

MCM's business model clearly places it in the business-to-consumer marketspace. The wide variety of merchants and merchandise being targeted also put it in a position to compete with almost all business-to-consumer Internet companies, within both Canada and the United States. This means that MCM must compete with Amazon.com, e-Bay, Toys Я Us.com, Chapters.ca, and others.

GETTING OFF THE GROUND

MCM started in January 1999 when Sodi Hundal prepared an Excel spreadsheet of the business plan and an outline of the Web site, and started talking about the concept to a few people that he knew in the technology business. He shared his idea with an old acquaintance, Rob Stocks, a software developer, who got very excited and soon became involved with the project. After this, Sodi discussed the concept with about forty retailers within the city of Vancouver, of which five confirmed their interest by providing the cash for the setup fee. Now, with five local retailers, Rob, and his personal money, Sodi began to build the company. As an accountant, he calculated that "the project would need about $3 million quickly just to get it off the ground." By this time, he had already quit his job and invested a substantial part of his savings into the venture. Working out of his home alone with encouragement from his family, he began his crusade to sell the concept to retailers, investors, and "anyone [he] could approach." With a half-grin on his face, he recounted, "I got a lot of advice, my network grew quickly, very quickly, but I wasn't getting the one thing I needed most—cash."

Undaunted, he continued to try to convince everyone he knew to invest in the venture. Sodi recalled creating a form that basically said, "The money you are giving me, don't ever expect to get it back because I don't know if this thing is going to work; it sounds interesting, and here is the business plan." Including his personal funds and those from family and friends, he managed to raise about $200 000 by June 1999. The investors were told that they would get their money back either when the business was sold or went public.

Rob Stocks started to build the Web site and the technology system that was needed to facilitate convenient online shopping, for both consumers and retail merchants. With limited finances and the need for more people to build the venture, Sodi contacted a former colleague, Gordon Heard, to get him involved in the venture. Gordon was the CFO of the company that he worked for and was recruited to help raise money. In addition, they needed someone to teach the local retail merchants how to use the Web site and the system. Fortunately, Sodi's brother, Jag Hundal, joined the venture, taking on the responsibility of teaching clients how to use the system and manage their day-to-day needs while Sodi was out on the road trying to recruit more local merchants and find other investors. The objective was to raise the C$3 million needed by October 2000 at the latest. To save on costs, Rob, Gordon, Sodi, and Jag all worked from their own homes and communicated primarily by email, telephone, and fax. Face-to-face meetings were kept to a minimum. Up until September 1999, none of them received a salary for their services and they were living on their own means. In October 1999, they began using the $200 000 to cover only their basic expenses. In September 1999, the MCM Web site was officially launched with five local merchants.

Realizing that they needed at least $3 million, Sodi and Gordon began meeting with venture capitalists "with very little success." In October 1999, two interested investors offered to operate MCM as a capital pool company (CPC), but after doing the due diligence on these investors, MCM management declined their offers. Reflecting on this experience, Sodi recounted that "Up to this point, I never knew what a CPC was, never raised money before, never did this kind of stuff before. We began to learn more about this process very quickly; in this business you grow up very quickly."

The next stop, in November 1999 was Spartacus Capital. Learning from their limited experiences, MCM management sought and got a financial commitment upfront from

Spartacus Capital. MCM's due diligence on Spartacus Capital revealed that they had very reputable people, the references were very positive, and they had a few Internet deals that were successful. However, the pace at which the negotiations were moving was very slow and they "had to have patience because everything took four times longer than anticipated."

THE STOCK MARKET

This delay did not bode well for MCM because it was around November 1999 when the stock market was having its first correction—the first downturn. They were thinking "Oh my God, what an awful time to lose your money." Fortunately, the market bounced back very quickly and by January 2000 the markets were "on fire again and I [Sodi] knew this was not going to last." Unfortunately, even at this time, MCM was not having any luck raising money for the business. Out of desperation, Sodi says he "sold a bunch of my own personal investments and put a substantial portion of the proceeds into the business. I got a good deal in the market. When the market crashed, the whole thing fell apart, so whatever chance we had to raise money went through the door, and at that point we began to slash our staff, cut costs, and try to survive. With very limited sales generating a bit of revenue and cash flow, we cut back our staff, down from a high of 13 people to 3. We limped along from March 2000 through to November 2000, with a few loans and some cash guarantees from Spartacus Capital."

By March 2000 they had over 20 local retailers subscribing to the service, but still had not raised enough money. Between October 1999 and March 2000 they had created a small sales force of about three people, and were moving aggressively to ramp up. "We didn't want to go out too fast because we knew the obstacles from going too fast. But we were being pushed to go fast, because we were being led to believe that without growth, without moving quickly, and without growing sales, we were not going to get any capital." In retrospect, the situation MCM found themselves in was just "dumb" money, because "smart" money "knows that this is not the case, especially, for early stage Internet companies—you've got to have the money if you want to grow fast. You need oodles of money upfront to get your name, your brand out. You need to buy your revenue to be successful. So we were being pushed into doing these things and we really felt that we didn't have a choice. We were tied into this agreement with Spartacus until September 2000."

One of the obstacles MCM did not anticipate was the substantial time investment required by the retailers to get their products online. Many were not willing or able to make such an investment, particularly since the initial estimate of online sales was about 1% of all sales. Another observation was that while they were having great difficulties recruiting local retailers, their U.S. competitors were recruiting retailers at a phenomenal rate. Canadian retailers had a wait-and-see approach. Consequently, MCM established an office in Seattle, created their Seattle Web site, and hired their Seattle team. As they were beginning to build their Seattle office, the market crashed. They pulled the plug on everything, fired everybody, and shut the office down, never having really gotten a good start in the United States.

On January 30, 2001, Spartacus Capital signed off for the process of a reverse takeover with MCM for an agreed 3.5 million Spartacus Capital's common shares. In addition, they also agreed to arrange for a brokered private placement of up to 3 000 000 special warrants and to raise gross proceeds of $1.95 million. Global Securities Corp. would be the agent for this financing. This additional financing would be used to fund the operations, expansion, and marketing of MCM into additional major centres across Canada and the United States. However, there had been some delays in completing the transaction, largely due to the soft market conditions over the past nine months in raising capital.

Since the announcement of the transaction between Spartacus Capital and MCM, MCM has been financed with loans and advances of over $430 000 and has reduced its operating costs to close to the breakeven point. These loans will be settled as part of the equity financing package and the lenders have agreed to accept shares in payment of their loans.

NEW STRATEGY

After the completion of the transaction with Spartacus, MCM will be looking to continue its growth, both through direct acquisitions of new clients as currently under way and through acquisitions of complementary e-commerce companies that may be undervalued in the current market. Any future acquisitions, of which none are planned at the present time, would be financed through future equity offerings and the targets would be acquired with payments made with shares. In addition to the financing provided by Spartacus, in the fall of 2000 MCM also received an injection of cash and services worth approximately $400 000 from two angel investors. This funding is being used to rebuild and refocus the company's strategy.

Instead of trying to aggregate retailers, MCM's new focus is on shopping centres. The objective is to partner with the shopping centres in the respective cities and provide those retailers with their solution. MCM's other objective is to get a national presence, because the strength of MCM is in providing consumers with convenient shopping from their favorite retail merchants at any time and from anywhere. By partnering with the shopping malls, MCM will have easier access to many of the large retailers that have a national presence, particularly in large cities. The benefit to consumers is that by using MCM, they can purchase any item from their favourite retailers, regardless of the city they are in. So the retailers can use the Internet to provide support for their bricks-and-mortar operations, which is a key objective of MCM. As of March 2001, MCM had approximately 40 subscribing retail merchants from the city of Vancouver.

Commenting on the new strategy, Sodi suggested that the weakness in the original plan was that, although it was an interesting and innovative concept, it did not address an immediate need. Therefore, in designing the new strategy, one of the primary objectives is to target an immediate need so that customers will buy it right away. Research undertaken by MCM indicates that shopping malls are facing increasing and intense competition from other shopping centres, amusement parks, theatres, home entertainment, and, to a lesser extent virtual stores, so they are looking for cost-effective ways to get more traffic through their stores. The research also indicates that an increasing number of consumers are planning to research their shopping online if they can do so conveniently. The new strategy has retained many features of the original strategy except for one aspect: instead of trying to aggregate individual retailers, aggregate the shopping malls with all of their respective retailers.

As part of the new strategy, MCM is partnering with two other companies. One is a national marketing firm that will help them to achieve a national presence; the other is a technology company that will provide the new technology they are lacking and cannot purchase due to insufficient funds. The technology is needed to increase MCM's ability to offer consumers greater convenience and to recruit local retail merchants. The arrangement with the new technology partner will allow MCM to offer local retail merchants its services at much lower price points.

KEY CHALLENGES

In evolving the venture, MCM faced several critical challenges. MCM's board of directors and advisory board included several well-known individuals; however, they were unable to raise the profile of the company within the investment community, and thus contributed little in terms of raising financing for the company. Also, because the board members were involved in several ventures simultaneously, it was extremely difficult for MCM's management to meet with them as needed, and some members were unwilling to take calls from people from the investment community and elsewhere. Thus, MCM was unable to use them actively to build the venture.

Commenting on the challenges of trying to raise financing from the venture community, MCM's president remarked, "I think that at any stage of your business people invest in people; not ideas, not concepts, but in people because they believe you can do what you say you can do." Further, he added, "The challenge was made so much more difficult because we did not have a big-name person behind us, or someone with experience who could walk in to a venture capitalist office and say, 'I did this already, I am going to take this one and make it work.'"

Another major obstacle MCM faced was their inability to launch an effective advertising and public relations campaign due to lack of money. This was compounded by the fact that MCM was launched in the peak of the dot-com frenzy when the media was inundated with dot-coms. Consequently, it was extremely difficult to get MCM's message out—"We just got lost in the shuffle," says Sodi. It seemed only the big players and cash-rich dot-coms who were able buy their way got the attention of the media at the time. It was also a time when business-to-consumer e-commerce was all the rage and MCM was unable to sufficiently differentiate itself from the rest of the players in the business-to-consumer space.

Lack of adequate financing also prevented MCM from acquiring and maintaining its technology infrastructure, which is critical to its ability to facilitate convenient online shopping. MCM was unable to add new functionality that was readily available in the market and was being implemented by some of its competitors. MCM did not have all the needed expertise in-house to integrate various key pieces of technology.

MCM's management felt Spartacus Capital was the big name that was going to propel them within the investment community and raise the financing they needed. They were disappointed because Spartacus Capital had linked up with a brokerage house in Vancouver that completely failed them and so they were unable to raise any money for MCM. Crouching over his chair with a smile on his face, Sodi Hundal said, "This is another lesson: If people are going to raise you money, then they have to do so very quickly, and if they can't do it quickly, they can't do it, bottom line—move on."

THE FUTURE

The evolution of MyCityMarket.com has been trying and difficult. MCM has been growing its customer base of retail merchants in Vancouver, its home city, but so far has been unable to execute its business plan of becoming a powerful player in all major Canadian and U.S. cities. MCM has refocused its strategy, and added two new partners who will assist in its marketing efforts and will provide much-needed new technology. The company continues to have the support of Spartacus Capital and a couple of angel investors. Is this enough to make MCM viable in the near future? Have market conditions changed so much that it is too difficult for MCM to penetrate other markets identified in its business plan? Is MCM's new strategy of going after shopping malls viable?

theme two overview

Customer Relationship and Service Management

The revolution within the New Economy has increased competition among buyers and sellers in e-business. To attract and retain customers, underlying tenets to success are convenience, personalization, and excellent service. Customer relationship management (CRM) is focused on providing and maintaining quality service for customers, by effectively communicating and delivering products, services, information, and solutions that address customer problems and requirements.

The application of CRM to an e-business strategy also includes the personalization and customization of customers' experiences and interactions with the Web site, call centre, or other method of customer contact with the e-business. To be effective, the CRM solution will take into account customer characteristics, how buyer decisions are made, and the systems most able to deliver the product, service, or solution.

An essential aspect of CRM includes support for customers and the establishment of trust and loyalty. Customer loyalty is the degree to which a customer will stay with a vendor or brand, and is increasingly the competitive advantage in the e-business world. It costs about five to eight times more to acquire a new customer than to keep an existing one, so the incentives are high to build sustaining client relationships. Considered another way, increasing customer retention rates by only 5% can translate into profit increases of 25 to 90%.[1] Despite the importance of e-loyalty, over the past decade customer loyalty has been decreasing. The introduction of e-business has hastened the trend to shop, compare, and switch in a Web-based environment.

Ultimately, loyalty is not sustained by technology, but rather through a consistently superior customer experience. Customer service, which is related to CRM, is a series of activities designed to enhance the level of customer satisfaction for a service or product. Customer service helps purchasers resolve problems encountered in the purchasing phase or during the after sales support process. Types of customer service functions and tools might include providing search and comparison capabilities, tracking of accounts or order status, ordering online, or real-time Web chat support.

The cases and readings in this Theme illuminate key characteristics of CRM development and how to establish loyalty with customers as it applies in B2C (business-to-consumer) and B2B (business-to-business) environments. Insights are provided about how to develop and retain customers, and the consequences of failed e-business client-customer relationships. The cases provide vivid examples of how CRM is expanding to include customized and comprehensive client solutions. It is important to note how strategy, as discussed in the previous Theme, impacts the form and function of CRM, and ultimately the success of each profiled company.

---

1. F. Reichheld and P. Schefter, "E-loyalty: your secret weapon on the Web," *Harvard Business Review*, 78(4)(2000): 106.

part one overview

Customer Relationship Management

This part of the book is focused on how to capture and develop e-loyalty in Internet-based businesses. The first case profiles the very successful Vancouver-based Pivotal Corporation, and how the company has innovated to enhance CRM for their customer base. Pivotal coined the term *eBRM*, for "electronic business relationship management"—a combination of CRM, e-commerce, business portals, and Internet business services. As such, eBRM encapsulates a wide range of services in which companies are involved to interact with clients using the Internet. Embedded within the case is how Pivotal's solutions are implemented in two client companies—North Shore Credit Union and Yorkton Securities. These client examples, and how a relationship-based strategy meets the client needs, can also be considered in the context of the previous Theme of strategy and business models.

In the case "Reflect.com: 'Burn the Ships,'" how the company sells a personalized line of beauty products and services only on the Internet is examined. Related to CRM, beauty-care expertise is leveraged on the Internet to create a unique experience unavailable in a bricks-and-mortar environment. The site is highly customized, allowing consumers to create more than 300 000 products and packages. Each consumer's needs are determined using an interactive question-and-answer format, followed by the creation of specialized products. Rare personal followup with each customer is provided at Reflect.com, making this a good example of how repeat business and order fulfillment are achieved.

The readings outline various facets of how to facilitate and reinforce CRM and customer loyalty. This includes focusing on the right customers, and then providing products and services that more than satisfy expectations. A key consideration is the rapid pace with which companies must improve products and services to retain loyalty. Key factors in building online customer loyalty are outlined, and provide a point for discussion related to how this is done in each of the companion cases.

case one

The Pivotal Solution: Beyond Customer Relationship Management

Dianne Cyr

Richard Lew

Thomas Lee

Since 1998 there has been explosive growth in the customer relationship management (CRM) market. Several companies have joined the original CRM players who provide business applications to manage complex sales, marketing, and customer service functions. The large number of solution providers has contributed to the confusion of end users, who are daunted by the plethora of choices and industry lingo. Above the din, there is at least one company that is rising to new heights with its solutions that take companies beyond customer relationship management. Canada-based Pivotal Corporation has emerged as one of the most respected CRM solution providers in the industry. The company has embarked on a worldwide strategy to help its customers capitalize on the Internet as a powerful business infrastructure for demand chain management.

Pivotal, located in Vancouver, British Columbia, is strategically nestled in the hotbed of the province's high-technological industry that includes such alumni as CreoScitex, PMC Sierra, and MacDonald Dettwiler & Associates. Pivotal enables large and medium-sized businesses (sales of $50-million+) to make, serve, and manage

The authors appreciate the participation of Norm Francis and Bob Runge of Pivotal Corporation, and Pivotal's clients including Neil Beube atYorkton Securities and John Allen and Chris Catliff at the North Shore Credit Union. Leslie Castellani at Pivotal excelled in the coordination of this project. Financial support was provided by the Technical University of British Columbia.

customers with superior speed and efficiency using demand chain management solutions which fuse the power customer relationship management with e-business technologies.

Pivotal's growth over the past five years has been nothing short of exceptional, with revenue growth of over 30 000% from 1995 to 1999. The company posted revenues of $52.9 million in the fiscal year 2000, an increase of 109% over the previous year. Pivotal has approximately 700 employees and a customer base of more than 1300 large and medium-sized enterprises in 35 countries. Pivotal solutions are available in a wide range of languages including English, French, German, Spanish, Portuguese, Swedish, Japanese, and Chinese.

Pivotal's extensive customer list includes such companies as KPMG Consulting, Yorkton Securities Inc., US Filter, Kimberley Clark, Deloitte & Touche, Intrawest Corporation, Dain Rauscher Wessels, Farm Credit Services of America, Atlas Copco, American Medical Security Inc., CIBC World Markets, Belgacom France, FLAG Telecom, ElectronicPartner, North Shore Credit Union, Crystal Decisions Corp., Blue Cross Blue Shield of Michigan, Nissan Motor Corp., Ericsson, and Deutsche Bank.

While Pivotal's industry leadership is indicative of the company's success, its ability to help its customers increase revenue, improve productivity, and increase customer retention is a driving force. Pivotal's customers, who are typically leaders in their respective industries, are leveraging the company's Internet-based solutions to improve their business processes, in particular sales, marketing, and service—and improve collaboration with key business partners, employees, and customers. Although the technology industry suffered a dramatic downturn after the dot-com meltdown in April 2000, Pivotal continues to demonstrate success with its long roster of established companies and deep focus on using the Internet as a business infrastructure for demand chain management.

Michael Porter, a professor of business administration at Harvard, was quoted in the May 13, 2001 *New York Times* as follows: "The real advantage established companies had was established brands, product lines, relationships. By setting up Internet operations as separate, they essentially walked away from those things." It is clear that companies using Pivotal solutions are prospering because they are strategically focused on using the Internet to improve sales, marketing, and service processes of their established businesses. The dynamic working relationship between Pivotal and its customers plays a key role in the successful integration of Pivotal solutions. North Shore Credit Union, a community-based credit union, and Yorkton Securities, a leading Canadian investment bank, are excellent examples of how Pivotal solutions are dramatically impacting their customers' ability to improve customer retention and increase revenues.

NORTH SHORE CREDIT UNION

North Shore Credit Union (NSCU) is headquartered in North Vancouver, British Columbia. Although it is British Columbia's third-largest credit union, the increasing competition from domestic and global financial services firms for market share is a major business challenge. More and more players are chasing after the same pool of customers and management of their assets. To this end, a variety of basic types of marketing strategies are deployed in the personal financial industry:

- Multi-line product marketing campaigns, which are often used by global players

- Mass marketing, which is extremely efficient in one or two markets and typically used by global firms
- One-to-one marketing, which builds personalized relationships with customers and tends to focus on particular customer segments; this is particularly suited for high-end and smaller organizations

NSCU decided early on that one-to-one marketing was the best relationship-building strategy for its business model given its size and its focus on local business.

Historically, NSCU was known for building and maintaining solid customer relationships, and the company enjoys a reputation for technological innovation and exceptional customer service. Since 1985, transactions were conducted through a variety of channels and relationships: call centres, ATMs, debit cards, credit cards, mobile sales, and branch-level transactions. Unfortunately, the information became localized and distributed within each business channel or centre, each having its own database for customer information. By creating silos of data, NSCU was unable to collaborate effectively between branches or financial representatives. As a result, information was often outdated, which made it difficult to provide exceptional, personalized service.

Chris Catliff, president and CEO, and John Allen, senior manager of Member Relationship Programs for North Shore Credit Union, are responsible for developing a strategic direction for the company that will take the organization to the next level of customer service beyond the year 2001. Chris and John often reminisce about the dynamic landscape of the banking and financial services industry. The July 1998 issue of the *Globe and Mail* Report on Business features an article that predicted that companies most affected by the information technology revolution would be in the banking, finance, real estate, hardware, software, and medical technology industries. Catliff cannot be sure if 50% of the world's GDP would ever be attributed to information-based technologies and services by 2020, but he does know that information technology is the foundation for the future success of North Shore Credit Union's business.

In the mid-to-late-1990s, the area of CRM undertook tremendous growth due to a number of synergies in computers, the Internet, demographics, demand for higher customer service levels, and explosive growth in financial services and product range. For the financial industry, which depends on establishing relationships with customers, CRM has become an important source of competitive advantage. Technical and social convergence has changed the mix and types of services and products, and now, how these services are being delivered is revolutionizing the financial services sector. It was not so long ago that only certain services could be obtained at selected branches, or access to accounts outside your local branch was a time-consuming and frustrating task. The adoption and integration of the latest information technologies has not only generated increased competition in the industry, but also generated growth for companies that supply these technologies.

With the increasing use of the Internet and other telecommunications media enabling global transactions, cross-channel conflicts were becoming a growing problem. Options such as bundling and anchor products were offered over the Internet to people with a computer. NSCU wanted to adopt a more holistic view of wealth management that linked service and product offerings to variables like demographics, individual and business needs, and other customer interests.

In response to the rapidly changing and competitive financial services industry, financial managers at NSCU realized they needed a more comprehensive and integrated understanding of their members. With customer relationship management becoming a focus for NSCU during 2000, they turned to Pivotal Corporation to help build an online infrastructure to streamline sales, marketing, and service processes.

Why Pivotal? It is a Canadian company that clearly understands NSCU's business issues and objectives. Solutions from other companies, such as Siebel, are too expensive, are extremely complex, and require substantial customization to operate in the Canadian business environment. In addition, the Pivotal solution suite is flexible, intuitive, and easy to customize, which allows NSCU to scale its technology to the expansion of the credit union.

Working together, NSCU and Pivotal incorporated the credit union's back-end banking systems into the Pivotal solution suite. Deployment of the Pivotal solution suite at NSCU lasted approximately five months, although the companies continue to work together on additional phases and capabilities. The results for NSCU have been nothing short of remarkable. Using the Pivotal Finance Demand Chain Network solution suite, NSCU has substantially increased sales revenue by delivering quick, intelligent customer service across all touchpoints, identifying member buying trends and service preferences, building extensive profiles that identify up-selling and cross-selling opportunities, and conducting marketing campaigns that are personal, precise, relevant, and timely.

Rather than waiting for a member to walk in to request a loan, mortgage, or financial consultation, NSCU uses Pivotal to create profiles that analyze factors such as age, family situation, life stage, and financial outlook to identify likely candidates for financial services. Through profiling, NSCU makes an intelligent assessment of who is likely to be considering a mortgage, life insurance, or a more comprehensive financial plan. Additional value is created by isolating gaps in the profile and using them to presuppose when an individual has mortgages, loans, or investments elsewhere.

Using profiling knowledge, NSCU conducts financial reviews that demonstrate the value NSCU can provide to its members through consolidation and enhanced financial services. In addition, NSCU can now ask its members how they want to be served. Do they want Internet banking, but prefer a face-to-face discussion about loans? Using the answers to these intricate questions, NSCU is directing resources and increasing value according to the needs of its members.

The return on investment is noted below:

- Increased investment sales activity by 25%
- Improved customer service by sharing up-to-date customer information between advisors and call centre staff
- Ability to provide instant, comprehensive customer profiling (member profiling)
- Increase of net business for financial managers by 16.9% from 4Q 1999 to 4Q 2000

"Using the Pivotal Finance Demand Chain Network solution suite, NSCU has realized a significant return on investment in a short time frame," comments Allen, "Our return on investment, achieved six months after deployment, is a testament that Pivotal is a smart, safe investment for financial services companies." Siebel Systems, a competing technology solutions provider, could not match Pivotal's offerings for NSCU.

YORKTON SECURITIES

Yorkton Securities is a leading Canadian investment bank that employs more than 600 people and has raised more than $12 billion for its clients since 1995. Investment bankers at Yorkton Securities probably didn't know a lot about customer relationship management software, but then again, they also had very little information on the interactions their colleagues were having with their clients. The company relied on email to communicate and collaborate on client activities, which created a daunting process of managing relationships. As a result, the company began an extensive search for a CRM solution that would address its business challenges, improve productivity, and increase client retention and revenues.

With the assistance of PricewaterhouseCoopers, Yorkton evaluated multiple CRM providers, including the largest player in the CRM market, Siebel Systems, and ultimately selected Pivotal to provide a solution that streamlined sales, marketing, and customer service processes. The Pivotal Finance Demand Chain Network solution suite was selected for several reasons including its Microsoft optimization, mobility, ease of customization, security features, and speed of deployment.

Optimization for the Microsoft platform was one of the top factors for Yorkton in selecting a CRM solution, since the company used Microsoft throughout the organization. Pivotal has an unwavering dedication to developing and delivering solutions on the Microsoft platform and as a result has worked closely with research and development teams at Microsoft Corp. on the Redmond, Washington campus. Pivotal's tight links with Microsoft enable the company to offer leading-edge solutions with advanced Microsoft technologies on a cost-effective platform. Pivotal's close relationship with Microsoft and Yorkton's exclusive use of the Microsoft platform by default eliminated several CRM vendors during Yorkton's selection process.

Integration with wireless devices was essential to Yorkton Securities where senior executives and research analysts can typically spend more time on the road than they are in the office. Pivotal Anywhere is mobile solution for demand chain management that provides access to mission-critical corporate information from anywhere, at any time, through handheld devices. The solution empowers business executives to make decisions with speed and intelligence. By responding to client requests and collaborating almost instantaneously with colleagues, Yorkton can accelerate the speed of deals and increase client service.

The evolving nature of financial services and the need to respond and adapt quickly to market demand are high-priority business challenges for Yorkton. As a result, Yorkton required a solution that was easy to customize and quick to adapt as business demands required. Pivotal solutions are designed to be flexible and highly customizable. Using Pivotal's customization capabilities, Yorkton can quickly adapt the solution to meet its needs.

By the nature of the financial industry, Yorkton keeps highly confidential investor capital information on record, so security features were a significant factor in the choice of a solution. The Pivotal solution offers a wide range of security options, which enables Yorkton to set access restrictions on its corporate database. Roger Dent, vice-chairman and director of research, notes, "The problem is, with one database of information, how do you restrict different people from accessing notes and communications without disrupting their access to all the contact records? The Pivotal solution suite allows Yorkton to customize security access right down to a very granular level." Using Pivotal, Yorkton can also build comprehensive audit trails. For example, if an employee makes an entry which is subsequently changed or deleted, the solution allows Yorkton to determine who and when made the change. Keeping records of communications with investors is critical, so the Pivotal solution keeps logs of all entries or access to the database.

Speed of deployment was another important factor for Yorkton in selecting a CRM solution provider. "Pivotal was put to the challenge," notes Dent. "We informed Pivotal that we would not buy the Pivotal solution suite until Pivotal could demonstrate to us what we wanted. Essentially, we wanted to see it work before they purchase it. It was amazing. Pivotal came in and developed and customized the solution in less than ten hours."

According to Dent, "As a leading technology investment bank, it is imperative that Yorkton Securities delivers fast, intelligent service and results to its retail investors and institutional buyers. Using Pivotal, Yorkton is accelerating its capital market initiatives and increasing revenue generation by delivering results and service that are personalized, precise, and timely throughout the entire investor lifecycle. The ultimate value of the Pivotal solution suite exceeds its cost. If the Pivotal solution suite avoids one deal falling through the cracks, it will more than pay for itself."

THE PIVOTAL VISION

Norm Francis, president and CEO of Pivotal Corporation, built his career by fusing his educational background in computer science and accounting—a unique combination in the business world. After a successful tenure as a senior executive at KPMG, Francis ventured out on his own to start Basic Software Group. His years as an accounting executive made him realize the massive market need for easy-to-use software that would automate and accelerate accounting processes. Francis, and his partner Keith Wales, hit the market with an accounting package, ACCPAC, which would soon make arduous accounting processes simpler for thousands of companies around the world. That software package was the embodiment of Francis' vision for efficiency and accuracy in accounting. And it allowed him to help companies operate their businesses more efficiently. In 1985, the company was acquired by technology powerhouse Computer Associates.

Francis' entrepreneurial spirit led him to another market opportunity. After reading about the breakthrough concept of "one-to-one marketing"—he realized that the market would soon be demanding technologies to automate their sales, marketing, and service processes. He teamed up once again with his longtime business partner Keith Wales to form Pivotal Corporation and create a strategy to attack this emerging technology market. In 1995, they offered one of the industry's first customer relationship management solutions—a market that would explode by the late 1990s.

The timing for Pivotal couldn't have been better. In the mid-1990s, the Internet was just beginning to emerge as an affordable and globally accessible network with vast commercial opportunities. In 1996 and 1997, the Internet wave gained momentum as a hub for commercial activity. Pivotal soon realized technology could be extended to more than just something that was being used by employees. It could be extrapolated beyond local area networks (LANs) to larger network communities. This was a watershed development for Pivotal, because the company was beginning to see much larger collaborative efforts between employees, customers, and partners, forming a much larger and interconnected business network. In the fall of 2000, Pivotal launched the Pivotal Demand Chain Network solution suite, an integrated solution that fuses CRM with e-business technologies across all Internet, wireless, and traditional communication channels. The launch of this first-of-a-kind solution offered companies the technologies and expertise to move beyond CRM and capitalize on improved sales, marketing, and service processes across all demand-driven communication channels.

THE CRM MARKET

Pivotal solutions were well established and positioned in the industry to catch the CRM tidal wave just as it was building momentum. According to AMR Research, the CRM industry is currently estimated to be worth $40 billion. In 1999 the market size hovered around $4.45 billion; it is expected to jump to $21.8 billion in 2003 (a growth rate five times that of the rest of the overall software market).[1] Large companies typically spend around $3.1 million on CRM hardware, software, and services with the expectation of seeing annual revenues grow by 8% within 12 months of CRM implementation.[2] Barton Goldenberg, president of ISM, a CRM research and consulting firm, notes, "the future of CRM is extremely promising with analysts forecasting more than a 40% growth rate per year for the next five years."[3]

When done effectively CRM can generate revenue growth through the building of customer loyalty, increasing customer retention, reducing client turnover, and improving revenue-forecasting capabilities. A recent IPSO-Reid survey commissioned by Microsoft found that the average return on equity for good knowledge management practices is 41%, or US$41 278.[4]

For Pivotal, CRM is only one component of its solution suite. According to an article by Rod Johnson in the *AMR Outlook EAS Alert*, November 2000, "Companies, especially large multinationals, will aggressively begin to invest in demand-driven e-business platforms. Pivotal is the only vendor to come to market with a vision and customers for its demand-driven, e-business platform. Pivotal has combined several new business strategies, including demand chain management, business communities, and shared e-business platforms."

PIVOTAL SOLUTIONS

Pivotal's demand chain management solutions help companies maximize their customer relationships and revenues by streamlining sales, marketing, and service processes. Demand chain management is best described in the context of what it is not—supply chain management. Supply-driven companies, which were in fashion during the heyday of ERP systems, are focused on streamlining costs through operational efficiencies of internally oriented, supply processes—such as inventory management, purchasing, and manufacturing. Such companies presuppose customer needs, negotiate deals with suppliers and manufacturers, build products that are cost-effective to produce, and offer them up to customers. In this scenario, customers are at the mercy of supply constraints—and therefore hold very few cards in the grand scheme of business dynamics. The goal is for companies to squeeze every bit of efficiency out of the supply chain.

Demand-driven companies, on the other hand, maximize revenue by focusing externally on the needs of the customer and on every component of the demand chain, such as customers, business partners, and employees. These companies concentrate on discovering the unique needs of every customer—and then tailoring demand-side processes (marketing, sales, service, and support), and integrating those processes with the supply chain, to fulfill customer expectations. As a result, demand-driven companies need to have flexible business models so that they can engage appropriate partners, suppliers, and employees to rapidly create personalized solutions and respond to changing market conditions.

The Pivotal Demand Chain Network solution suite is a set of advanced technologies for demand chain management. By fusing CRM and e-business, the solution suite synchronizes all the elements—the people, processes, activities, touchpoints, and devices that go into making, managing, and serving customers. It allows companies to extend their enterprise to tightly incorporate partners into all demand chain processes in order to create a seamless customer experience. The solution suite leverages all Internet, traditional, and wireless communication channels to create a dynamic business infrastructure that allows companies to respond to customer and market demands quickly and effectively.

DEMAND CHAIN MANAGEMENT

> The Internet enables people providing sales, marketing and service to collaborate in better ways with the customer. It's analogous to what's going on in the supply chain side, which is how components flow up; but in demand chain management there are business processes that revolve around the customer.
>
> —Norm Francis, December 2000

Pivotal and its advanced solution suite have won international recognition. The company's long list of honours includes: named to the Aberdeen List of Top Ten Significant CRM Applications for 2000, ranked on the ISM "Top 15" CRM Software Selections, selected as the best Integrated CRM/eBusiness Solution of 2000 at the Microsoft-sponsored Industry Solution Awards, named as the fastest-growing technology company in the 2000 Deloitte & Touche Canadian Technology Fast 50, ranked as the ninth-fastest-growing technology company in the 2000 Deloitte & Touche North American Technology Fast 500, selected as Microsoft's North American "Packaged Application Partner of the Year," and awarded the 2000 "Company of the Year" by the British Columbia Technology Industry Association.

BUSINESS STRATEGY AT PIVOTAL

Pivotal now caters to more than 1300 companies in 35 countries worldwide supplying expertise and technology-based solutions across all verticals including health care, finance, technology, manufacturing, retail, and telecom. Approximately two-thirds of its revenues come from the U.S./Canada market, and the remaining one-third comes from its overseas operations.

Pivotal believes its success derives from three sources: technological innovation, customer success, and human capital. According to Francis, the company remains "at the leading edge of technological innovation and it is 'constantly pushing the envelope' of what is possible." Second, the company's success very much depends on the customer's success. Third, the company has managed to thrive due to its ability to attract and retain top talent. Recruitment is a key activity or "process," as Francis describes it, in a company that selects executives who have the experience and the knowledge to rapidly expand a company on a global basis. Key employee attributes include entrepreneurial spirit, a great sense of urgency, and ability to adapt quickly and take ownership in their roles—people who, in Francis' words, "run hard, run fast."

The company realizes top talent drives the company, not good ideas. According to Francis, "good ideas don't last very long." Innovation is the key to ensuring continued success, and the company needs to remain "one step ahead of the game." To ensure that the highest calibre of talent is hired and retained, the company offers stock options, bonuses, and employee referral fees as inducements to employee loyalty and commitment.

In 1998 it was decided that, in order to facilitate growth, a presence in the United States was required. Accordingly, an extension to the Vancouver corporate headquarters was added in the Seattle suburb of Kirkland, Washington. This has proved instrumental in enabling the company to recruit exceptional management talent to the Seattle operations—people who would otherwise have avoided the prospect of working in Canada.

Growth is integral to Pivotal's future success, and the company is actively embarking on expanding market opportunities through the sale of vertical solutions through acquisitions, and by selling into large enterprises on the basis of its strategic alliances with well-known companies such as Microsoft, Hewlett-Packard, and Siemens Business Services.

PARTNERSHIPS FOR GROWTH

Pivotal's partnership strategy allows the company to quickly expand its global reach by working with market leaders to market, sell, and/or implement the Pivotal Demand Chain Network solution suite. Pivotal has strong, strategic relationships with world-leading companies such as Microsoft, Hewlett-Packard, KPMG, Deloitte & Touche, Compaq, Siemens Business Services—and many others. By leveraging the expertise and recognition of these global partners, Pivotal has been able to increase its presence in the global market. Pivotal also works very closely with Microsoft from a development perspective as well, which allows the company to consistently be ahead of the market in terms of market trends and technological capabilities. Pivotal will continue to expand its partnership strategy to meet the needs of its fast-growing company and market.

> We're deepening our relationship with Pivotal to accelerate an entirely new way of doing business of the Web. By combining Pivotal's breakthrough solutions with the power of new technologies like XML and Microsoft.NET enterprise servers, we will enable companies to achieve an unprecedented level of business agility and integration with customers and partners. We're very excited to work with a pioneer like Pivotal to open up tremendous revenue opportunity for companies around the world.
>
> —Steve Ballmer, president and CEO of Microsoft, December 5, 2000

ACQUISITION STRATEGY

Pivotal's acquisition strategy enables the company to increase its market presence by enhancing its ability to sell into important geographies, to advance its industry-leading capabilities in demand chain management, and to implement Pivotal solutions on a global basis. In 2000, Pivotal acquired Exactium Ltd, an Atlanta-based company that produces intelligent e-selling solutions, and Simba Technologies, a company that developed e-marketing solutions. The previous year saw the company purchased Transitif S.A., a French e-business solution provider. In addition, the company made a number of other significant acquisitions, including the CRM Division of Software Spectrum, Project One Business Technologies, Inc., and Ionysys Technology Corporation. Acquisitions will continue to play a major role in Pivotal's corporate growth strategy.

THE FUTURE

> In the next ten years, the demand chain management market will surpass the supply chain management market by the very nature of the way we do business today. Consider all the people within an organization that use financial, human resources, or other ERP systems. Now consider all the people within an organization that interact in some way or another with customers. The latter is at least three times more predominant. As a result, the business need for demand chain management solutions that optimize sales, marketing, and service processes to streamline our interactions with customers will grow incredibly in this worldwide customer-focused economy.
>
> —Norm Francis, CEO of Pivotal Corp., December 5, 2000

Pivotal has clearly set itself apart from the crowd by performing well in a market that is undergoing considerable consolidation. The market for CRM and demand chain management technologies continues to grow—and Pivotal is positioned well to capitalize on this massive market opportunity. Norm Francis sees increasing demand for Pivotal solutions as companies are realigning their businesses to become more customer-focused. Not only are companies becoming more customer-focused, but they are also building extended enterprises that tightly network business partners into demand chain processes. Companies that fail to do so will be unable to adapt quickly to the market demands of this competitive, global environment.

As with the growth and acceptance of fax machines in the 1980s and 1990s, solutions that improve sales, marketing, and service processes are no longer an option. Customers are demanding personalized interactions and exceptional experiences. According to Francis, "The company of the future will allow customers to move fluidly and seamlessly through all channels of communication, including phone, fax, email, Internet, and partner channels—to allow them to receive the fastest, most responsive and intelligent service possible at any given moment in time."

Pivotal Corporation is taking further technological strides by leveraging XML and Simple Object Access Protocol (SOAP) and Microsoft.NET technologies. The importance of the Internet is rising for virtually every enterprise. Whether it's transacting business with customers or external partners or communicating with distributed employees, the Internet has a role to play in every enterprise, no matter what its size. The concept of supporting multiple operating systems and multiple data formats is just getting too costly and inefficient, and simply doesn't work in a globally connected world. By offering solutions on the Microsoft.NET platform and leveraging XML as a standard for communication, Pivotal is able to offer advanced solutions in a world in which enterprises can communicate with customers, partners, and employees anywhere, any time, and on any device. According to

Francis, XML will become the future Internet standard—systems that are not XML-compatible will be left behind.

Has Pivotal made the right forecast on future needs for technological and business developments? As Norm Francis fully knows, innovations in software products "don't last very long" because they are readily copied by competitors. What must Pivotal do to capitalize on future opportunities, and to continue to develop leading-edge solutions ahead of the market to remain an innovative and industry leader? What should their strategy and positioning be? Will the new .NET products being offered by Pivotal be appealing enough to North Shore Credit Union and Yorkton Securities to justify upgrading their systems? Will demand chain management solutions be able to help Pivotal maintain the high growth and levels of achievement that have marked the early years of the company? If not, what must Norm Francis do to position the company for the next stage of growth?

NOTES

1. Roxane Richter, "Newly arrived and already on its way out? Why experts say CRM needs to go ERM," *Electric Light & Power*, May 2000, p. 30.
2. Cap Gemini and International Data Corporation study.
3. See note 2.
4. "New way to track client needs: Customer relationship management," *National Post*, April 2, 2001, p. E7.

case two

Reflect.com: "Burn the Ships"

Jean Pierre Divo

Margaret Higgins

Molly Milano

Juan Montoya

M. Anne Wickland

> At Reflect.com, your state-of-the-art skin care, hair care and cosmetic products don't exist until you create them. Simply create your beauty profile and our scientific process then blends your requests with the best technology to custom make your products. Delivered free. Unconditionally guaranteed.[1]

It was a warm October day in San Francisco as Ginger Kent, CEO of Reflect.com, sat at her desk and pondered whether or not the company would receive its recently requested second-round financing. Kent and her colleagues felt that the funds were desperately needed to redesign the Web site and improve the consumer purchase process. Reflect.com, an e-commerce site that allows women to customize beauty products, was about to celebrate its first anniversary. At this time, however, it needed a capital infusion from its original investors, which included the consumer packaged goods leader Procter & Gamble. While Reflect was hitting its monthly sales targets, it was difficult to ignore the turmoil that was ravaging the online beauty industry. Ingredients.com, Eve.com, Beautyscene.com, Beautyjungle.com, and countless others

MBA candidates Jean Pierre Divo, Margaret Higgins, Molly Milano, Juan Montoya, and M. Anne Wickland prepared this case under the supervision of Professor Christopher L. Tucci, for the purpose of class discussion rather than to illustrate either effective or ineffective handling of an administrative situation.

had closed down business, and it was rumored that others were not far behind. Reflect.com's business model was unique, however, and Kent felt it was superior to other online third-party retailers. However, the question loomed: Was it strong enough? Would women ever feel comfortable enough to buy their cosmetics and beauty needs online without a chance to touch, smell or see them first?

COSMETIC INDUSTRY OVERVIEW

The health and beauty care industry, a $24 billion market, has been one of the fastest-growing and most profitable sectors in the United States over the past 50 years. It is expected to top $29 billion in 2003. According to Jupiter Communications, online beauty sales are projected to reach $100 million this year and perhaps $360 million by 2003.[2] The total cosmetics market (approximately $10 billion in sales) comprises two segments: the mass market and the prestige market. Mass products are sold through drugstores, grocery stores, health and beauty stores, and mass merchandisers. According to Information Resources Inc., mass cosmetics sales (excluding the nail segment) rose 10.5% to $2.8 billion for the 52-week period ending May 21, 2000. Including the nail segment, sales were $3.2 billion. Prestige products are sold through department stores and upscale retailers. In 1999, prestige beauty market sales were $6.5 billion in the United States. Overall growth for the market was 3%.[3]

Online Consumer Trends

Both mass and prestige products are sold on the Web, either directly by manufacturers or through third-party vendors. By 1999 a Media Metrix/NPD E-Visory Report estimated that more than one-third of Internet users had ventured onto a beauty e-tail site, with women making up the majority of beauty buyers. The most popular purchases were in the bath and body category, while colour cosmetics was the least-purchased category. Women's scents led sales dollar shares.[4] The study also found that buyers are not very experimental: only 6% said they bought things they had never tried before. The Web sites that have the highest recognition are "pure-plays" (i.e., Web sites without offline operations) that focus on health and beauty.[5] Nevertheless, the outlook was promising. Women made up nearly half of Internet users in 1999, representing 27 million women online in the United States. Approximately 58% of these new Internet users were women, up from 44% in 1998.[6]

Competition: Chaos in Online Cosmetics

Reflect.com competes on multiple levels within the beauty industry. Reflect.com competes for the same wallet share as all of its competitors, mass, prestige, online, or offline. However, first and foremost, it competes against traditional manufacturers and marketers such as Procter & Gamble, L'Oréal, and the Estée Lauder Companies. (See Exhibit 1 for a list of the top 20 global beauty companies.) Only one year ago the beauty e-tail scene was thriving. Site after site opened, each better than the last. Recently, however, the industry has undergone a shakeout with many of the sites that once seemed promising shutting their virtual doors.[7]

EXHIBIT 1 Top 20 Global Beauty Companies

Name	HQ	Sales ($ billions)	Subsidiaries/ Main Brands
L'Oréal Group	Clichy, France	$11.20	L'Oréal Paris; Laboratoires Garnier; Gemey; Maybelline; Club des Createurs de Beauté; La Scad; Laboratoires Ylang; Soft Sheen; Lancôme; Biotherm; Helena Rubenstein; Lanvin; Parfums Armani; Cacharel; Ralph Lauren; Paloma Picasso; Kiehl's; Guy LaRoche; Vichy; La Roche-Posay; L'Oréal Technique Professionelle; Kerastase; Redken; Inne; Matrix; Galderna; Sanofi-Synthelabo (20%); Carson Inc.
Procter & Gamble	Cincinatti, USA	$7.50	Olay; SK-II; Cover Girl; Max Factor; Physique; Pantene; VS Vidal Sassoon; Head & Shoulders; Pert; Rejoice; Old Spice; "G" Giorgio; Hugo Boss; Red; BOSS; Reflect.com
Unilever	Rotterdam & London	$6.92	Elizabeth Arden; Calvin Klein Cosmetics; Parfums Karl Lagerfeld; Parfums Cerruti; Parfums Valentino; Scherrer; Helene Curtis; Cheeseborough Pond's; Elizabeth Taylor; Elida Gibbs; Fabergé Brut; Atkinsons; Timotei; Clear; Sunsilk; Organics; Rexona; Sure; Axe; Lynx; Vaseline; Impulse
Shiseido Co. Ltd.	Tokyo	$4.90	Shiseido; Carita; Beauté Prestige International; Jean Paul Gaultier; Issey Miyake; Clé de Peau; Tony & Tony; Ayura Co. Ltd.; D'ici la Co. Ltd.; Et Tu Sais Co. Ltd.; Zihr International; Nars; Za; 5S; Inoui; Auslese; Naturals; Qiora; Praudia; Pureness; Vital Perfection; Bio-performance Super Revitalizer; Basala; Féminité du Bois
The Estée Lauder Companies Inc.	New York, USA	$4.20	Estée Lauder; Clinique; Aramis; Tommy Hilfiger; Prescriptives; Origins; MAC Cosmetics; Jane; La Mer; Donna Karan; Aveda; Stila; Jo Malone; Bumble & Bumble; Kate Spade

EXHIBIT 1	Top 20 Global Beauty Companies (continued)		
Name	**HQ**	**Sales ($ billions)**	**Subsidiaries/ Main Brands**
Johnson & Johnson	New Brunswick, USA	$3.40	Neutrogena; Clean & Clear; Purpose; pH5.5; RoC; Aveeno; Penaten; Johnson's; Renova; Retin-A
Avon Products Inc.	New York, USA	$3.20	Anew; Avon Techniques; Avon Beyond Color; ColorTrend; Perceive; Women of Earth; Far Away; Starring; Josie Sweet Honesty
KAO Corporation	Tokyo	$2.60	The Andrew Jergens Co.; Goldwell; Guhl; Ikebana; Biore; Curel; Qualité; Jergens; Trendline; Merit; Blaune; Levenus; Sofina; Aube
Biersdorf AG	Hamburg, Germany	$2.53	Cosmed Division; NIVEA; 8?4; Atrix; Basis pH; Labello; Gammon; Juvena; La Prairie; Medical Division-Dermatology
Wella Group	Darmstadt, Germany	$2.43	Wella; Cosmopolitan Cosmetics; Sebastian International
Bristol-Myers Squibb	New York, USA	$2.40	Clairol; Aussie/Redmond Products; Hydrience
Kanebo Ltd.	Tokyo	$2.28	Kanebo Cosmetics Europe; Kanebo Home Products; e'quipe Ltd./Kanebo Silk; Exclusive Bio; Sensai; Cosmetia; IB; Mild Coat; Medicated Shidenkai XD; Dada; Testimo; Kanebo Bio; Revue; RMK; Twany; Fila; Naïve
Intimate Brands Inc.	Ohio, USA	$2.05	Bath & Body Works; Victoria's Secret Beauty; White Barn Candle Co.
Alberto-Culver Co.	Melrose Park, USA	$1.97	Alberto-Culver; Cederroth International; Alberto VO5; TRESemmé; St. Ives Laboratoires; Sally Beauty Company; Molnlycke Toiletries; TCB; Pro-line; Motions
Henkel KGAA	Dusseldorf, Germany	$1.92	Schwarzkopf & Henkel; Poly Color; Fa; Schauma; Drei Wetter; Taft; Gliss Kur; Diadermine; Aok; Schwarzkopf Professional; Schwarzkopf & Dep Inc.; L.A. Looks; Morris

EXHIBIT 1	Top 20 Global Beauty Companies (continued)		
Name	**HQ**	**Sales ($ billions)**	**Subsidiaries/ Main Brands**
Revlon Inc.	New York, USA	$1.86	Revlon; Colorstay; Ultima II; Streetwear; Almay; Flex; Charlie
LVMH Moët Hennessy Louis Vuitton	Paris, France	$1.81	Christian Dior; Guerlain; Givenchy; Parfums Kenzo; Parfume Loewe; Hard Candy; Benefit Cosmetics; Make Up Forever; Urban Decay; Bliss
Coty Inc.	New York, USA	$1.80	Coty Beauty; Lancaster Group/Vanilla Fields; The Healing Garden; Stetson; Addidas; Calgon; Davidoff Cool Water; Jil Sander; Exclamation; Vivienne Westwood; Isabella Rossellini; Rimmel; Yue-Sai
The Boots Company PLC	Nottingham, England	$1.60	Boots the Chemist; Boots Retail International; Boots Opticians; Halfords; Boots Properties; Boots Healthcare International; E45; Nobacter; Solubacter; Boots Contract Manufacturing; Handbag.com.
Colgate-Palmolive Company	New York, USA	$1.50	Colgate; Palmolive; Speed Stick; Lady Speed Stick; Skin Bracer; Afta; Protex; Caprice

- Beauty.com was acquired by Drugstore.com in February 2000; in late October 2000, the site terminated 10% of its workforce and announced that it would close its New York office.[8]
- Beautyjungle.com laid off 60% of its staff and undertook a review of its strategic operations in late October 2000.[9] The site closed its doors for business by mid-November 2000.
- Beautyscene.com went out of business in late November 2000.
- Bliss/Blissworld.com, a growing spas and cosmetics company, has developed successful lines of skin care and home spa products under the brands Remede and Bliss, which are distributed in selected locations. Bliss also distributes a wide variety of its distinctive beauty products through its Blissworld.com Web site.
- Eve.com shut down operations on October 20, 2000, less than 24 hours after its parent, Idealab, pulled financing from the site.[10] Eve.com's domain name and remnants have been acquired by competitor Sephora.com.

- Gloss.com is on target to be relaunched in March 2001. It will feature all of the Estée Lauder Companies brands as well as Clarins and Chanel. Industry sources believe Estée Lauder's presence may have a significant impact on the online industry by drawing more customers online.
- Ibeauty.com, a certified AOL merchant, has recently hired a new CEO, Gabriella Forte.
- Lab21.com is an online laboratory that custom formulates skin care products to a customer's specific needs and requests. The site claims it is capable of formulating 21 million unique skin care products. Customers answer an online questionnaire about their skin and its needs.
- Sephora is an international beauty retailing venture owned by LVMH, which has drawn wide client and industry praise for its innovative store design and fresh approach to merchandising presentation. Sephora.com, launched in October 1999, extends the Sephora retail beauty concept to a worldwide audience.

PROCTER & GAMBLE

Procter & Gamble, started in 1837 as a soap manufacturer in Cincinnati, today offers over 300 brands of consumer packaged goods in nearly 140 countries. P&G, a global leader in the industry with sales topping $38 billion annually, manufactures products in a wide range of categories, including Fabric & Home Care, Baby Care, Feminine Care, Tissues & Towels, Beauty Care, Health Care, and Food & Beverages products. With leading market shares, P&G's Beauty Care segment represents approximately 20% of P&G's total sales, or $7.5 billion annually. This category includes three cosmetic labels, each targeted toward a different segment of the mass market.

- *Cover Girl.* P&G's Cover Girl line of cosmetics, launched in 1960, caters to girls and young women 14 to 24 years of age who are concerned with clean skin, a natural look, and having fun.
- *Max Factor.* This line started as a line of theatrical makeup in 1909 created by Max Factor, Sr., who began as a makeup man for the Royal Ballet in Czarist Russia. Today, Max Factor is positioned as a cosmetics line used by makeup artists, but it is available to consumers through mass channels. Brand promotions centre around Hollywood themes such as blockbuster movie hits like *Titanic*.
- *Oil of Olay.* The Oil of Olay brand is the youngest of P&G's beauty lines. Launched as a full cosmetics line in 1999 as an extension of the popular moisturizer used by many women, this line is targeted to middle-aged women who want to look and feel younger. Benefit claims include reduced wrinkles and younger skin.

The Beauty category also includes non-cosmetic brands, such as hair care, including VS Vidal Sassoon, Pantene, and Physique. Distribution for these products is almost exclusively in drug, grocery, or mass merchandisers such as Kmart and Wal-Mart.

Project Mirror

A corporate behemoth known for innovation and brand marketing prowess, P&G has long been a leader in new product development. However, in the early 1990s, the consumer giant began to stumble. The new product development process itself had become too bureaucratic and too slow to market. With so much time and money at stake, P&G could not afford another debacle like Olestra, the fat substitute that took 25 years and $250 million to develop. P&G began an initiative to foster more innovation and to shorten the new product development cycle. Major changes in their product development process included:

- Implementing new collaborative technologies that promote sharing ideas and information
- Instituting global email systems that link 93 000 users
- Creating virtual libraries and "collaboration [chat] rooms"
- Developing an internal innovation fund
- Providing desktop videoconferencing capabilities

All of these corporate initiatives have aided in reducing product development time and bureaucracy at P&G. As of late 2000, product development time was down 50%.[11] In addition to revamping its product development process, P&G pursued another important initiative: embracing the Internet age. At a 1995 advertising industry meeting, P&G's CEO Ed Artzt warned, "Our most important ad medium, television, is about to change." Artzt believed that if marketers did not keep up with new digital media, years of brand-building would be lost. Keeping up was vital for P&G. Artzt issued a mandate: "We have a lot of work to do. Let's get going."[12]

P&G reacted by building Web sites for virtually every brand they offered, even trying to sell products over the Web. However, much like the company brand structure, the attempt was uncoordinated and lacked a unified corporate vision. The company was simply "not uniquely prepared to capitalize" on Artzt's vision and had not harnessed the power of the Internet.[13] Additionally, P&G could not risk alienating its traditional distribution channels.

During this time, P&G's Interactive Marketing Team, a group of ten or so brand managers who received corporate funding to execute interactive projects with select brands, was quietly developing an idea in Cincinnati. Within a few months, the team came up with a plan, developed technology to customize products, and created a prototype Web site.[14] Thus, the idea of Project Mirror was born: a mass customization Web site that would allow women to make their own formulations of makeup, shampoo, and fragrance, complete with their own personalized label. What began as a skunkworks project with $1 million from an internal innovation fund quickly ran into P&G's limited knowledge about the Internet.[15] P&G began to look outside its doors for help.

Armed with a list of venture capital firms from P&G's investment bankers, Denis Beausejour, P&G's worldwide vice-president of marketing for beauty care, Nathan Estruth and other P&Gers flew to Silicon Valley to talk to the top venture capital firms. They grilled executives and venture capitalists about the secrets of Web success. The executives also learned the benefits of stripping out extra layers of management and increasing the pace of innovation and decision-making.

REFLECT.COM

Reflect.com was financed with $35 million from Procter & Gamble and $15 million from Institutional Venture Partners (IVP), the investment firm famous for backing Excite Inc.

(See Exhibit 2 for description of IVP.) IVP's Geoff Yang summed up his enthusiasm for the deal saying, "What energized us was that this wasn't just another e-tailing deal. They were going to do something no one's done before."[16]

However, there were some sticking points in ironing out the details of the partnership. Where IVP was used to conducting informal negotiations with young entrepreneurs that were finalized quickly with a handshake, the P&G lawyers went over every detail.[17] IVP's typical negotiations lasted just one day, whereas with Reflect.com they took three weeks. Issues arose regarding equity, control of future financing events, and the new company's governance. "Yang wasn't interested in being a mere midwife for a P&G development project. He wanted to build a killer freestanding company that could pursue its own best interests. He put forward an argument he remembers this way: 'If you guys want control, it might as well be inside P&G. We can't allow you to call the shots. If we can't take this company public, then you're capping our upside.'"[18]

Despite the sticking points, P&G "threw caution to the wind on some key points." The investors agreed upon the 65-15-20 split (for P&G, IVP/Redpoint Ventures, and Reflect.com employees respectively). IVP received the same number of board seats as P&G, as well as "an equal say over such pivotal issues as whether and when to take Reflect.com public." P&G, however, retained control over any reorganization or sale of the company.[19] A. G. Lafley, then president of Procter & Gamble's global beauty care division and interim CEO of the new company (now P&G CEO), summed up P&G's feelings about the site, "We very strongly believed we had to get out in the middle of the start-up environment and see if we could deliver innovation and speed at that rate."[20]

EXHIBIT 2	Institutional Venture Partners (IVP)

IVP has been venture investing since 1974 and has funded more than 200 companies. It now manages more than $1 billion. IVP has marshalled 60 IPOs and over 25 successful "IPO-like" acquisitions. The company has consistently funded companies that have become dominant players in new industries:

- *Internet.* Excite, Mpath, Ask Jeeves, Concur
- *Communications equipment.* Bay Networks, MMC Networks, Aspect Telecommunications
- *Enterprise software.* Clarify, Concur
- *Semiconductors.* LSI Logic, Altera, Atmel, Cirrus Logic
- *Storage.* Seagate, Exabyte
- *Computing.* Stratus, Sequent
- *Life sciences.* Aviron, Biopsys

IVP's investments have combined revenues of more than $20 billion and a combined market value of more than $30 billion, and employ more than 125 000 people.

Source: "About IVP," Institutional Venture Partners Web site, accessed August 19, 2001 <www.ivp.com/about/overview.html>.

Independence Day—"Burn the Ships"

In order to make the Web venture more authentic, P&G forced employees to resign from the consumer goods giant, take pay cuts in exchange for stock options, and move to San Francisco. On October 1, 1999, a team of 15 people left P&G to join Reflect.com. The night before, Denis Beausejour hosted a sendoff party at his home, ceremoniously presenting each team member's spouse with one share of Reflect.com stock. "You don't have a lifeline back to P&G," Beausejour told the troops. "All you've got left now is your Reflect.com stock and your teammates. Now make it happen." The lifeline bit was no joke. A. G. Lafley decided that the 15 people sailing off on the Reflect.com lifeboat would not have the option of returning to P&G. "Burn the ships"—a reference to the conquistador Cortès' decision to stay in the New World—became a Reflect.com mantra.[21]

The Site

The Reflect.com site launched in December 1999 as a personalized line of beauty products (including skin and hair care and cosmetics) and services created for and available solely through the Internet, using a patent-pending system for a mass customization model. With access to P&G's global supply chain and R&D facilities, the site has the capability to create more than 300 000 different products and packages. By asking the consumer a series of questions and letting her control the experience, the site creates customized products and packages. Additionally, Reflect.com owns its unique manufacturing process that resembles a virtual plug-and-play. The company is able to produce in very small lots (25 versus competitors' 10 000), and has reduced changeovers to 5–7 minutes. (The industry average is 90 minutes.)

The site capitalizes on P&G's beauty care expertise while leveraging the Internet's capabilities to create a consumer experience that cannot be duplicated in a typical bricks-and-mortar environment. Using an interactive question-and-answer process to determine each woman's needs and P&G's research and development lab, Reflect.com creates unique products for each customer.

The product creation process begins on the site and ends with a fulfillment centre in Cincinnati called Direct Site.[22] Sourcing from multiple suppliers along with technology as a delivery tool dictate order fulfillment. This process, from front to back end, is proprietary and currently pending patent approval.[23] Reflect.com also enjoys the benefits of lower inventories and reduced cost of sales.

The company allows a customer to build her own brand of upscale beauty products that are created, manufactured, packaged, and distributed on an individual basis. "Reflect.com acts as a channel to serve the high-performance sector of the beauty product market. Its target customers are 'beauty involved,' meaning that they are willing to invest the extra time in designing their own beauty product solutions. They're also experienced Internet buyers who are comfortable with e-commerce and online interaction."[24]

In September 2000, Reflect.com launched a patent-pending online process that allows women to create their own perfume. Women are guided through the creation of their signature scents by answering questions that reveal the components of their ideal fragrance. Each selection is made through "an interactive visual experience designed to capture both her imagination and her scent preferences to create the perfect fragrance."[25] The customer is sent three samples of her creation from which to choose.

Three days after a customer's order is shipped, first-time buyers receive a live orchid as a "thank you." Browsers who register on the site and create a product but do not buy it receive a surprise "delight sample" with their name on the bottle. If a customer is not satisfied with the product, Reflect.com will customize it until she is. The site, however, does not accept returns.

THE CROSSROADS

Regarding the site, Lafley has stated, "even if it flops, we will have learned a lot, and it would have been worth it."[26] Lisa Allen, an analyst with Forrester Research, believes that P&G is more interested in information than sales. She explains, "Procter & Gamble sees Reflect.com as one big-time, real-time market research tool. They can get information directly from consumers on a range of products, then feed it back to the mother ship in Cincinnati. ... Even if they lose money in direct sales, they gain value in market research."[27]

By November 2000, Reflect.com had sold more than 250 000 customized skin, hair, and cosmetics products since its December 1999 launch.[28] However, in order to succeed, P&G's new customized beauty site will have to create a loyal following among the industry's brand-conscious upscale consumers. In fact, it is commonly acknowledged that "brands help people get over the hurdle of buying online."[29]

As Kent sat at her desk, she could not help but wonder, could Reflect.com shift the NPD process to consumers, and still build a loyal consumer base? Would this new business model ever amount to more than a multimillion-dollar learning experience for P&G?

The company had already applied for second-round financing that it needed to redesign the site; but given the tumultuous market conditions, it was uncertain whether they would receive it. Kent had to decide what course to chart the Reflect.com ship. If Reflect.com received the funding, how would the company improve its site, and would this redesign prove pivotal in attracting and keeping loyal customers? If Reflect.com was denied financing, would the company attempt the redesign anyway, or would it close its virtual doors forever?

EPILOGUE

Two days shy of its first birthday, Reflect.com received a $30 million round of financing, in which its original investors returned. (While the details of the second round were not made public, the terms are reported to be similar to the first-round financing.)[30] "Our investors are pleased with what we've achieved in the time we've been up and the response we've been getting in terms of orders and reorders," says Richard Gerstein, vice-president of design and marketing.[31]

Reflect.com officials claim that they did not need the second-round financing, because the site had burned through the first, but that it was necessary to invest in infrastructure and to further build the business. One of the first projects with the infusion was a relaunch of the site in response to customer feedback. As of November 2000, the site offered a more streamlined system and additional shopping benefits. For example, the site still profiles customers' needs, but the customer has the ability to start customizing her product as early as the first page. Previously, she had to navigate through several screens before reaching this step. Another new feature enables shoppers to see aspects (e.g., package selection, choice of graphics) of their product as it is being created. Customers can also window-shop, viewing what types of products can be made, in what sizes, etc., before starting the creation process. In this browsing section, the shopper may click on the creation area any time she wants if she sees something she likes. The site incorporates a navigation bar across the top of each screen that provides visitors with more flexibility to move around the site.

EXHIBIT 3 Average Price Points for Reflect, Lancôme, and Oil of Olay

	Reflect.com	Lancôme	Oil of Olay
Lipsticks, shampoos, conditioners	$12.00	$18.50	$8.29
Foundation makeup	$16.50	$32.50	$10.99–$12.99
Moisturizers	$19.50	$36–$77	$7.59
Facial mask	$24.00	$22.50–$27	N/A
Eye gel	$28.00	$44.00	$9.99
Night cream	$29.50	$59	$9.99
Fragrance	$40.00	$32–$80	N/A

Sources: Reflect.com Web site, accessed July 29, 2001 <www.reflect.com>; Lancôme Web site, accessed July 29, 2001 <www.lancome.com>; local drugstore.

EXHIBIT 4 Management Team

Ginger Kent, Chief Executive Officer

Diane deCordova, VP, Business Development

Don Donovan, VP, Fine Fragrances & Strategic Planning

Richard Gerstein, VP, Marketing & Design

Jonathan Grayson, VP, Engineering

Alex Zelikovsky, Chief Logistics Officer

EXHIBIT 5	Investors' Strengths
IVP	**P&G**
$15 million	$35 million
Extensive Silicon Valley network	Branding/marketing expertise
Ask Jeeves Inc. execs meeting	
Internet startup experience	Extensive R&D infrastructure
High-tech recruiting muscle	Launch team
Speed	Existing cosmetic business with formulas
Credibility with Net establishment	Credibility with media and Wall Street

NOTES

1. Reflect.com Web site, home page, accessed October 2000 <www.reflect.com>.
2. Kerry Diamond, "Taking stock of Beauty's net worth," *Women's Wear Daily*, November 3, 2000, p. 6.
3. Laura Klepacki, "The Star report," *Women's Wear Daily*, May 19, 2000, p. 2.
4. Janet Ozzard, "Understanding Beauty's Web appeal," *Women's Wear Daily*, August 11, 2000, p. 10.
5. See note 4.
6. Alev Aktar, "Women on the Web," *Women's Wear Daily*, January 28, 2000, p. 9.
7. See note 2.
8. See note 2.
9. See note 2.
10. See note 2.
11. Marianne Kolbasuk McGee, "Culture change: come together: the idea behind collaboration rooms," *Information Week*, October 5, 1999, accessed July 29, 2001 <www.informationweek.com/758/prga3.htm>.
12. Dale Buss, "Procter & Gamble faces the future," *The Industry Standard*, April 3, 2000, accessed July 29, 2001 <www.thestandard.com/article/0,1902,13264,00.html>.
13. See note 12.
14. Himelstein Linda and Peter Galuszka, "P&G gives birth to a Web baby," September 27, 1999, p. 87.
15. Jerry Useem, "Can these marriages be saved?," *Fortune*, November 8, 2000, p. 102.
16. See note 15.
17. See note 14.
18. See note 14.
19. See note 14.

20. Scott Herhold, "Web site a thing of beauty for P&G," *San Jose Mercury News*, September 14, 1999, p. 1C.

21. See note 15.

22. Richard Karpinski, "Beauty site gets personal—Reflect.com delivers fully personalized Web customer service," *Internetweek*, November 29, 1999, p. 33.

23. Ramin P. Jaleshgari, "An alternative culture: Reflect.com's unique approach," *Information Week*, October 25, 1999.

24. David Ticoll, "The beauty of the Internet—letting customers create their own brand results in 'ultimate stickiness,'" *Teledotcom*, June 5, 2000, accessed July 29, 2001 <www.techweb.com/se/directlink.cgi?TLC20000605S0067>.

25. Beth Cox, "Ah, the sweet smell of eau de e-commerce," *Ecommerce Guide*, September 6, 2000, accessed July 29, 2001 <ecommerce.internet.com/news/insights/trends/article/0,3371,10417_454021,00.html>.

26. See note 15.

27. Betsy Spethmann, "Beauty treatments," *Promo*, August 2000.

28. See note 27.

29. Arent Lindsey, "Procter makes up a gamble," *Wired News*, September 17, 1999, accessed July 29, 2001 <www.wired.com/news/print/0,1294,21795,00.html>.

30. Colleen O'Connor, "Venture-backed Beauty site reflects potential," *IPO Reporter*, September 18, 2000. (No page number from Lexis/Nexis.)

31. Christopher Heun, "Per$onalizing cosmetics," *Information Week*, September 18, 2000, accessed July 29, 2001 <www.informationweek.com/804/04fmcos.htm>.

part two overview

Customer Service in E-Business

In the euphoria following the use of the Internet for e-business, the general perception surfaced that if you build a Web site consumers will flock to it and shop. Within a few years, many e-businesses have come to realize that selling anything online is indeed a difficult and daunting task involving more than just establishing a Web site. In the early days of e-commerce, the key metric was Web site traffic, that is, the number of hits or visitors to the site. Today, the key metric is "conversion," a statistic that captures the proportion of "browsers-turned-buyers." As with traditional customers, online shoppers demand and expect a high level of customer service, especially since their loyalty is just a click away. Clearly, e-business companies must pay close attention to both their customer attraction strategy as well as their conversion and retention strategy.

Although customer service is a critical component of enticing buyers, and establishing a loyal clientele, it is often neglected or mishandled. The cost of providing superior customer service can be measured easily, but the resulting revenues are not easily visible or measurable, and this is the reason why it is often neglected. However, if e-businesses are to capitalize on the opportunities the Internet provides as a marketing channel to attract and retain loyal customers, they must ensure that the quality of the experience they provide is closely aligned to what customers expect. That is, everything from the Web site to values, strategies, tactics, processes, products, and customer support should be consistent with, or exceed, what customers expect. However, to accomplish all this, companies must be able to develop a deep and personal relationship with their customers, and this is a complicated endeavour, as outlined in the readings in this section of the book.

case one

Onvia.com: Grow Your Business!

Ajax Persaud,
School of Management,
University of Ottawa

Jasbir Dhaliwal, Norwegian
School of Management

ONVIA: ON THE ROAD

In 1996, Glenn Ballman, a graduate from the prestigious Richard Ivey Business School, sold ice cream from his truck, worked as a telemarketer for an Internet service provider selling Web services to businesses, and started his own company, Sun Commerce Corporation—all in one year! At Axion Communications, the Vancouver-based Internet service provider, Ballman tried to become a partner in the company but his hopes were soon laid to rest after being rebuffed by Axion's management. Disappointed, he left to form Sun Commerce Corporation, and, as he puts it, "I took with me all the people I wanted [from Axion]."

Sun Commerce Corporation targeted small companies with turnkey, e-commerce solutions, designed exclusively for the Web. Essentially, small e-commerce companies hosted their Web stores on Sun Commerce servers for a setup and monthly fee. A year later, Ballman questioned himself, asking that if he had such a great technology, then why not use it to set up his own e-commerce store? Ballman, a true entrepreneur, along with his business partner, Rob Ayer, founded MegaDepot.com (MD) in August 1997.

This case was prepared with the assistance of Gary Meehan, for class discussion purposes rather than to illustrate either effective or ineffective handling of a business or administrative situation.

His idea was that MD would serve as "the window to the warehouses of the world, selling anything that can conceivably be ordered over the Internet, paid for by credit card, and shipped by normal means." MD sold a wide range of items including grass seed, horse feed, gold chains, computer hardware and accessories, and software. MD was positioned partly as a consignment store that small businesses could use to extend their sales channels by simply listing their products with MD. When MD received an order, it set the price and collected the payment, then sent the order to the supplier, who shipped it directly to the customer. MD received the difference between what it charged the customer for the order and the invoice received from the supplier.

Ballman's dream was to make MD into something big, but he needed "money, oodles of money quickly." He and Robert Ayer were unable to find investors in Canada to fund MD because either the "investors wanted to have majority control of the business, wouldn't provide enough funding, or simply did not understand the business." Unwilling to give up majority control of MD, Ballman decided to open a U.S. office and began looking for financing in the United States. In June 1998, he packed up, rented a truck, and moved to Seattle to find office space. Four months later all of MD's eight staff had moved to Seattle, which then became its new headquarters. Gary Meehan, who joined MD in June 1998 as vice-president of operations, was appointed president of the Canadian operations later the following year.

The move into the United States marked a fundamental shift in the company's strategy and name. MD shifted its focus from being the "window to the warehouses of the world" to helping small business operate and grow. MD completely overhauled its Web site to reflect the new focus on small business. According to Gary Meehan, "we targeted small business because of our own frustrations trying to create, operate, and grow a small business, and our customers, the majority of whom are small businesses, were asking us for help. Also, the research that Kristen Hamilton, Onvia's Chief Strategy Officer, had done in the small business market suggested that a big opportunity existed since the needs of small businesses were largely untouched and the Internet had the potential to even the playing field vis-à-vis big business." It was also felt that the name MD sounded more like a mass-consumer brick-and-mortar operation and did not resonate with small businesses as a company that could help them operate and grow their businesses. So in the summer of 1999 MD changed its name to Onvia.com—"Onvia" translating loosely from the Latin for "on the path" or "on the road."

Onvia.com ("Onvia") has become the leading online exchange helping small businesses succeed and grow. Small businesses can now sell their products and services to other businesses and government agencies through Onvia's Web site. Also, it increased the services offered through its Web site to help business owners grow their businesses; that is, it has become more than just a marketplace for buying and selling business goods and services. As of April 2001, Onvia had just over 1 000 000 registered users and over 700 000 customer accounts. In Canada, there are over 100 000 registered users of the Web site. Originally started by one person, the company grew to 500 staff and now employs over 200 employees in both Canada and the United States. On March 1, 2001, Onvia's market capitalization on the NASDAQ was just over US$600 million. The company has been the recipient of numerous awards, including Forbes Magazine's Top 100 Technology Companies (February 2001), Forbes' Best B2B Site (June 2000), and one of Washington Software Alliance's three Most Innovative Service Providers (2000).

ONVIA'S PRODUCTS AND SERVICES

The strengths behind Onvia's offerings are the versatility and services offered on its Web site, **www.onvia.com**. The Web site points to thousands of products and services, including professional services, which small businesses can purchase to help them grow and operate more efficiently. Within a matter of seconds, purchase orders can be expedited, requests for quotes can be submitted, business advice can be obtained, and links to a wide array of companies can be made. Through Onvia's trading hub, customers obtain quotes and information on products and services directly from the sellers, while at the same time selling products and services to interested buyers. In addition, customers can access the latest business news, information, worksheets, business forms, business calculators, and other tools. Through the *online forum*, its customers can share information, know-how, expertise, contacts, and business opportunities.

Specifically, Onvia offers the following services:

- *Request for quote network.* This service provides businesses with access to a network of more than 54 000 suppliers across more than 100 service categories. Interested buyers submit requests for a desired service and sellers reply with pricing and fulfillment information to the purchaser. Through this service, customers can get estimates from a large number of bidders quite quickly.
- *Business to government exchange. DemandStar* by Onvia gives small business sellers access to state, local, and regional governments' tendering and procurement opportunities.
- *Buy products system.* A marketplace of more than 100 000 business products can be bought quickly and conveniently.
- *Productivity tools.* A collection of downloadable business forms, worksheets, checklists, and how-to advice for businesses to grow and manage their operations.
- *Digital community.* A forum for business owners to exchange ideas, advice, and opinions, and build networks of relationships.
- *News and tools.* Bringing the latest business news.

The guiding principles that form the cornerstone of Onvia's value proposition to its customers are as follows:

- *Superior customer service.* This begins with hiring the right people who not only understand small business, but also deliver top-quality service levels to customers. In fact, as Ballman puts it, "delivering value over and over again" is what Onvia tries to provide its customers.
- *One-stop shopping.* This begins with creating a Web site that provides small business owners with all that is needed to help them to build up and manage their businesses—products and services, customer-lead generation, productivity tools, breaking news, and expert advice. "We work very hard to ensure that all our products and services are timely and seamlessly integrated, and our Web site is user-friendly. We have done our usability testing," says Gary Meehan, president of Onvia Canada.
- *Return on investment for customers.* Strong, life-long customer relationships are what Onvia is pursuing. According to Ballman, "this means that when a small business

pays me $3 for a lead, I want to make sure that lead is worth $3000 to them." Every customer must be satisfied at all times.

Where Onvia sees its primary value-added offering is its ability to offer its customers a complete range of services that are required to operate and grow their businesses quickly and easily. Realizing the importance of content and presentation to its business, Onvia employed its own team of journalists, headed by Mark Pawlosky, who had won a Pulitzer Prize for his work with the *Kansas Star* and worked as an editor with MSNBC and the *Wall Street Journal*. According to Geoff Davenport, Onvia's vice-president of sales and marketing in Canada, "our customer feedback indicates that our Web site is user-friendly, intuitive, content-rich, and the products and services offered are well integrated; even customers who are not Web-savvy say they can use the site quite effectively—our Web site offers convenience, speed, and choice."

FINANCING

From October 1998 to February 1999, Mark Calvert, Onvia's chief financial officer, Glenn, and Kristen spent a lot of time trying to convince angel investors and venture capitalists (VCs) to invest in Onvia. By the end of January 1999, they had raised approximately US$1.1 million in seed money from angel investors. This allowed the company to continue to operate while the trio continued to look for more financing. Then, in February 1999, Onvia secured its first round of venture capital (VC) financing from two VC firms, the Internet Capital Group (ICG) and Mohr Davidow Ventures. Together, these two firms provided approximately US$11.5 million. Again, in August 1999, Onvia secured a second round of financing to the tune of approximately US$25 million from ICG, Mohr Davidow, and a couple of other large investors such as GE Capital. Over the summer of 1999, the company also secured US$11 million in debt financing.

Successful in raising venture financing, Onvia moved aggressively to ramp up its operations and execute its business plan. The company moved both its Seattle and its Vancouver operations into substantially larger facilities, hired more staff, including some very-high-profile people, improved its Web site, and launched an aggressive marketing campaign to increase its subscriber base. Satisfied with the progress it had made, gauging market sentiments—and realizing that it was a race among its competitors as to who would be the first to obtain public financing and a listing on the NASDAQ—Onvia, in October 1999, began preparing the documentation required to file for an initial public offering (IPO). On December 21, 1999 the company filed its IPO application with NASDAQ. Onvia's next-closest competitor filed for their IPO three weeks later. Prior to filing its IPO application, Onvia secured one final round of funding when some of its major investors wanted to increase their shares in the business. In the end, the company raised about US$71 million prior to IPO.

Onvia made its IPO on March 1, 2000. Meehan recalls, "Initially we planned to price our stock at $11 but just before the offering, we repriced it at US$21 per share and sold all 8 million shares we offered. We raised about US$230 million net on that IPO event. It was certainly the largest war chest among independent online B2B companies." Commenting on the race to IPO, Gary Meehan noted that "because of our success and the market volatility, our key competitors decided to put their IPOs on hold and waited for the market to settle down but this never happened. Instead, the market crashed, and so none of our competitors ever got out and most of them have now gone under, are struggling, or have been acquired or merged with other companies." The cumulative effects of these events have been to help catapult Onvia to be the leader in this particular marketspace and have given it the flexibility to move its business into new strategic directions. It was also the first to brand itself in the marketspace.

Reflecting on the financing process, Meehan observed, "it took much longer than expected to get angel and VC financing. The key challenge was to get them together as a group in one place rather than individually." According to Ballman, "finding the right investors creates a double win: 'They're paying you money to help you.'" Although it was still challenging, "having an operating business and an experienced management team [see Exhibit 1] with great connections definitely helps." Also, timing was critical. According to one of Onvia's executives, "we were fortunate because it was just around this time that the venture capital community started to warm up to the idea that small businesses are going to become an important market for those involved in the Internet. So angels and VCs were much more receptive and eager to invest in some of the ventures that were emerging." In addition, Onvia acted swiftly trying to be the first within its space to launch its IPO. It was a risk that paid off.

EVOLVING STRATEGY

During the fall of 1998 as Ballman was crisscrossing the United States trying to secure financing, he met up with a former classmate from the Richard Ivey School of Business,

EXHIBIT 1	Onvia's Management Team as of January 1, 2001

Gary Meehan, President, Canadian Operations

Leonard Brody, Vice-President, Corporate Development Canada

Geoff Davenport, Vice-President, Sales

Sean Neighbors, Senior Director of Marketing and Exchange Operations, Canada

Mike Pickett, Chairman, Chief Executive Officer, and President

Kristen McLaughlin (formerly Hamilton), Chief Strategy Officer

Rob Ayer, Vice-President, Strategic Development

Don Bowler, Vice-President, Investor Relations

Clayton Lewis, Vice-President, Marketing

Dusty Routh, Vice-President, Onvia Solutions Group

Gretchen Sorensen, Vice-President, Corporate Affairs

Clark Westmoreland, Vice-President, Operations

Glenn Ballman, former Founder, President, Chairman, and CEO (resigned on April 3, 2001)

Source: "Management," Onvia Web site, accessed July 29, 2001 <www.corporate.onvia.com/management.xml>; David Akin, "A dot-com comet fizzles out," *Financial Post*, May 5, 2001, p. E12.

Kristen Hamilton, who joined him in his efforts to raise financing. Kristen had worked with a consulting firm assisting several major corporations (e.g., Compaq, Microsoft, Oracle, and MSN) to help them develop their strategies toward small businesses, since it was believed that small businesses would become a major market with the coming of the Internet. In addition to her high-level contacts in these corporations, she was well known in the investment community, especially in the Pacific Northwest and California. Kristen had also done a lot of research on the role of small business in the Internet economy, so she brought a solid understanding of these issues. Within a few months of joining Onvia, Kristen helped to recruit Mark Calvert to the management team. Mark had extensive experience as an investment banker and in startups. The experience, knowledge, and connections of Kristen were very influential in convincing Ballman that Onvia needed to refocus its strategy away from being the "window to the warehouses of the world" to being an online exchange for business products and services targeted to small businesses. Ballman, Kristen, and Mark played a crucial role in the early success of Onvia.

Convinced of the tremendous opportunity from a largely untouched market for online services to help create, operate, and grow small businesses, Onvia redesigned its Web site, making it a comprehensive "one-stop shopping" site where small businesses and entrepreneurs could obtain much of the information, products, services, and tools needed to run a company efficiently. The primary target market was the emerging small e-business marketplace. Onvia's goal was to help entrepreneurs "who are always trying to do more with less, grow faster, and express their visions through sustained, Web-enabled customer relationships and services." Initially, Onvia positioned its Web site as a destination for business products and services. Later, with the launching of its Request for Quote service—whereby small businesses sell their products and services and generate new business leads—the company repositioned its site as more than just a destination for business services, but a new marketplace. The objective was to emphasize the transactional nature of its offerings, which allow companies rapid and cost-effective ways of conducting business online.

In the beginning, when there was far less competition, Onvia's strategy focused on helping small businesses *operate* efficiently. For example, if an entrepreneur wanted to set up a new business, Onvia's Web site would provide much of the products and services needed to register and incorporate the business, prepare a business plan, and find market research data, and provide advice on where to get the best deals on office supplies, and so on. However, as competition intensified from highly specialized niche players, Onvia had refocused its strategy to stay ahead. Onvia's new strategy focused much more strongly on trying to help small businesses and entrepreneurs *grow* their customer base and revenue streams. In this regard, Onvia has strengthened its offering in areas such as helping small business owners generate new business opportunities, including helping small businesses with the marketing and financing for these. The most recent incarnation of Onvia's strategy focused largely on helping small businesses participate effectively in the very lucrative business-to-government (B2G) sector by helping with the government tender and procurement process. Intending to be a major player in the B2G space, Onvia acquired two key B2G players—GlobeOne in August 2000 and DemandStar in March 2001. Through these acquisitions, Onvia secured some key technology and personnel. According to Meehan, "the DemandStar acquisition provided us with software solutions which we can leverage for efficiency gains using the Internet." Onvia's acquisitions have been concentrated in the United States, "since it has a larger market, and a land grab there is certainly critical for success."

In addition to acquisitions, Onvia has established partnerships with media companies, banks, associations, and other organizations that target small business, in order to build its market share, extend its brand, and advertise. Onvia has made strategic alliances with major companies including Visa, U.S.A., the California Small Business Association, the American Subcontractors Association Inc., AOL Canada, Canada.com, The Globe & Mail, Profit Magazine, E*Trade Canada, CNC Global, Women's Entrepreneurs of Canada, IBM, and Visa Canada (visit **www.corporate.onvia.com/alliances.xml** for a more comprehensive list of partners).

With an eye to increasing its customer base, Onvia has also been forging strategic partnerships with close to two dozens chambers of commerce across the United States to promote Onvia's services in exchange for member discounts. Onvia also has deals with companies and associations that have high hit rates on their Web sites, increasing Onvia's exposure. The importance of Onvia's strategic alliances and partnerships cannot be underestimated, especially when the market is typified by the highly fragmented nature of the e-marketplace.

REVENUES

Onvia makes its money through various means, including product sales or commissions on products, sponsorships, ad sales, subscriptions, and transaction fees. In 1997, revenues were approximately US$210 000; in 1999, revenues increased to US$27.1 million; and in 2000, revenues increased by 443% to US$147.6 million.

Profitability has remained elusive for Onvia. In 2000, the company posted a loss of US$117 million on revenues of US$147.6 million.[1] It lost US$43 million in 1999. However, Onvia's management is confident that their new strategy, which focuses on helping small businesses to grow instead of helping them to operate more efficiently, combined with its foray in the lucrative B2G market and strategic partnering on several initiatives will propel it to profitability by 2002, its internally set goal.

THE MARKET AND COMPETITION

Gary Meehan, president of Onvia Canada, believes that the market opportunity facing Onvia in both Canada and the United States is huge. He estimates that there are approximately 1.9 million small businesses in Canada and about 28 million small businesses in the United States. Small businesses in the States spent approximately US$25 billion in goods and services over the Internet in 1999. Forrester Research predicts that the size of the business-to-small-business market in the United States alone will be in the neighbourhood of US$107 billion by 2002.[2] This figure does not include the small-B2G transactions.

According to Statistics Canada, the Canadian e-commerce industry for 1999 was C$4.4 billion, and is expected to grow to C$151.5 billion, 3.9% of the world's e-commerce market, by 2004.[3] IDC Canada predicts that the business-to-business (B2B) market will reach C$272 billion by 2005 due to the pressure on businesses to increase their usage of sophisticated supply chain and customer relationship management tools to stay competitive.

Onvia believes that as the number of businesses using the Internet increases, the demand for the types of services it offers will increase substantially. This would in turn attract a growing number of competitors; however, it is well positioned to take on the competition. According to Gary Meehan, "when Onvia first started out, there were no clear competitors, and to this date no other company has been able to match Onvia's offerings as a one-stop shopping mecca for small business products and services. While companies exist that offer similar products or services, they lack the ubiquity and breadth Onvia has." Onvia describes itself as a destination site for all types of small business products and services, unlike many of its competitors, who operate like Web portals. In addition, in the U.S. market, Onvia is differentiating itself by adding new business opportunities for small business through its aggressive expansion into the B2G space.

In Canada, BellZinc, CIBC's BizSmart, and TD MarketSite are Onvia's three primary competitors in the business-to-business space. Other notable competitors include Procuron, a consortium of five companies (CIBC, Scotiabank, Mouvement des Caisses Desjardins, Bell Canada, and BCE Emergis) that is focused solely on B2B procurement, beginning with Big Business, MasterCard's Small Connections Portal, and Royal Bank's TradeMC. The United States has a number of niche players that compete with Onvia in some, but not all, areas. They include Staples (office supplies), ConnectSpace (business cards, buying and selling of goods/services, advice), Works.com, DigitalWorks.com, and Allbusiness.com.

BellZinc.ca is Bell Canada's B2B portal designed for small and medium-sized businesses. The portal offers businesses a wide array of products and services to help them save time and money. Among its offerings are its *Electronic Tendering Service* that receives requests for proposals and submits quotes, and connects buyers and suppliers. A *buy section* allows businesses to buy products and services and become their own authorized sellers of products and services. The *Business Information Center* answers questions about managing business. This section has plenty of practical, relevant information that is very accessible. There is a *Trade Directory* that allows companies to search for suppliers and register themselves as suppliers. Bell ActiMedia is the company in charge of Bell Canada's Internet gateway strategy. It provides e-commerce solutions to small and medium-sized enterprises, and provides database services, electronic delivery services, and print directory services. The company owns the Yellow Pages trademark in Canada and has a clientele of over 320 000 advertisers in Quebec and Ontario.

TD MarketSite is the B2B e-commerce arm of TD Bank Financial Group that was launched in July 2000 to link buyers and suppliers in an open real-time Internet-based trading community. It was designed to aid the buying and selling process between companies. The site allows customers online access to a global marketplace, and the business and financial services required to undertake online transactions. The services offered include a buy site, a supply site, an auction service, TD services, business services, and global trading. The site was developed using TD Bank's financial services technology and the B2B software solutions produced by Commerce One of Pleasanton, California. TD MarketSite is located in Toronto, Ontario.

The major thrust behind TD MarketSite was to utilize the scale of the bank's customer and technology bases to bring about new banking opportunities. Part of this development was to help banks make up for decreasing profits in the retail sector, add new revenue streams, and enhance relationships with existing clients and form new ones. Revenues are generated from transaction fees. Basically, buyers can automate their purchasing and inventory processes, choose which suppliers to purchase from, lower cost through price comparisons, enhance control over spending, and reduce purchase ordering processing cycle times and costs. CIBC's BizSmart is partnered with Staples in Canada, and its primary objective is to promote and sell CIBC's financial products, while providing other SME services.

In the U.S. B2G space, Onvia is a major player, since it has acquired DemandStar, which was among the earliest companies to take the government tendering and procurement business and make it Web-enabled and accessible. In Canada, Merx is the dominant player in the federal and provincial market, and Electronic Tendering Network similarly in the regional and local markets. In the United States, there are a number of players in this space with varying levels of service.

In assessing the competitive landscape, Meehan noted that "most of our competition did some of what we did but not all of it. They outsourced a lot of offerings on their site, for example, by simply linking out, because they only had competencies in limited areas themselves. Commenting on Onvia's offering, Marilyn Muller, a research analyst with Summit Strategies, observed, "Onvia's secret is tying all the ends together. They execute very quickly and have left no feature uncovered."

THE FUTURE

The dot-com shakeout of 2000 has rocked the world of "pure play" Internet companies in fundamental ways. Many very large dot-com ventures have closed shop and many are struggling to remain viable, as the investment community has all but withdrawn from this sector of the new economy. This has been both a blessing and a curse for Onvia. Within weeks of Onvia successfully completing their IPO, which raised US$230 million, the NASDAQ started its downward trend, making it very difficult for its competitors to go public. In fact, those of Onvia's competitors who still hope to go public have put their IPOs on hold indefinitely, waiting for the market to normalize, an event yet to take place. This development has meant that Onvia has gained access to a substantial amount of capital, which its competitors did not have, over the past 12 months. On the negative side, the downturn in the market and the negative perception of pure Internet companies have made it increasingly difficult for the likes of Onvia to raise additional capital. Additionally, investors are demanding that these companies go beyond revenue generation to achieve profitability much quicker, thereby putting a tremendous amount of pressure on them to rethink their business plans and strategies. This is a challenge which Onvia is addressing. The decline of Onvia's shares from US$61.50 per share when it went public in March 2000 to US$0.50 just over a year later (April 5, 2001) resulted in a tremendous decline in Onvia's market capitalization. Although this decline has more to do with general market conditions and investor nervousness about Internet companies, it makes it increasingly difficult for these companies to execute their business plans according to schedule.

Although Onvia is the leader in the B2B market in Canada and is a major player in the B2G market, it has been unable to replicate the level of success it achieved in the United States. This may be partly due to the almost exclusive focus on the much larger U.S. market, where it is much easier to sell its services. However, in order to become a major player in North America, Onvia must find ways to extract a larger share of the Canadian market. According to Forrester Research, the volume and scale of the U.S.-based electronic marketplaces will make it hard for Canadian-owned and -operated electronic marketplaces to prosper unless it targets Canadian buyers or Canada's strength in natural resources. And owing to the increased competition in the United States, some B2B portals/destinations are already curtailing operations or merging with competitors. Canada could face a similar situation—U.S.-based portals also pose a threat to Canadian operations if they decide to pursue market opportunities in Canada.

Highly specialized niche players that are offering only a part of what Onvia offers are increasingly invading the competitive landscape in the B2B sector. Also, very rich and financially stable companies, for example the banks, fund many of the competitors as a means to enhance and consolidate their relationships with existing customers and to attract new customers. Because these specialized niche players are closely integrated to their bricks-and-mortar sponsors (e.g., BellZinc to Bell Canada and TD MarketSite to TD Bank), they have the ability to offer their services at very competitive rates and are in a better position to compete with Onvia on prices. Thus, Onvia must continue to find ways to remain competitive and maintain its strong position in the industry. In fact, it may be advisable for Onvia Canada to partner with one of these large Canadian organizations in order to leverage its technology, strong Canadian brand, and small business market leadership, to capitalize on the partner's direct channels, market reach, and existing small business customers and products. Recently (May 29, 2001), Bell Zinc[4] announced that it is buying Onvia's Canadian operations. Financial terms of the agreement were not released.

The future will be littered with mergers, acquisition, shakeouts, failures, and successes. The one to lead the pack not only will have the largest subscriber base, but also will be able to include wireless access and hassle-free utilization (i.e., bringing useful products to market). More and more, B2B portals and destinations are carving highly specific niches as the nature of competition force players and would-be entrants to pursue particular segments of the B2B, business-to-consumer (B2C), and B2G markets. In the United States, Onvia plans to focus on the B2G e-commerce marketplace, which means that it must quickly develop the capability to be a major player in this space and set up significant barriers to entry. Becoming the dominant player could lead to spillover effects, which include being recognized by governments around the world as the leader in this market thus making it easier for Onvia to penetrate overseas markets.

In 2000, Onvia posted a loss of US$117 million on revenues of US$147.6 million.[5] During this time, the company discovered that moving products through a Web site was a low-margin, high-risk business. And so the push toward a new revenue model, deriving income from higher-margin services, for instance, was implemented. Onvia's original prediction was that it would become profitable by 2004; however, investors' expectations are that the company must turn a profit much sooner than that. In addition, the difficulty of raising additional capital means that the company must turn a profit before exhausting its existing available funding. The company has made a number of strategic changes aimed at increasing its prospects of achieving its goal of becoming profitable by 2002. Changes made by Onvia include outsourcing its products' business, divesting some of its business units, developing the capability to sell to government clients, lowering the company's spending rate, and acquiring some additional capabilities by purchasing GlobeOne and Hardware.com. Achieving profitability by 2002 remains a significant challenge given the current downturn in both the U.S. economy and the Canadian.

CONCLUSION

The challenges and opportunities facing Onvia are huge. In many respects, the company is ahead of its closest competitors and has been quick to refocus its strategies when necessary. However, the competitive landscape is not likely to become less intensive, but rather more, with new players entering and targeting highly specific niches. It would be extremely challenging for Onvia to compete equally with all the various specialized players; therefore, it is critical for the company to adopt strategies that will help it to maintain and increase its existing customer base, create effective strategic partnerships and alliances, and provide the best customer service and support. New revenue streams need to be generated for the company to achieve profitability by 2002 and to remain viable. Onvia will also have to address whether it has the vision, drive, and management team to lead it in the next few years. Onvia has so far been quite successful in meeting these challenges (Exhibit 2 gives milestones in the Onvia story), but the question is: Can it repeat its past successes and what would it take for this to be realized?

EXHIBIT 2	Milestones in the Onvia Story
June 1996	MegaDepot founded by Glenn Ballman in Vancouver.
July 1997	First MegaDepot.com Web site launched.
June 1998	U.S. Web site launched; Vancouver HQ relocated to Seattle, WA.
January 1999	US$1.1 million angel financing secured.
February 1999	First-round venture funding received—US$11.7 million.
April 1999	U.S. site relaunched as Onvia.com.
November 1999	Canadian site relaunched as Onvia.com.
March 2000	Onvia's IPO, 8 million shares of common stock, worth US$230 million.
March 2000	Onvia traded on NASDAQ as ONVI. Shares finish trading at US$61.50 on day 1.
June 2000	GlobeOne, a B2G e-commerce company, acquired.
October 2000	Hardware.com purchased.
March 2001	DemandStar, an established B2G company, acquired.
April 2001	Shares traded at US$0.78.
April 2001	Glenn Ballman, founder and CEO, resigns from company.
April 2001	Michael Pickett succeeds Glen Ballman.

NOTES

1. Announcement by Onvia, February 5, 2001.
2. Onvia.com, Inc. Web site <www.corporate.onvia.com/overview.xml>.
3. "Canadian businesses gear up for hypergrowth in e-commerce," *Silicon Valley North*, January 2001, pp. 9–10.
4. "Bell Zinc Corp. to acquire Onvia's Canadian operations," *Brockville Recorder and Times*, May 29, 2001, accessed July 28, 2001 <www.recorder.ca/cp/business/010529/b052927.html>.
5. See note 1.

theme three overview

E-Business Operations and Supply Chain Issues

Many of the innovative business models of the e-business sector capitalized upon recent managerial ideas and approaches that represent a trend toward the greater adoption of the scientific approach to the management of business operations. In many ways, and especially in the context of e-business dot-com startups, these ideas were pushed to their limits in terms of operational implementation. For example, consider the idea of focusing on core competencies in operations and outsourcing support functions that has been popular in business management since the late 1980s. Many e-business startups exploited this approach to an extreme extent as a means of getting "off the ground" quickly with the minimal amount of investment in operational infrastructure. Many such ventures tried to remain completely "virtual" as informational intermediaries while relying completely upon third-party manufacturers, distributors, warehousing partners, and application service providers (ASP) for their total physical and technical operations. This was advantageous as it minimized the investment tied up in operational infrastructure, gave them flexibility to change their business models and operations on the basis of the feedback of their "experimentation," and protected them from the day-to-day realities of managing physical business operations. However, this outsourcing approach to business operations necessitates a newer and different set of operational managerial skills that focus on cross-functional project management and interorganizational coordination through strategic operations partners. Thus, in a sense operations management in e-business requires quite a different approach. Managers still need the traditional focus on operational detail and optimization and this has to be combined with a more pronounced strategic understanding of the various aspects of operations and the ability to work through other organizational units as well.

While emphasizing the operational challenges of e-business innovation especially during the e-business implementation stage, the cases in this Theme also capture the entrepreneurial orientation of such efforts. This is done irrespective of whether the organizational context is that of a large Old Economy corporate hierarchy or that of a new startup e-business venture. This theme of the book also attempts to demonstrate that success at entrepreneurial innovation requires paying careful attention to operational details from both intra- and interorganizational perspectives. The readings and cases of this Theme also highlight the role that information technology and business processes play in e-business innovation. It is argued that the high failure rates of the business process reengineering (BPR) revolution of the early 1990s can be attributed to the immaturity of the technology solutions that could help meet the ambitious productivity targets of BPR projects. These technology solutions are now much more sophisticated, and mature enough to help make the large productivity gains of e-business operations possible. There are now suggestions that a third-generation process reengineering revolution is currently under way, one based on innovation in e-business processes and operations. The ShoppeShoppe, iQLinux, and FishMarket cases of this Theme emphasize these aspects by focusing on how they are transforming existing business processes and supply chains.

Another key aspect of e-business innovation is the close link between e-business strategy and e-business operations. All the cases in this Theme attempt to explicitly illustrate the various dimensions of this link. Innovation processes necessitate market-based experimentation in terms of e-business models and operations especially in a new and dynamic field such as e-business. Readers of the book are encouraged to use the contextual data of the cases to explore how e-business strategy impacts e-business operations and how feedback from e-business operations helps reshape e-business strategy.

part one overview

Managing E-Business Operations

This Part focuses on the operational challenges involved in managing e-business operations. The first case describes the situation of an e-business startup in the business-to-consumer retailing area. It focuses on the operational challenges the company faced with dealing with its third-party warehousing and distribution partner and the challenges of trying to manage complex business operations with a skeletal combination of staff. It also draws attention to the multidisciplinary set of skills that are brought to bear on the operations side of business operations: merchandising, marketing, inventory management, financial management, and distribution management. It also shows that while e-businesses may overcome the problems associated with the silo orientations of traditional businesses, this does not mean that they are immune to the cross-functional disagreements and tensions that characterize business operations in the old economy. This lends support to the argument that the business-model innovations of e-business need to be complemented with organizational and operational innovations as well. The case also emphasizes the importance of order fulfillment and logistics as key issues for success in e-retailing.

The second case considers the operational rollout of e-business at a large banking organization with a long history of corporate success. It poses questions such as who should take responsibility for e-business planning, coordination, implementation, and operations in a large corporate hierarchy organized into strategic business units along the dimensions of traditional banking processes. This case also provides the context for exploring the role of the corporate information technology unit in e-business planning and implementation as well as traditional line versus staff functional roles; discusses a set of critical success factors that were found to be instrumental to the deployment of e-business operations; highlights the managerial challenges faced by e-business executives in carrying out their operations; and provides a good basis for analyzing how large companies can organize themselves to harness the entrepreneurial energies of e-business startup ventures in an effort to experiment with e-business models while sheltering their click-and-brick businesses and brands. This is an area of growing importance for 21st-century management that emphasizes business innovation; it is often termed *corporate entrepreneurship* or *intrapreneurship*. The case provides a rich background for exploring the link between e-business strategy and the operational implementation of e-business in the form of specific e-initiatives.

The readings provide background material and conceptual ideas that can be explored within the contexts of the cases. Key concepts that should be considered include the key drivers impacting e-business operations, synchronization of business processes, order fulfillment planning, virtual warehousing and inventory management, and distributed and partner fulfillment operations. The cases should also be used to understand the operational implications of the shift from the traditional "buy-hold-sell" to the new "sell-source-ship" model for e-business operations.

case one

ShoppeShoppe.com: Home of Affinity-Based Shopping

Jasbir Dhaliwal, Norwegian School of Management

Ajax Persaud, School of Management, University of Ottawa

It was November 1999 and Simmi Willis, CEO of ShoppeShoppe.com sat looking out of his 18th-floor glass-walled office in the Yaletown District of Vancouver, and reflected on the Weekly Operational Resource Meeting (WORM) he had just come out of that afternoon. He was determined to find a way to put to an end the ongoing conflict between his chief technology officer (CTO), Jens Watersberg, and Rosetta Wilcocks, his chief operations officer (COO). He knew that if he did not act soon, it would affect the morale of all the employees at ShoppeShoppe.com and lead to operational breakdowns. He also knew that he would have to find better ways to communicate to the principals of the firm, led by David Sidhu who held 35% of the total equity, the operational and resource issues that the organization faced.

Simmi had initiated the weekly WORMs as a way for him to bring Jens and Rosetta together to discuss common operational and resource problems that were cropping up as ShoppeShoppe was rolling out its business-to-consumer site. However, instead of bridging the gap between Jens and Rosetta, the meetings were largely disintegrating

Many of the names of organizations, persons, and locations in this case have been disguised to protect the confidentiality of the organization that was the focus of this case study. Any resemblance to real organizations or persons is purely coincidental. This case was prepared for class discussion purposes rather than to illustrate either effective or ineffective handling of a business or administrative situation.

into finger-pointing grudge sessions with individuals at the next level of the organization having to take sides behind either the CTO or the COO. The latest problem focused on what had happened during the prior week ever since the shopping site was launched the week before. Goods had been shipped to the customers who had filled up their shopping carts on the Web site but payment had not been received from any of them due to a breakdown in the payment process.

Once customers had provided their credit card information for payment at the time of purchase, the information had been electronically sent for processing through CyberCash and ShoppeShoppe's bank. As was standard practice in the industry, the validity of the card was checked and the total amount for the purchase was transferred to an intermediate account to be held by the financial intermediaries until shipping notification had been received. This amount could only be held for seven days and if shipping notification was not received, the amount was credited back to the purchaser under the assumption that the order could not be or had not been fulfilled. For all of the week's customers, this shipping notification had not arrived in time and the money had been credited back to the customers' credit cards. Given that the payment process was supposed to be fully automated, nobody at ShoppeShoppe had realized the problem until an honest but confused customer had called the company's 1-800 customer service line. She had informed the operator that while she had received the goods, her card had not been been charged for the purchase.

The logistics and shipping functions of ShoppeShoppe's supply chain had been outsourced to a medium-sized third-party warehouse in Chicago that was not fully Internet-enabled. As was the operating procedure at the third-party warehouse, shipping notifications were only sent out in batch model by email in spreadsheet format at the end of each week. The first week's email had been received by a customer service supervisor at ShoppeShoppe (who reported to the COO) but who had not acted upon it as she had not known what to do with the information. Both she and the COO had assumed that this was a weekly summary report and had no knowledge about the criticality of the shipping notification for the CyberCash payment process which had been arranged and implemented by the CTO and his group.

The problem had been discussed at WORM and the CTO and the COO blamed each other for causing the breakdown. Simmi had finally stepped in and instructed that the CTO should immediately fly to Chicago and resolve the electronic transmission of shipping order information with the third-party warehouse operator. Rosetta had then informed the meeting that ShoppeShoppe was the only e-business client of the third-party warehouse who mainly dealt with old-economy clientele and who did not understand the real-time informational requirements of e-business. It was then decided that in the event that the third-party warehouse was not able or willing to send the shipping notifications on a real-time basis through a live Internet connection, the fallback position would be for the warehouse to fax or email daily shipping notification information to ShoppeShoppe every evening for input into the payment system. There had been disagreement as to who would be responsible for handling this data entry task, as both the CTO and the COO had argued that it did not fall into their operational jurisdiction and that they did not have the manpower to handle the task.

HISTORY AND ORGANIZATIONAL STRUCTURE

Save2Shop had been the brainchild of David Sidhu, an ex-stockbroker and successful technology entrepreneur who specialized in taking startup companies public. He had made his fortune by setting up and growing a stockbrokerage firm in a rural town in southern Alberta and had become a millionaire by the time he was 30. He had then sold the firm and moved to Vancouver where he worked as a stock promoter and investor. Together with a band of other promoters and co-investors he had successfully taken another startup technology-based company public on the NASDAQ market in 1997. Following up on this success, David had become interested in business-to-consumer electronic commerce after hearing about the successes on the capital markets of companies such as Amazon.com, eBay.com, and Onsale.com. He discussed the idea with his partners, sought the advice of technology experts, and did his own research on the potential of e-retailing. A friend of his who worked as a university professor at a business school advised him that the key to success in the B2C sector was having a *critical mass* of potential customers who could be targeted at a significantly low customer acquisition cost. David then set about finding a strategic partner who could provide him access to such a critical mass of consumers. A business associate from the capital markets industry in New York soon introduced him to Timothy Lee, a successful businessman from California. Lee too had heard about the success of e-commerce retailing Web sites, and was seeking competent partners in electronic commerce for his marketing company, Concept2100 Marketing Inc.

Concept2100 had been set up in 1983 for the purposes of handling membership development and benefits package management for large and medium-sized affinity groups in the United States. The company was very successful and the total membership of all the affinity group organizations contracted to it was about 16 million. Concept2100 had expanded its own reciprocal benefits and rebate shopping network to these members, many of whom held affinity group membership cards that doubled as Concept2100's *CONCEPT* reciprocal rebate shopping card. Cardholders could use the card for rebate purchases at over 92 product suppliers (having an arrangement with Concept2100) who carried a total of about 1.1 million products at preferred prices. Total rebate purchases using the *CONCEPT* card totalled a few hundred million dollars annually and yielded revenues for the affinity groups (a small percentage), the product suppliers, and Concept2100 Inc. which developed and coordinated the operation. Concept2100 had developed the operation using point-of-sales (POS) systems functionality as well as debit card and cheque transaction processing much earlier, before the advent of the Internet. Lee was now interested in porting over his operations to be Internet-enabled and also wanted to exploit the growing popularity of e-commerce for B2C. Some of his larger affinity group customers, including unions and some religious organizations, had also been sounding him out about the possibility of setting up their own Web-based e-shopping malls for increasing their non-membership-fee revenues.

At a meeting in Seattle, David Sidhu and Timothy Lee struck an agreement to set up ShoppeShoppe.com. In exchange for equity in the new venture, Save2Shop would be able to leverage all of Concept2100's resources and business relationships and immediately access a large aggregated customer base to achieve "critical mass" in its operations immediately. The company was registered in Delaware and through the reverse takeover of a dormant company immediately acquired over-the-counter trading status on the OTCBB market. David had promoted the venture to his associates and this had yielded a startup fund of close to US$2 million.

Rosetta was the first person hired by David Sidhu to get the venture off the ground. She had a bachelor's degree in social sciences and an MBA from a prestigious university in central Canada, and had worked for 15 years in various managerial capacities pertaining to marketing with a large company in the telecommunications sector. An energetic and resourceful personality, she had also completed a part-time diploma program in electronic commerce offered by a local university just a year before taking up the ShoppeShoppe challenge. In the opinion of Sidhu, "During a time when there were very few e-commerce-trained people around, she was the first prospect I met who impressed me with her knowledge about the new e-commerce sector, her energy to get going, and her willingness to learn. All she asked for was for me to hire a strong technical person to assist her on technology issues and to get out of the way." For three months, Rosetta single-handedly got the organization off the ground. She found an office, hired a couple of programmers just out of college to build an investor relations Web site, arranged for T1 line connection to the Internet, and fleshed out the details of the business plan. She also used her connections to assist Sidhu with the building of a board of directors that had profile and credibility in electronic commerce. She also built up a very loyal team of mostly junior employees (two programmers, two operations assistants, and a receptionist) who regarded her as the de facto CEO of the organization.

Sidhu had a largely hands-off day-to-day role and concentrated on the investor relations activities and legal matters with U.S. lawyers. As the organization, its Web site, and the detailed business plan took form, Sidhu felt that there was a need for a high-profile and experienced CEO who could lead the company toward an IPO and a technically competent CTO who could provide technological leadership to the organization. He felt that Rosetta was not the ideal person for either of these roles during the next phase of rapid expansion. Soon he announced the hiring as CEO of Simmi Willis, a 52-year-old English engineer and technology entrepreneur who had experience in setting up and growing his own companies in the telecommunication networks area. Sidhu had known Simmi for some years and had been a junior angel investor in one of Simmi's earlier ventures. In Sidhu's opinion, Simmi's lack of experience about e-commerce or the retailing sector was made up for by his maturity, general managerial experience, entrepreneurial sense, and vast contacts in the investment banking and capital markets sector.

Within a few days of starting work, Simmi asked Rosetta to join him at a lunch meeting with Jens Watersberg, who in his mind would be suitable for a role as information technology manager. Simmi told her that Watersberg "was a very energetic and bright 27-year-old fellow who had dropped out of high school in Austria, immigrated to Canada, and self-taught himself into a programming and systems development wizard. He now worked as a technical contractor for various dot-com startups while running a small personal computer suppliers distributorship from his girlfriend's garage." Simmi had met him at the bar during a promotional event organized by a technology vendor at a local hotel, and had found out through his network that he had quite a sound reputation as a technical programming and implementation expert. At the lunch meeting, both Rosetta and Simmi were impressed with Watersberg's mastery of the technical side of e-business infrastructure and Simmi immediately offered him a post as information technology manager for the venture. Jens responded immediately that he would only come abroad if he was appointed chief technology officer with complete control over technology decisions and if an appropriate options and remuneration package could be agreed upon.

A few weeks later, the first formal organizational chart of the company was produced; it is shown as Exhibit 1.

In addition to the two programmers who had been hired earlier by Rosetta, Jens was instrumental in hiring three more junior staff for technical and programming roles, and he insisted on the term "architects" being included in their job descriptions. Very soon he had built a highly motivated technical team who generally started work at 11 o'clock in the morning and worked long hours that usually lasted late into the night. Rosetta's team, on the other hand, worked regular hours and handled virtually all non-technical matters pertaining to operations, customer service, and logistics.

THE SHOPPESHOPPE VALUE PROPOSITION AND BUSINESS MODEL

ShoppeShoppe is an online shopping supersite that capitalizes on the explosive growth of Internet-based shopping by consumers. Its retail section emphasizes "lowest price" online shopping, easy-to-use functionality, and expedient product delivery for its customers. ShoppeShoppe offers a multitude of products on its own Web site and also acts as an individual consumer's online shopping sleuth as it searches other sites with similar products to make sure that its shoppers receive the lowest price. It utilizes background technology that continually runs Internet-wide price checks, and automatically adjusts prices below the competition. If ShoppeShoppe cannot beat a competitor's price, it may even inform the customer of the name of the competitor, and provide a link to that competitor's site.

EXHIBIT 1 Organization Chart of ShoppeShoppe.com

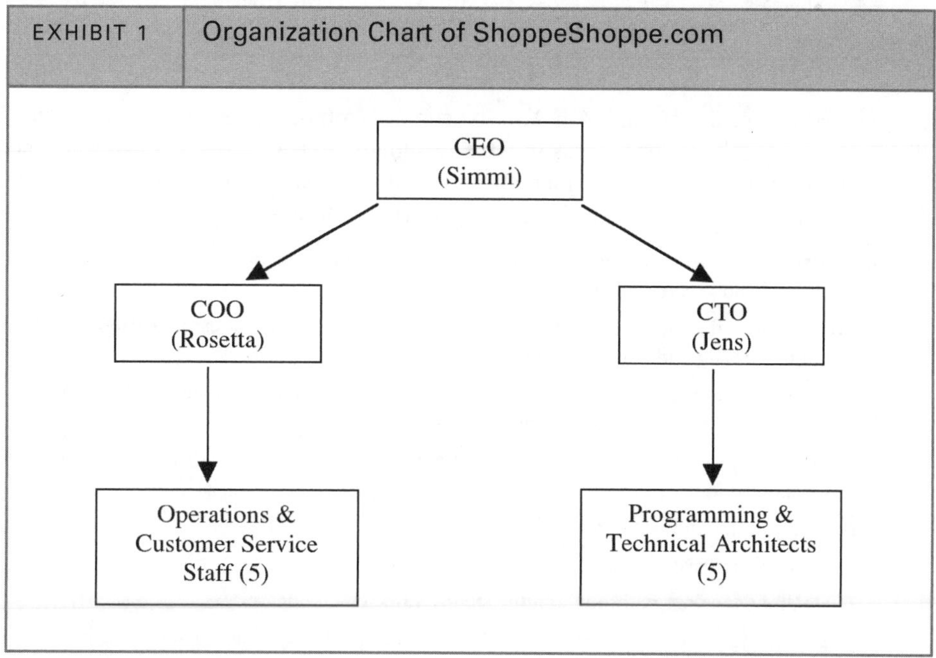

Furthermore, it offers its customers the opportunity to become rebate shopping club members at little or no cost, entitling them to substantial rebates on many of the products made available through its online shopping mall. This is in addition to the rebates received for being members of partnering affinity groups. All in all, its strategy is to become the logical place for consumers to begin their search for the best value when making a purchase. In addition, the site would also provide many free content-related services such as consumer reports and product testimonials to its customers.

The business plan of ShoppeShoppe called for an aggressive rollout strategy based on meeting an ambitious set of financial goals. Details of these are shown in Table 1, which captures the pro forma financial information. Top management realized that meeting these financial targets would require coordinated action and much innovation given that it only had a limited amount of resources at the startup phase of the venture. A key strategy here was to build strategy alliances and partnerships with other organizations both to move as fast as possible and to minimize capital requirements for operations. A large part of Simmi Willis's time was spent identifying and building such strategic partnerships in operations. Once he had set up the partnership, he passed the task over to either Rosetta or Jens, who would then manage the operational implementation of the relationships.

TABLE 1 Financial Projections of ShoppeShoppe.com Inc.

	Year 1	Year 2	Year 3
Revenue	$14 563 111	$128 860 506	$479 671 660
Net income	(929 413)	8 116 973	41 962 001
Total cash flow	4 234 761	7 926 239	39 588 518
Total assets	10 659 357	31 786 070	100 603 538
Total liabilities	2 816 170	16 325 910	44 181 357
Total owners' equity	7 343 187	15 460 160	56 422 161

On the basis of the examples of Amazon.com, the top management team understood that the primary criteria for success in the e-retailing sector were operational excellence and customer service. They had therefore adopted the mission statement "Operational Excellence and Customer Delight." This was clarified as follows:

> Our mission is to become a world-class E-business, engineered to constantly re-optimize its processes and add greater value by:
>
> - Creating deep functional excellence and depth of skills in customer care, distribution, transaction processing and E-business management;
> - Utilizing world-class information technology—applications, data management, communications, and analytical & decision support tools;
> - Incorporating virtual logistics management technologies to lever the distinctive capabilities of specialized logistics providers;
> - Building strong and lasting customer & supplier relationships by
>   - Establishing trust;
>   - Maximizing synergy throughout the supply value chain;
>   - Leveraging our core competencies with those of our strategic partners, and suppliers.

COMPETITION

ShoppeShoppe was competing with a number of other retailers with similar concepts. These competitors can be broadly segmented into three groups:

- Traditional "bricks-and-mortar" megastores (e.g., Target, Wal-Mart, Kmart, Sam's)
- Online megastores (e.g., Valueamerica.com and Worldspy.com)
- Online specialty stores (e.g., Furniture.com, Jewelry.com, Electronics.com)

Traditional Stores

These represent bricks-and-mortar megastores that offer the same product types and large selections of low-priced products. Many of these stores not only operate bricks-and-mortar outlets but also have online shopping capabilities (e.g., Shop.target.com, Wal-mart.com). These stores may have some distinct advantages in that they are able to offer both types of shopping experiences, online and offline. Many customers had developed a loyalty to these stores based on historical experience, financing options (e.g., many customers carried store credit cards), excellent customer service (e.g., the unquestioned return policies), etc. These stores also had a significant reputation and presence in many communities and access to substantial funds for additional marketing and advertising.

Online Megastores

The company viewed its two key competitors in the online megastore/shopping mall arena as being ValueAmerica.com and Worldspy.com. These Web sites, and a growing number of similar ones, sold a large number of products in many different categories such as home improvement, electronics, toys and games, home furnishings, footwear, pharmacy, jewellery, general merchandise, houseware, and gifts. Many of these sites were also starting to offer services similar to those of ShoppeShoppe, including comparison shopping and easily accessible product information/research (e.g., consumer reports). Like ShoppeShoppe, these sites also had esthetic appeal, sticky content, and ease of use. Most of these competitors tried to draw consumers on the basis of convenience, low prices, excellent selection, and additional services that might not be available from a bricks-and-mortar retailer. This included chat rooms to discuss product purchasing experiences, free e-mail, and electronic announcements regarding sales or special deals. However, unlike ShoppeShoppe, none of them were yet offering a shopping search agent and very few of them offered cash rebates on the purchases that customers made. It was felt that while ShoppeShoppe had competitive advantage over other sites in marketing to rebate shopping club members (those who will receive rebates on their purchases), it would also face growing challenges from competitors who offered coupons and special discounts, which might offset the savings gained through membership-based rebates.

Specialty Stores

There were other online retailers who competed with ShoppeShoppe in niche product categories. Retailers such as Furniture.com, who specialized in only one type of product category and who were able to offer a greater selection and better prices in the particular category than ShoppeShoppe, were also major competitors. Many of these specialty retailers were well capitalized, had significant budgets for marketing, and had developed mind share (branding) for their niche markets (e.g., Amazon.com, CD-Now.com).

Despite the competitive landscape, ShoppeShoppe.com was confident of being able to meet its revenue targets. This was because of the revenue potential arising from the 16 million locked-in critical mass of potential customers who were affinity group partners. (See Table 2.) It meant that, unlike other independent Web shopping malls that were starting to appear, it would not have to fork out the industry average of about $56 that was needed to acquire each new customer. It also avoided paying the average cost of about $1 being charged in the online advertising industry for each potential customer who arrived at one's site through a link placed on another site.

TABLE 2 Revenue Model for Affinity Group Target Market

Projected Numbers	Explanation
16 000 000	Total membership of affinity groups
× 27%	Percentage of U.S. adults that used the Internet
4 320 000	Approximate number of affinity group members with Internet access
× 7.77%	Capture rate of affinity group members
335 664	Affinity group members purchasing from ShoppeShoppe.com
× $144	Average amount purchased per person per year
$48 335 616	Pro forma revenues from affinity group members

OPERATIONS AND TECHNICAL ISSUES

David Sidhu and the board of directors of the company had decided that one of ShoppeShoppe management's main goals was to construct a "virtual" company. That is, it was to make every effort to keep its manpower and asset needs to a minimum, as it leveraged the operations of its strategic partners. ShoppeShoppe's current management team was qualified to launch the business and to address initial operational needs.

As the business grew, ShoppeShoppe was to keep its staff requirements constant and to maintain consistency and continuity of quality in its management. Its first operational focus was on its Web site's user interface. The company had to ensure that the software functioned properly and offered a reliable and appealing environment to search for and select merchandise at competitive prices. And this had to happen regardless of the number of users who logged on at a particular time. ShoppeShoppe had to monitor the level of service and quality in the areas of product fulfillment, transaction processing, and customer assistance provided by its partners to continuously identify areas for operational improvement. This was a difficult task given its small and specialized staff size.

ShoppeShoppe had two offices, one in Vancouver and the other in San Francisco, and it had servers in multiple locations. Main servers were housed either at ShoppeShoppe's head office or at qualified co-location facilities in the form of third-party-operated server farms. Backup servers were also housed in independent server farms across many locations. The plan was to add servers seamlessly as capacity increased. Although ShoppeShoppe purchased some of its own servers for security and reliability reasons, it also leased others to maintain flexibility and reduce its capital requirements. Setting these up was a challenge to Jens Watersberg, and he had to spend a lot of time on the road. It was also difficult to predict the regional breakdown of Internet traffic to the site and coordinate this with the supply chain and customer service side of the business. He often joked about having to "hit the road again to visit his [server] farms" to deal with technical operations and maintenance issues. Significant redundancy and capacity was built up to ensure smooth operational efficiency and Jens alone understood the complex overall technical architecture which was in large part undocumented.

The principle of making every effort to keep corporate overhead to a minimum and avoid tying up cash in hard assets and inventory extended to all operational sides of the business, technical and non-technical. The company's many strategic partners (who often received equity participation opportunities) provided it with access to technologies and operational expertise to help architect, build, and implement the online mall. Such partners assisted with the following internal operations and technical applications:

- Web mall and back-end database management
- Call-centre help desk
- Tracking of product fulfillment
- Credit card authorization
- Sales transaction processing
- Database management for 1.1 million items (currently 50 000 online)
- Adding of new merchandise
- Intensive comparative pricing research
- Network architecture
- Rebate card administration (outsourced)
- Product fulfillment (outsourced)
- Credit card transaction processing

Timothy Lee's Concept2100 Marketing Inc. provided ShoppeShoppe with rebate cards and card administration services for all new members signing up for online rebate shopping privileges. Each rebate card had a separate number and all transactions associated with it were tracked through ShoppeShoppe's databases. Concept2100 was also responsible for all rebate payments made to ShoppeShoppe rebate card customers after validation by ShoppeShoppe. Through the shared databases ShoppeShoppe was able to access all data related to its rebate card customers for the purposes of marketing, auditing, accounting, and other internal operations.

Product fulfillment involved the ordering and shipping process that was coordinated by Rosetta's group, who used third-party supplier chain brokers and jobbers to source and supply products at the best prices. The third-party logistics and warehouse operator in Chicago handled product fulfillment operations. Yet another partner provided a group of people dedicated to answer telephones and chase jobbers but were coordinated by Rosetta's customer service staff. These included operating a level-one help desk for a potential customer's first Web search, product search, and purchase. Other product fulfillment tasks included contacting jobbers, expediting orders, changing orders, and tracking orders.

UNRESOLVED OPERATIONAL CHALLENGES

It was now September 2000. Simmi scanned the minutes of the last few WORMs and open-agenda items for the next WORM to identify some of the major operational challenges facing the firm at this time.

Lack of Merchandise and Promotion Management Expertise

ShoppeShoppe's Web site now featured close to a million products. While the company had a good handle on interface design issues, it lacked experienced personnel in merchandise management who could lead efforts at structuring the various products that were for sale in a manner that made sense from both a marketing and a supply chain perspective. Simmi had tried to interest an experienced merchandising manager from a large retail chain to join ShoppeShoppe without success. Currently, one of Jen's database design staff handled merchandising in an ad hoc manner largely on the basis of database design considerations. This often led to conflicts with members of Rosetta's group who were responsible for product promotions. Successful retailing companies like Wal-Mart, Sears, and the Bay had significant merchandising and promotions departments.

High Cost of Visual Digitals and Multimedia Design

For the ShoppeShoppe shopping experience to be appealing and competitive with other sites, it was imperative that an increasing amount of graphic and multimedia content be sourced, modified, and featured on the site. While many product manufacturers were increasingly providing visual "digitals" for their products, it was still costing ShoppeShoppe an average of about $175 to source, modify, and feature the digital of each product on its site. Given the lack of internal multimedia design skills this function was currently outsourced to a local digital media and graphic design organizations. Given its scarce resources, ShoppeShoppe could only feature the visual digitals of a very small segment of its total product line on its Web site. This did not bode well for its conversion ratio (of site visits to items purchased) as some of its competition was from physical retail stores where customers could touch and inspect products before deciding on purchasing them.

Shortage of Technical Competencies

While the bulk of its customers were in the United States, ShoppeShoppe had decided that its systems development offices should remain in Vancouver because of the difficulties in getting competent technical personnel in the United States. It had advertised for a systems administrator position to be based in Seattle and received just two qualified applications. One of these individuals had not shown up for the scheduled job interview, and the other, while being eminently qualified, had informed Simmi on arrival that he was not interested in a formal employment offer as was advertised, but could take on the whole function as a contractor; he had also asked for an equity and options package that, in Simmi's view, was unreasonable given what he had to offer the firm.

Need for a Real-Time Link to Product Inventories

The fact that ShoppeShoppe did not maintain its own inventories in any significant way was seriously impacting its ability to meet customer service requirements as well as its operational cost objectives. The lack of a direct online real-time link between a product offering on the Web site to an inventory master of on-the-shelf products, meant that significant human intervention was required to source for products and to arrange for their delivery through the third-party warehouse. Simmi had also read about problems other e-commerce companies had experienced in relation to thousands of a featured "sale" product being sold online in just a few minutes when there were only a limited number available for fulfillment purposes on the warehouse shelves. He constantly reminded Rosetta's staff to be careful in this regard when planning product promotions.

Customer Returns (Reverse Logistics)

It was also becoming clear in the e-retailing sector that the rate at which customers returned (or did not accept) goods that they purchased was higher than that in the bricks-and-mortar retailing sector. This meant that ShoppeShoppe had to set up complex business processes for reverse logistics. These involved the transportation partner (who had to pick up the goods to be returned), the third-party warehouse, the original manufacturers (to whom defective goods had to be returned), and the financial partners for re-crediting customers with payment. Currently, one of Rosetta's staff coordinated this time-consuming procedure, which was still significantly error-prone. The delivery partners who were supposed to pick up the returned goods were often unreliable, and quite often the staff at the third-party warehouse did not know what to do with the goods brought back.

Communications Issues with Logistics Staff

Another operational challenge for ShoppeShoppe was that its customer service staff had a severe communications problem with the logistics staff at the third-party warehouse. While it was largely a "white collar/blue collar"–oriented communication gap, the problem was made worse by the fact that ShoppeShoppe was one of the smallest customers of the third-party warehouse (in terms of volume) and its only e-commerce customer. The warehouse staff often complained that the small order sizes and the large range of stockkeeping units (SKUs) were uneconomical in terms of efficient and effective stock picking, packing, and shipping. They had even suggested to ShoppeShoppe that it consider consolidating its orders on a weekly basis for picking and delivery to generate greater economies of scale in the supply chain.

Multitasking and Lack of a Defined Organizational Structure

Given that ShoppeShoppe was trying to replicate virtually all the functions that are performed in the traditional retail industry, it found that its limited number of staff often had to multitask. For example, database programmers often had to help with Web design or even customer support over the phone, while marketing staff helped with data entry of product-line information during critical stages. While this was inevitable given its startup phase and represented a standard practice at many e-commerce dot-coms, it caused a lot of conflict because of the reporting structure in the organizational chart. While Rosetta argued that formal job descriptions had to be developed and followed, Jens argued that multitasking was inherent to e-commerce and that all staff must pull together and contribute during crunch times to all tasks. This led to an extremely fast turnover of staff at the junior levels and an inefficient use of staff skills and training.

Seasonality Factor of B2C Retailing

The seasonality factor of business-to-consumer retailing also exasperated the operational planning and resource utilization at ShoppeShoppe. Table 3 presents a breakdown of the seasonality variance in sales activity. For example, sales activity during December was more than six times that of July. This was especially problematic for the customer service and support staff who in Rosetta's words were "drowning" in December with no extra support due to resource constraints.

TABLE 3 Seasonality Adjustments

Month	Percentage of Baseline Sales
January	60%
February	96%
March	84%
April	84%
May	96%
June	72%
July	48%
August	48%
September	96%
October	96%
November	120%
December	300%

As the implementation and market role of the ShoppeShoppe site proceeded, the initial excitement of the staff was tempered by the practical realities of operations management, a tightening in resource availability, and morale problems.

NEXT COURSE OF ACTION

Reflecting back on the past 15 months, Simmi Willis thought about how different his experience at ShoppeShoppe had turned out to be from what he had expected. In many ways, the challenges he faced during his prior experiences with startup telecommunications and networking companies paled in comparison to the day-to-day operational challenges confronting an application-oriented e-business such as ShoppeShoppe. He found that it was very difficult for him to concentrate on the strategic aspects of the company's development unless he found a better way of handling operational challenges that kept cropping up. In his opinion, while other e-business companies were constantly evolving their business models and strategic orientations, he was too burdened by "firefighting" in operations. He also knew that the future success of ShoppeShoppe was going to be dependent on success in handling operational customer service details. However, this required significant investment in human and physical resources such as warehouses, transportation equipment, and inventory. This was inconsistent with the organization's strategic goal of trying to remain a virtual organization in an effort to minimize capital requirements. He needed to find a way of communicating this to David Sidhu and his backers. With the recent drop in the stock prices of technology companies on the public markets and the drying up of the market for e-commerce IPOs, he wondered if he should signal to the investors that it was time for the company to pursue alternative exit strategies. These included partnering with a bricks-and-mortar supply chain company who could provide the physical infrastructure for operations as well as established practices for operational excellence. He decided that he would make a presentation to the board of directors at their next meeting about the operational issues facing the organization as a means of getting them to appreciate the need for a change in strategic orientation.

case two

Den norske Bank: Corporate Entrepreneurship at Work

Jasbir Dhaliwal, Norwegian School of Management

Ajax Persaud, School of Management, University of Ottawa

It was May 2001, Siri Røsberg, general manager for e-business at Den norske Bank (DnB), sat in her office close to the Oslo Fjord in downtown Oslo contemplating the latest development in the implementation of her organization's e-business strategy. This had involved the corporate communications unit of the bank taking on the responsibility for quality assurance of the organization's Web presence to ensure an accurate and consistent projection of the bank's communications to its customers and stakeholders. This also signalled that content management issues were going to be a critical managerial portfolio in the continuing implementation of the bank's e-business strategy.

The bank had been an early starter at utilizing the Internet for transforming itself into a leader in e-banking. This had been driven by national as well as strategic business considerations, as the Norwegian government was a significant investor in the DnB. This was articulated by Svein Aaser, the group chief executive officer of Den norske Bank ASA, as follows in an address entitled "The Future of the Norwegian Financial Services Industry" on October 9, 1999:

> ... a technological revolution is taking place, where banking technology and financial expertise are in a process of dramatic change. Every month, for example, an estimated 15 000 to

This case was prepared with the assistance of Siri Røsberg, for purposes of classroom discussion rather than to illustrate either effective or ineffective handling of a business or administrative situation.

> 17 000 Norwegians are switching to Internet banking. Technological developments are managed from banks' head offices. A country left with no head office within the financial services sector risks entering the new millennium completely lacking in the core competencies of tomorrow's financial services industry. The transformation into a country of branch offices will have consequences for customers, but will also have an impact on the IT sector, the rest of the financial market, and even on the Norwegian securities market.

It was well understood by DnB management that the connectivity of the Internet was going to exert a strong centralization or consolidation effect in the technological transformation of banking in addition to the decentralization and "buyer power" effects that were well publicized in the mainstream media. They knew that it was just a matter of time before their strong competitive edge in the Norwegian market would be challenged by larger foreign-based entities. This required them to act fast to stay at the leading edge in utilizing the new technology to protect their traditional markets in Norway. The Nordic banking sector had a strong history of using technological innovation for competitive purposes and Norway had been one of the first countries to adopt a centralized clearing system for the whole banking sector.

ORGANIZATIONAL AND OPERATIONAL BACKGROUND

The DnB was the largest financial services group in Norway with close to one million retail customers. It had 130 000 customers participating in customer benefits programs, and was also the largest Norwegian issuer of debit and credit cards. It served as principal banker for over half of Norway's 300 largest companies and had 30 000 corporate customers that represented a 25% share of the Norwegian corporate market. It also handled payment flows that were close to 50% of Norway's international trade. Through its strategic business unit DnB Markets, it was also Norway's largest investment firm with substantial market shares within trading in foreign exchange, interest rate, and equity instruments. The DnB group offered loans, deposits, asset management, payment and trade finance services, financial advisory services, foreign exchange and capital market products, and life, pension, and non-life insurance products and services to its customers. Over its history spanning over a century, the bank had succeeded in maintaining its traditional strengths and markets despite the competitive nature of the Norwegian banking sector. Norway's 4.5 million inhabitants had close to 130 banks to choose from for their financial needs, and the financial market for small and medium-sized companies in Norway was divided between many competitors. Some years earlier the DnB had successfully merged with Postbanken, the state-owned post office savings bank in Norway with a significantly large retail deposit base.

The recently announced financial results of the DnB group show that it recorded a healthy rise in profits during the first quarter of the year. Profits after taxes amounted to 1149 million Norwegian kroner (NOK) for the quarter, up from NOK 331 million from the same quarter of 2000 (US$1 was approximately NOK 9.0). The strong performance shows that DnB's strength lies in its broad range of products and services as weak developments in stock markets were offset by increased income on foreign exchange and interest rate instruments, and in other areas. The DnB Group's operations were also streamlined during the quarter and this saw its cost-to-income ratio declining from 63.6% in the first quarter of 2000 to 60.0% in the comparable quarterly for 2001. Return on equity rose to 18.8%

from 14.8% a year earlier. Its earnings per share also increased from NOK 1.05 to NOK 1.48 from the year before. Total income from its strategic business unit Vital, which focuses on mutual funds and pensions, also rose by 29% from the year before. The total combined assets of the DnB Group amounted to NOK 463 billion as at March 31, 2001, up NOK 18 billion from the end of December 2000.

Exhibit 1 presents the organizational chart of the bank and its various business units. The e-business development unit, led by Nikolai Stefanovic, as director for e-development, had been set up in 1999 and was currently not part of any of the bank's five strategic business units. Rather, it reported directly to the group managing director and CEO, and Nikolai was part of the top management level of the organization, which comprised the group executive vice-presidents (see names in Exhibit 1) who led the five strategic busi-

EXHIBIT 1 Organization Chart and Business Units of the DnB Group

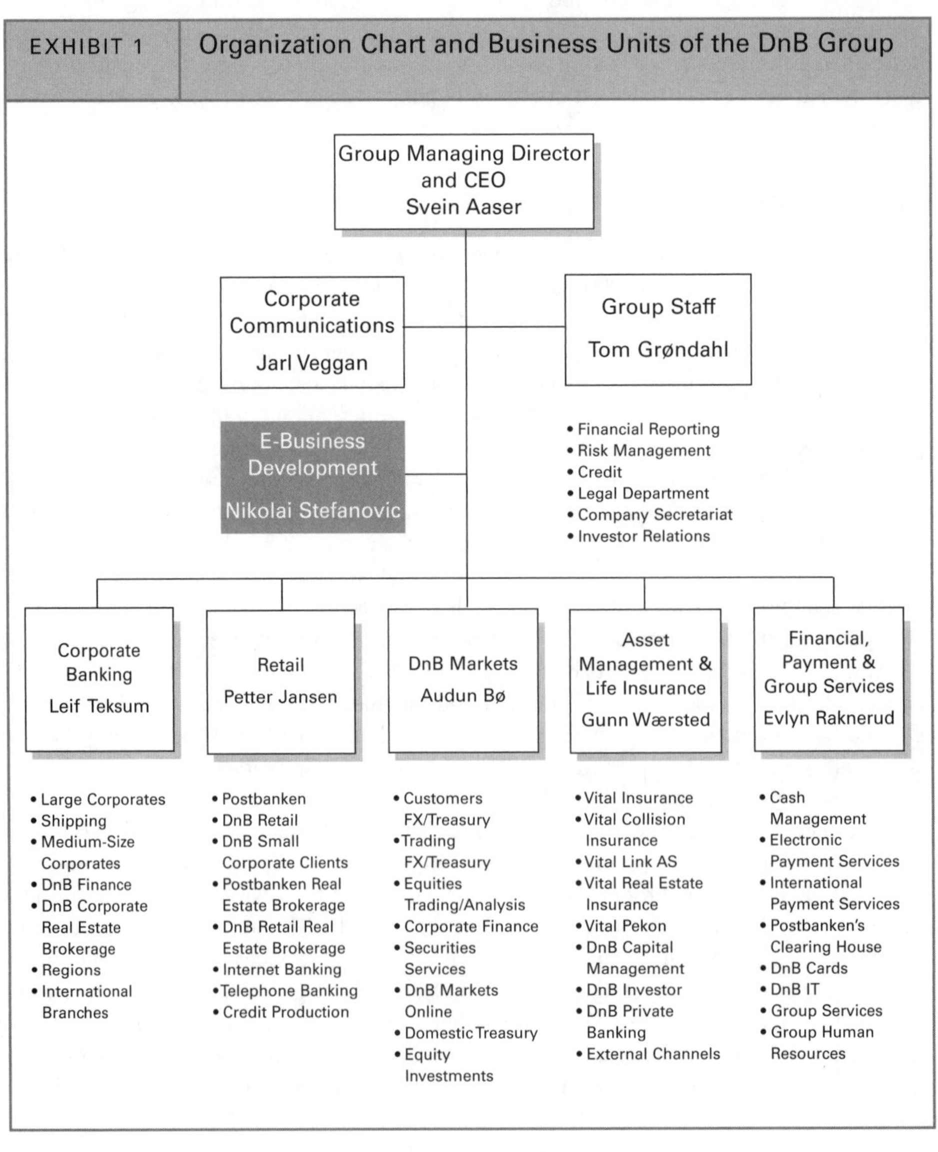

ness units of the bank. The e-business development group comprised five members who were experienced in the core areas pertaining to DnB's e-business operations such as IT development, banking processes, customer relationship development, business development, and Internet consultancy. Major functions led by the group included e-business strategy development, market surveillance and intelligence, management of e-business strategic alliances, and coordination of the implementation of the bank's various e-business ventures and initiatives. The e-business development unit of the bank was a distinct operation from the information technology (IT) development division of the bank. It had a direct link to, and was an integral part of, top management. The IT development division was a part of the strategic business unit Group Services, and reported to Evlyn Raknerud. The technical, operational, and implementation responsibilities pertaining to e-business initiatives were held by the various strategic business units of the bank such as DnB Markets, Corporate Banking, Retail Banking, DnB Markets, Financial Payment Services, and Asset Management. In Siri's opinion, this structure was a major factor that contributed to the success of e-business at the bank. It ensured that ownership for the e-business initiatives remained at the functional business level that emphasized bottom-line results and customer servicing while the planning of the initiatives was integrated into the bank's overall strategic business planning at the senior management level.

As the bank continued aggressively with its e-business development strategy, it had recently announced that it was outsourcing its IT operating services to external partners as part of its efforts to streamline operations to generate cost savings. Svein Aaser had explained the significance of this to shareholders as follows:

> An important step in our efforts to streamline operations is the letter of intent signed with Telenor/EDB Business Partner today for the outsourcing of IT operating services. This is consistent with DnB's strategy, which includes outsourcing certain operations when this proves profitable. Annual cost savings for DnB are estimated at around NOK 150 million from the time the transfer of these operations is completed. I emphasize that the agreement concerns the operation of IT systems, while systems development will remain within DnB.

This action was in accordance with trends in the local IT industry. Organizations were realizing that IT operations and systems maintenance were taking up an increasing proportion (often as high as 70%) of the total IT budget and that this was impeding the ability of their IT division to innovate in new systems development through the use of new technologies. Outsourcing these functions helped to cut costs, because of the economies of scale offered by the third-party service providers, while ensuring that the internal technology groups stayed focused on technological innovation through new systems development.

DNB'S E-BUSINESS STRATEGY

The essence of DnB's e-business strategy is distilled in Exhibit 2. It is conceptualized as being an e-business marketspace of banking formed by matching three buyer roles (consumers or retail customers, corporate customers, and banks) against two seller roles (the bank and corporate sellers). The bank believes that, over the medium to longer term, it has to innovate and compete in all the six segments of its e-banking market space. The challenge to the bank is to innovate in terms of the appropriate e-business models and applications that are required for each of the segments.

EXHIBIT 2 DnB's Strategic E-Marketspace of Banking

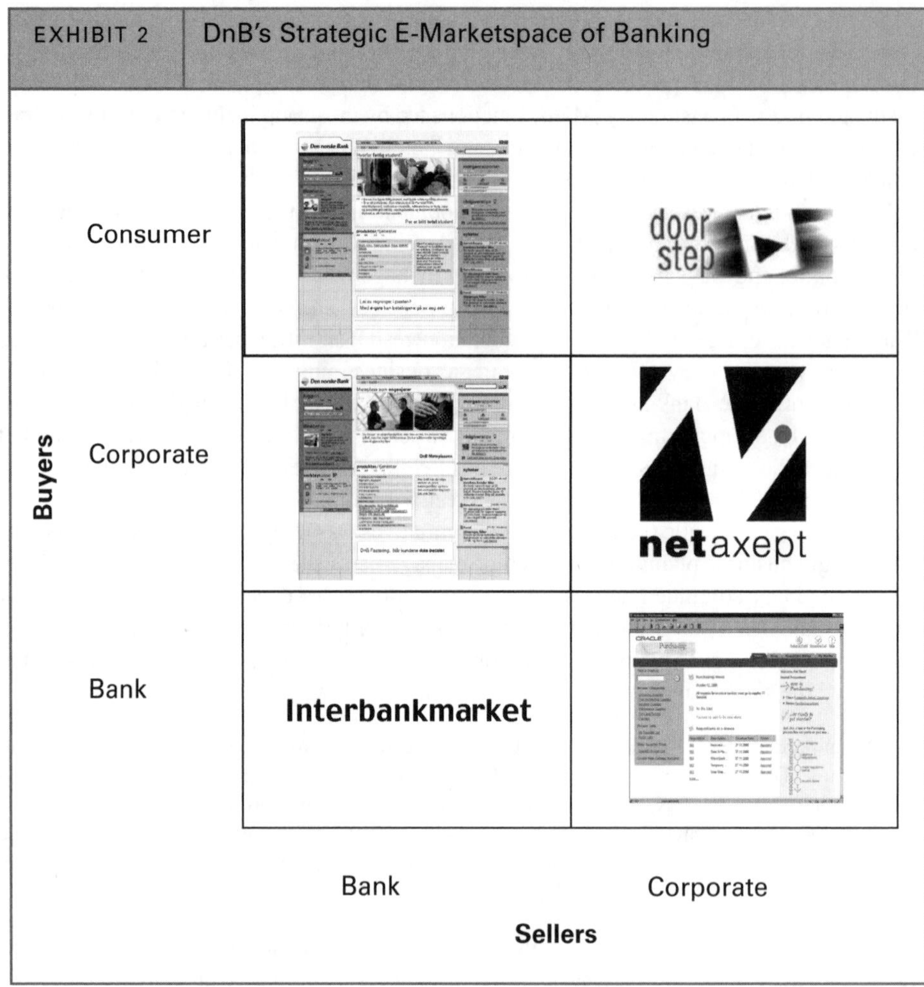

The three items of the left column represent the Internet-based services that it can provide (sell) to its three customer categories: retail customers, corporate customers, and other banks and financial intermediaries. The three items of the right column represent Internet-based services and products that its corporate partners can provide to consumers, other businesses, and banking organizations.

From the perspective of branding strategy, the bank decided to nurture and grow four distinct brand names in its e-business endeavours. These capitalize on its preexisting brick-and-mortar brands and are: dnb.no, postbanken.no, vital.no, and amex.no. The fourth represents DnB's business as the Norwegian franchise of the American Express credit card. From the very beginning, DnB has avoided trying to build newer dot-com-type brands but has instead focused on nurturing its existing brands and transitioning them to the digital economy. Despite the global orientation of the Internet, its e-business branding strategy has focused on strengthening its hold on the Norwegian financial market rather than pushing for growth in international markets. This is a key reason behind its adoption of the ".no" suffix for its e-business branding. For example, it does not hold the rights to the "dnb.com" domain name which instead belongs to Dun & Bradstreet.

DnB's e-business strategy also recognizes that there is a need for an integrated approach to competing in the e-business sector that goes beyond the mere development of e-business applications. It has also been implementing various other programs that are aimed at transforming DnB into an e-business entity. For example, jointly with a local business school it has implemented a postgraduate-level, e-business executive training program that has the objective of upgrading the e-business knowledge of all managerial and key staff. In coming up with an integrated approach to e-business transformation, DnB has identified four key operational areas that are critical for success in e-business implementation leading to a Net-ready infrastructure and a Net-ready organization, as follows:

1. *Information technology infrastructure.* How adequate is the IT infrastructure in supporting and enabling e-business processes?
2. *Human resources and training.* How adequate are human resource skills for effectively driving e-business operations?
3. *Customer and external linkages.* How effective are relationships with customers and external partnering organizations in facilitating and improving e-business operations?
4. *Organizational design and policies.* How effective are organizational structures, practices, and reward systems for ensuring effective e-business operations?

DNB'S E-INITIATIVES

Based on the strategic e-marketplace perspective depicted in Exhibit 2, DnB had by May 2001 started work on six distinct e-initiatives, and five of these had been successfully implemented. With the exception of the inter-bank-market segment, it was now active in all five of the other strategic segments of Exhibit 2. Its two e-initiatives in the left column, where it was the seller, were its retail banking portal and its corporate banking portal.

1. Retail Banking Portal

This was a full-service portal offering e-banking services to the retail customers of the bank. It was the responsibility of the strategic business unit Retail Banking. As Norway had the highest penetration of Internet banking (as a percentage of population) in the world, this portal was significant to strengthening DnB's current role as the market leader in the Norwegian retail banking sector. Some of the services offered by the portal to retail customers include account balance verification, inter-account transfers, bill payments, loan applications, foreign exchange transactions, and financial planning tools.

2. Corporate Banking Portal

Similarly to the retail banking portal, this full-service portal for the bank's corporate customers had been internally developed and managed by the bank. The strategic business unit Corporate Banking had integrated all its traditional services with the portal to exploit the Internet as a new service channel for corporate customers and to provide seamless service between Internet and traditional channels. Some of the services offered by the portal include trade payments, international transfers and letter of credit applications, corporate loan applications and processing, and sophisticated financial planning and risk management tools. From a corporate banking perspective, the bank was interested in facilitating e-business for its customers by playing both an enabler and an intermediary role. The enabling role of the portal focused on providing the infrastructure, tools, and trust services to support the e-business transactions and interactions of its customers. The intermediary role focused on creating customer-relevant communities (e.g., for procurement purposes) and market-making through operating e-business marketplaces. The idea was to have the corporate banking portal provide direct links to the e-business marketplaces that were relevant to corporate customers. The corporate banking unit of the bank was also currently working on enhancing the informational content of the portal to make it more user-friendly and valuable to its customers, and was starting to recognize that "content management" was a key aspect of managing e-business operations.

3. Netaxept

This initiative focuses on building the operational and fulfillment infrastructure for providing secure settlement and delivery for e-business transactions. Both the bank itself and its corporate clients can subscribe to these services for their e-business operations. It has been developed as an independent business unit in partnership with the state-owned Norwegian postal service, Posten, and the consulting organization Accenture, who also hold equity interest. One of the first corporate clients of the bank that has signed up to use the Netaxept service is Coshopper.com, an e-commerce firm with international operations based on the demand aggregator consumer-to-business (C2B) business model. Netaxept capitalizes on the regional post office network of Posten to provide efficient door-to-door delivery and flexibility in dispatch options and a reverse logistics process for goods that are returned by consumers. It also aims to become the standard for online shopping in Norway and represents an extension of established payment systems (debit cards, credit cards, GIRO) to online shopping. Netaxept is positioned as a trusted third party for Internet transactions and offers consumers full choice in banking and dispatcher selection. Consumers also do not require a special bank connection to be able to use Netaxept. In its second stage of development, Netaxept has plans to extend its service to provide a solution covering all of Scandinavia. It also has plans to provide electronic IDs, e-billing services, and factoring/reconciliation services to business clients.

4. Doorstep

Doorstep was the bank's business-to-consumer (B2C) venture that had the objective of building up an open cyber city and e-mall where businesses can offer e-business services to Norwegian consumers. This venture is also an independent business unit and is developed as a 50-50 equity partnership with Telenor, which is Norway's largest telecommunications company. Doorstep has recently developed a mobile computing and multi-access orientation to its operations and is positioned to become Norway's leading marketplace for electronic shopping offering a wide range of goods and services for all the different population groups. Security and accessibility are key features of Doorstep, which provides secure payment and delivery, digital certificates, electronic signatures, and quality screening of suppliers and contractors. Doorstep is currently actively recruiting businesses to set up shop within its cyber city. It has targeted upstart Net shops, traditional shops with a desire to get into e-business, service institutions, and entertainment outlets as supplier partners who can offer their services and content on its site. Customers will be able to use the integrated site for all their banking and bill payment needs, mail and email communications, news and informational requirements, and Internet-based education and training purposes, in addition to shopping. The revenue model of Doorstep is based on rental fees from businesses joining the cyber city, annual user fees from consumers, and commissions on shopping transactions. The venture had a startup capitalization of NOK 100 million and has the objective of breaking even by the end of 2002. The orientation of the venture was changed in April 2001 to deemphasize the business-to-consumer marketplace and to strengthen its multi-access and mobile computing focus.

5. B2B Marketplace (Atento.no)

This represents the bottom item of the right column of Exhibit 2. Together with Accenture, the ErgoGroup of Posten and Telenor, the bank was also in the process of developing the largest Nordic e-procurement portal for B2B (business-to-business) purchasing. This marketplace would provide integrated services to facilitate e-procurement, especially for the purchasing of maintenance, repairs, and operating supplies (MRO) which had become the killer application of B2B e-business. All three of the partners intended to use the purchasing portal for their own procurement needs and it was the strategic intent of DnB to be the preferred financial partner for all other large and medium-sized parties who joined the purchasing portal.

6. E-Venture Capital

The company had also set aside a significant amount of resources, as a venture capital fund managed by the e-business development unit, for purposes of taking equity interest in both internal and external e-business ventures that were deemed strategic to the bank's future interests and markets. A few investments have already been made in startups that underpin DnB's e-business strategy. In March 2001, the bank invested in Coshopper.com, a company focusing on building demand fulfillment communities. In May 2001, it took a position in FishMarket, a leading e-business marketplace for the trading of fish.

The framework for such e-business investments and the decision processes are well defined within the e-business development unit of the bank. Any venture has to fall into one or more of the following categories before it is recommended by the e-business unit to top management for consideration: (1) the venture is technological unique from an e-business perspective; (2) it provides DnB an advantage from a market perspective; (3) it gives DnB access to requisite e-business competence; and/or (4) it provides DnB with a cost advantage in tackling a particular market segment. The potential investment candidate also has to meet all the following criteria:

- The management team must be well qualified for developing and growing the company.

- It must have a track record and an established network in place.
- A well-documented business plan including financial forecasts must be available.
- There must be commitment from other co-investors besides DnB.

DnB's first three e-initiatives had served to ensure that it was well positioned to use the Internet as a core distribution channel to provide integrated service with its traditional channels. It was now using this foundation to develop new service concepts to enhance its customer relationships and to innovate in terms of value-added products that could serve niche or specialist markets. For example, it was currently nurturing internally and investing in external initiatives focused on providing value-added products and services to the shipping and fisheries sectors that represented markets in which it had historical strengths.

As can be seen in Exhibit 3, the bank was also taking new strategic roles in supporting all the various steps of the new value chains that were developing as a result of the expansion of e-business in the economy. These had forced it to go beyond the main areas that were the focus of traditional banking. For example, it was now developing its role as the owner and operator of new business models and marketplaces. It was also cognisant of the e-business requirements for a secure infrastructure and a tight link to the physical flow management aspects of delivering goods. For the future, it was also investigating how it could play a value-adding role in the growing customer relationship management (CRM) activities of its customers. It was also interested in how intelligent-agent technology could assist in enhancing its role as an agent or advocate in buyer-seller relationships.

EXHIBIT 3 Role of DnB's E-Initiatives in Supporting New Value Chains

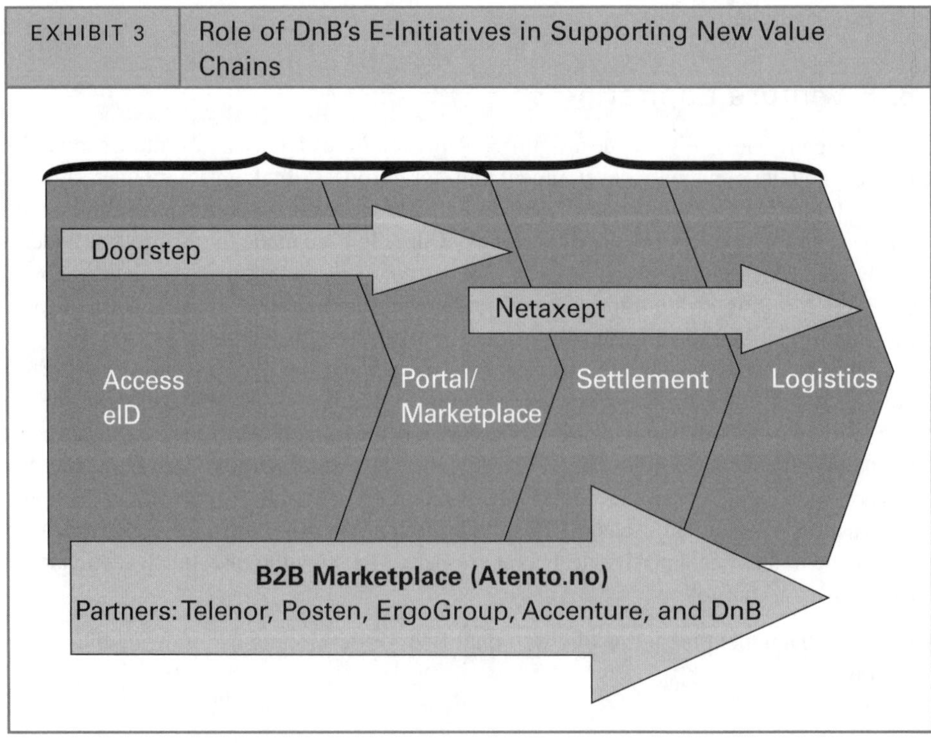

OPERATIONAL CHALLENGES IN E-BUSINESS IMPLEMENTATION

Table 1 provides a brief summary of the timeline for the operational rollout of e-business implementation at DnB. The first task of the e-development group on initiation was to go about developing the organization's e-strategy. This can be characterised as a top-driven, bottom-up development process that was supported by an international management consulting firm using an idea workshop format focusing on industry best practices. Managerial-level representatives of each of the strategic business units and the IT development unit of the bank participated in the exercise. Key managerial challenges during this stage were the tight schedule adopted and met for developing the e-strategy and the limited exposure of participants to the rapid changes occurring in the e-business marketplace. After adoption of the e-strategy by senior management, the head of the e-development unit announced it to the financial markets during the bank's capital markets day when the

TABLE 1 Operational Rollout of DnB's E-Business Strategy

Timeline	Activity or Event
November 1999	"E-development" unit established as part of Organizational and Group Services division of the Bank.
January 2000	E-strategy development process initiated.
March 2000	E-strategy announced to financial markets.
April 2000	Doorstep Cyber City B2C joint venture between Telenor and DnB announced, with emphasis on mobile computing and accessibility. Netaxept joint venture between DnB, Posten, and Accenture initiated, with focus on physical flow fulfillment and integrated payment functionality.
May 2000	E-business development unit re-designated as a separate organizational unit within the bank and part of top management.
June 2000	E-venture capital initiative set up to support DnB's e-strategy and capitalize on relevant external entrepreneurial ventures.
September 2000	Development of B2B procurement marketplace announced as a joint venture between DnB, Posten, Telenor, and Anderson Consulting (later Accenture).
October 2000	Internet-based transactions at Dnb.no and Postbanken.no grow to 855 100 from 334 670 in December 1999 (an increase of 156%). Average of 3.5 monthly e-transactions per customer.
November 2000	Netaxept service is launched. Number of e-customers who use the Internet for transactions grows from 97 650 in December 1999 to 273 260 (an increase of 180%).
April 2001	Doorstep marketplace put on ice but development of mobile access and payment functionality continued.
April 30, 2001	Second-round investment into FishMarket.no announced.
May 2001	European Commission approves B2B procurement marketplace venture (Atento.no).

bank's preliminary results were announced. The presence of the CEO, COO, and vice-presidents of the strategic business units at the announcement provided a strong signal to both internal and external parties of the organization's commitment and sense of urgency in pursuing the development of e-business. Subsequently to this, the various strategic business units of the bank took responsibility for initiating their own e-business initiatives and projects in concert with the e-business development unit.

The e-business development unit of the bank faced significant managerial challenges during the implementation. Exhibit 4 shows nine major categories of operational and environmental issues that were identified by Nikolai Stefanovic's e-business development team as being critical to the success of e-business implementation at DnB.

EXHIBIT 4 Factors Impacting the Success of E-Business Implementation at DnB

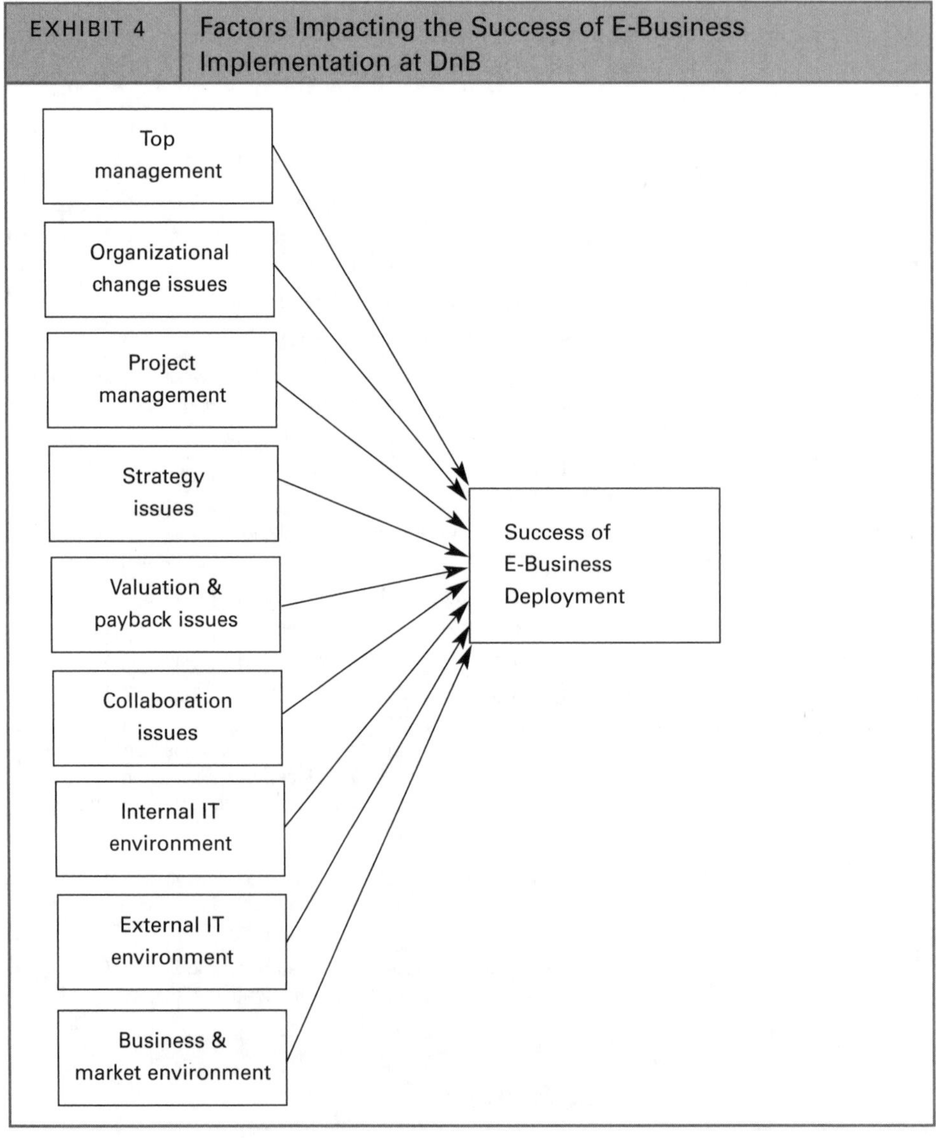

1. *Top management.* Senior management's early recognition of the potential benefits of e-business applications and their ongoing support contributed significantly to the mobilization of DnB staff for the e-business implementation. From an e-business management perspective, it was just as important for the e-business development group to work with top management to shape the strategic vision for utilizing Internet technologies as to work with the strategic business units of the bank to shape the appropriate business models for e-business operations.

2. *Organizational change.* Deployment of e-business operations at the bank required significant changes in its organizational culture and internal business processes. In Siri's opinion, e-business implementation was 80% about change management. Focusing on the larger issue of making DnB an Internet-ready e-business organization through skill upgrading, training, etc. helped prepare the bank's employees for the change management effort. The fact that DnB was going through a major strategic reorientation in terms of its relationship with the government, rationalization arising from merger/acquisition activity, and a major cost-cutting exercise involving the outsourcing of non-core competencies helped prepare the staff for the change as well. The fact that banking in general traditionally had a risk-averse organizational culture (in direct contrast to the rapid-change-and-experimentation orientation of e-business) meant that the bank had to pay careful attention to the change management opportunity. Siri also found that e-business operations required a diverse set of knowledge competencies that were a combination of new as well as old competencies. She characterized this aspect of her responsibilities as being an exercise in knowledge management, constantly innovating in terms of coupling newer competencies with the valuable older competencies that were abundant in the bank.

3. *Strategy-related issues.* The process by which the bank's e-business strategy was developed also contributed to success in e-business deployment. The strategy was focused enough to provide guidance to the organizational e-business efforts but broad enough to allow flexibility in operational tactics. This was critical given that Internet technologies and applications were constantly changing in the marketplace. As well, it was to be expected that a certain amount of experimentation was necessary for figuring out the best business model for e-business operations. In Siri's opinion, it is not necessary for an organization to develop a detailed long-term e-business plan similar to the five-year business plans used by traditional organizations. Rather, the focus should be on the strategy development process and on a mechanism for constant reevaluation and reorganization based on technological developments.

4. *Project management.* The e-business development unit spends a lot of time and effort to build dedicated project teams, appropriate communication structures, project management skills and methods, and pools of external project resources and expertise, in order to successfully deploy the various applications. Working in teams and emphasizing cooperation across different business functions in the bank was a significant challenge to the organization. Much of the e-business development unit's time and effort was spent playing a project coordination role for multiple concurrent projects.

5. *Valuation and payback.* With an increasing level of investment in e-business, sorting through the payback and valuation methods for e-business projects was a major operational challenge. Having the strategic business units take ownership for the various

applications ensured that only value-added e-business projects were undertaken and that cost justification discipline was maintained. This also relieved the e-business unit from the competitive pressure of having to compete for organizational resources against other, less strategic but more defined initiatives. In a sense, the bank relied upon its tried-and-true internal managerial processes for evaluating, justifying, and rationalizing e-business investments.

6. *Collaboration factors.* DnB's experience has been that successful deployment of e-business requires active support from suppliers, customers, and other, related business partners. Its early decision to collaborate with strategic industry partners such as Telenor, Posten, and Accenture meant that it could rely on the skills and competencies of these organizations to complement its internal skill base. This, however, required the e-business group to quickly develop collaboration mechanisms with these partners for supporting day-to-day e-business operations. In a sense, the e-business development unit felt that it was running an e-business incubator from the outside. The challenge was to harness the entrepreneurial nature of e-business development while retaining the corporate perspective of the bank.
7. *Internal IT environment.* Internet-based banking services necessitated that the bank's "back-end" processes and systems had to be linked to the Web site on an online storage and real-time processing basis. This resulted in enormous demand for high data quality and systems coordination to ensure consistent and seamless "multi-channel" servicing of customer needs. Thus, while Web site development could be carefully managed on a modular basis, ensuring application integration was a demanding managerial challenge. The fact that the bank had upgraded its information technology infrastructure some years before in preparing for the Y2K challenge helped ensure that an appropriate technical integration, communications, and database infrastructure was in place to support cross-channel and bank-wide e-business operations on a "24 hours/day by 7 days/week" basis. Integration of the bank's systems with those of its other e-business partners was facilitated by the availability of the requisite technical expertise.
8. *External IT environment.* Coping with the rapid developments in the external technology environment also proved to be a major operational e-business challenge. In the design and development of the e-business applications, the e-business development unit of the bank was constantly faced with "balancing act"-type decisions. These often involved trading off the requirements for creating functional e-business applications that met current needs against the need to be innovative in developing high-risk e-business solutions for the future. Other issues arising from the external technological environment included reliable payment mechanisms for interorganizational transactions, security and encryption problems, and data protection in interorganizational data transfers. As was the case with its Netaxept e-initiative, DnB worked with its strategic partners to develop a solution to these issues in the face of uncertainty and unreliability in the external technology marketplace.
9. *Business and market environment.* Market excitement and overreaction about the significant potential of e-business had raised internal and external expectations to unrealistic levels. As the e-business development of the unit proceeded with the implementation, it found that managing these expectations required intensive effort as

e-business implementation conformed to the age-old, trusted principle that "things take time." There was also a large category of unresolved questions that had to be dealt with on "an interim basis" as the external business and legal environment changed. These included taxation issues pertaining to online payments and sales, legal issues in electronic document transfer across organizations, and international trade barriers for conducting global e-business. A key market-oriented issue was the e-readiness of consumers to utilize the bank's e-business applications. In Siri's words, "the first challenge was to ensure that customer needs were the basis for the development of innovative e-business applications. This was followed by the challenge of working to ensure that a critical mass of customers migrated over successfully to these new applications."

part two overview

Supply Chain and Logistics in E-Business

Supply chain management represents a major managerial innovation of the 1990s. It has transformed our traditionally intrafirm orientation toward the management of physical flow operations into a strategic interorganizational perspective. The advent of e-business has helped to further extend the supply chain and operations management concepts to a global and real-time level. Many e-businesses ventures used the connectivity of the Internet to innovate in terms of transforming the global supply chains for both digital and physical products. The first case of this Part describes the context and entrepreneurial efforts aimed at the transformation of the supply chain of a service industry: Linux technical support. It also introduces readers to the growing "community-based" open-source movement for software development and to the operational business processes required for service provision over the Internet. The case can be used to illustrate how operational supply chain processes shape the functionality of the e-business engine developed to serve as a Web-based marketplace. The case also illustrates technical and managerial issues involved in the operational development of the e-business engine.

The second case focuses on the operational processes, technical development, and change management aspects of reengineering the supply chain practices of the fish and seafood industry. It provides a rich context for investigating trading models for business-to-business transactions over the Web by detailing the operational intricacies of Web cataloguing, auctioning, and contract sale business processes. Additionally, it discusses some of the legal and privacy issues involved in e-business operations and illustrates how these influence the design of the user interface and business processes. It also brings a process perspective to the supply chain to clarify the systems development approach used for developing the technical architecture. Given that change management issues are an integral component of e-business operations, the case provides material that can be used to explore the major risk factors in the implementation of e-business operations designed to transform an industry's supply chain.

The readings for this Part provide a conceptual model and integration framework for exploring various issues pertaining to the link between e-business and supply chain management. These include demand and supply chain integration, information integration and the bullwhip effect, and supply chain collaboration activities pertaining to shared demand forecasts, capacity plans, production schedules, inventory status, and shipment schedules. Another key aspect that can be explored is the intertwined operational relationship between marketing, customer relationship management, and demand-supply chain management in e-business organizations.

case one

iQLinux.com: A Supply Chain for Open Source Technical Support

Jasbir Dhaliwal, Norwegian School of Management

Ajax Persaud, School of Management, University of Ottawa

THE ENTREPRENEURIAL ROOTS OF THE VENTURE

Peter So, a Canadian of Chinese ancestry, grew up on a First Nations reservation in the Pacific Northwest of Canada. In that environment, he met and developed an affinity for many people who did not fit into "mainstream society" and who went about their community-oriented affairs without regard to the preponderance of wealth and opportunities. This upbringing and exposure had a big influence on his later development of the technology and business model underlying iQLinux.com.

After university, he started his career in research and development by implementing real-time computing and control systems using Unix platforms. He ventured out on his own after a decade of working for a large forestry company where he held various positions in information technology. Running his own company, he undertook a lot of software development and consulting projects with Microsoft platforms and tools. Work was abundant and demand for his skills was high. After more than four years of building solutions with mainstream technology, and accepting daily personal computer reboots as being the norm, he realized that "most of the world seemed to have been sold on Microsoft marketing and technology." Triggered by the coming birth of his son, he

This case was prepared with the assistance of Peter So, for purposes of classroom discussion rather than to illustrate either effective or ineffective handling of a business or administrative situation.

reflected upon his tough upbringing and asked himself "if there was a better, more innovative way for building, sharing, and commercializing software?"

Over the next two-and-a-half years, he returned to his early computing roots and began to explore the Linux operating system and the underlying ideas and philosophies of the open source movement. Open source, with its roots in scientific and academic information sharing, is a software industry tradition through which source code (the underlying code of a program) is made freely available for use or modifications by a community of developers. In those early days of the technology, which were just a few years ago, Linux had been created, amazingly, by a unique breed of developers; but a Linux solution in business computing was a hard sell. He found that while the situation has been changing more recently, it was still a challenge in the business world to get enough experienced Linux people to work with, when a project becomes available. His discussions with friends in the systems development industry and with captains of the local IT industry suggested to him that the unavailability of a coordinating mechanism for Linux technical support and components was the single biggest obstacle holding back the mass adoption of the Linux technology.

It was then, in the year 1999, that he started work on an e-business model that would provide such a supply chain for Linux technical support and components. This led to the birth of iQLinux.com. The objective was to help accelerate the introduction of Linux to the mainstream business computing market, to small and medium-sized businesses, and to the public sector computing market by providing an efficient and viable supply chain for technical support and components. Peter realized that this was necessary because in these markets it was difficult and/or insufficient to just hire a group of Linux experts for the task. He also felt that many "free agent" independent Linux consultants were currently exploiting the lack of an open marketplace by charging high rates for technical support consulting, to the overall detriment of Linux adoption on a large scale. He also saw the need for a Web-enabled site that would bring "free agent" independent Linux consultants together for Linux projects of a larger scale. Such a site would enable them to work together on projects or opportunities and set their own terms for participation in line with the open source philosophy. The site would contribute to Linux adoption on a large scale.

Having been an independent consultant for a long time and an entrepreneur behind various small technology businesses, he realized that such a site had to provide other support tools besides market-making and coordination. These included billing functionality, account settlement, bad debt resolution and mediation, complex client handling features, and marketing. He therefore set about designing iQLinux with these features in mind and to make Linux technical support consulting and component development both practical and viable as an independent business in a global setting.

A SUPPLY CHAIN MECHANISM FOR OPEN SOURCE DEVELOPMENT

The supply chain for open source products, such as Linux-based firewalls, is very different from that of proprietary software products. From the perspective of users of Linux products, providing access to pools of high-quality Linux technical support personnel and Linux components is a key role of the supply chain. In the case of proprietary software like the Microsoft Windows operating system, the software vendor has set up such a supply chain to support users' needs for technical support and components required for application development, customization, configuration, and maintenance. The chain often comprises its resellers, education partners, certified support partners, and the like. The vendor often spends considerable time, resources, and effort ensuring that this supply chain is large and efficient enough to support the rapid adoption of the software. Given that the intellectual capital of open source products lies with the community at large, there is no such benevolent vendor who takes ownership of this role involving setting up and maintaining the supply chain.

Some Linux companies have tried to fill this gap using a niche strategy focused on the high-end high-margin segment of the marketplace by branding their services and variations of Linux, even though its founder Linus Thorvald held the rights to the original source code. By and large, however, the demand and supply sides of the Linux technical support and components market were much too diffused and disorganized to support the mass adoption of the software. Chief information officers of large IT departments have often suggested that the lack of a reliable and reasonably priced technical support source for Linux was a major reason that held back their use of the operating system and Linux-based software products. Independent Linux consultants and software component developers (often termed "free agents" in the Linux jargon) also found that the diffuse nature of the market hindered the growth of their businesses beyond serving primarily local needs. This was despite the fact that close to 70% of Linux technical support (implementation-oriented support, problem resolution, and maintenance) could be provided remotely over the phone or the Internet. Peter So realized that the advent of the Internet was rapidly changing the cost and scale dimensionalities of creating a market coordinating mechanism to resolve this gap on a global scale.

THE OPEN SOURCE PHILOSOPHY OF IQLINUX

In Peter So's opinion, the growth in the trend toward "free agents" extended beyond the Linux and open source communities and was part of the large trend toward home-based entrepreneurship (single owner, home office) as the basis for work in our society. The spirit of the underlying philosophy is captured by Dan Pink in his statement:

> There's a new movement in the world. From country to country, in communities large and small, people are declaring their individual independence and drafting a bill of rights. An authentic grassroots spirit has appeared and infused the world.

Peter estimated that there were roughly 25 million such "free agents" in the United States and Canada. These are people who move from project to project and who work on their own, sometimes for months, sometimes for days. They too did not fit into the mainstream of our working society that was characterized by a rigid corporate life. The philosophy and business model of iQLinux was designed to serve the specific working and lifestyle needs of these free agents of the Linux world. Mark Kuharich of Softwareview.com, an independent voice in the open source Linux community, has characterized the company's philosophy as follows:

> One of the most compelling sub-plots in the Free Agent World story is unfolding at iQLinux.com. Throughout the world, small groups of free agents are helping one another succeed professionally and survive emotionally. These groups belie another of the central myths

> about free agency: that without that office water cooler, free agents become isolated and lonely. Working solo is not working alone. iQLinux.com provides you a Linux community on the Internet. ... This group—at once hard-headed and soft-hearted—is creating a new community. One part board of directors, another part group therapy, this small, self-organized cluster is part of the emerging free-agent infrastructure. It is helping to form the new foundation of our economic and social lives.

It was for these reasons that the features and functionality of iQLinux.com's Web site emphasize community empowerment, relationship building, virtual development and support teams, fair business practices, and dispute mediation by peers. It provides a marketplace where open source products, solutions, and support services can be negotiated and acquired. This business model and its underlying technology engine and business processes could be applied universally to many other communities as well.

THE IQLINUX BUSINESS MODEL AND FUNCTIONALITY

iQLinux.com offers a unique vertical market portal for relationship building and makes pertinent business services available on a contingency basis to the open source community, particularly the Linux community. Its Web site provides great value to its members, who can be both customers seeking to acquire Linux products, solutions, and services and consultants who are offering them. Member consultants are able to collaborate and form remote virtual teams that work together to most effectively meet the customer's requirements and needs.

The Web site can be thought of as both a meeting place and a marketplace; and it has been described as a combination of e-Bay and Onvia. It brings members of the open source Linux community together and helps them to meet their business objectives with as little overhead costs as possible. Customers are able to post their needs ("requests") and consultants are able to post the products and services they are making available. The Web site supports the negotiation and establishment of contracts between customers and consultants. Consultants are also able to identify subcontractors and form teams collaboratively through the vertical market portal. If required, the site also coordinates the acceptance of deliverables and the closure of contractual agreements. Should discrepancies arise in the course of delivery, dispute mechanisms are provided to resolve them in a negotiated fashion. When an unresolved dispute arises between a customer and a consultant, there is a "jury of peers" business process available, one that captures the essence of the community-based ideas underlying the open source philosophy. In this process, the respective cases of the two parties are heard online by a number of "jurors" selected from within the Linux community and a collective decision is rendered to resolve the issue. Closed professional mediation is also available online as an option if the one of the clients desires privacy.

iQLinux.com offers its members a powerful and flexible mechanism to join and collaborate. Members may assume one or more roles, simultaneously, if needed. When they first sign up, they are considered by default to be customers who may avail themselves of the technical support products or services offered through the Web site. Once a member has defined a profile of products and services of interest, the member may also take on the role of consultant—forming teams, bidding on other requests for proposals posted by other customers, and accepting service requests made directly to them by customers. Members may also make themselves available as subcontractors to other ("lead") consultants for the purpose of forming virtual technical support teams. They may also appoint other, trusted members to resell their offerings, product components, expertise, or services, either as standalone items or as part of a larger solution. Commission settlement and relationship management services for such contexts are also provided on the Web site.

The net effect of the iQLinux.com portal is that a technical support consultant is able to participate at a Web site associated directly with the open source Linux community, and thereby market his or her products and services to Linux customers on a worldwide basis. The consultant can effectively publicize the experience and capabilities of his or her team and describe the functionality and properties of his or her products and components. Just as Linux customers regularly visit the site to post their needs and requests (project and technical support requirements), the consultant is now able to browse at any time to search for work opportunities as they arise in real time.

E-BUSINESS ENGINE AND BUSINESS PROCESSES

The underlying business model of iQLinux' business-to-business and community engine was designed to provide a business community framework and structure to both processes and transactions on the Internet. The engine enables users to create a structured community marketplace where safe e-commerce transactions take place. Besides utilizing the engine for building iQLinux for the open source Linux vertical market, the engine and business processes have also been licensed to other community-oriented domains. This high-growth emerging market for community-oriented marketplaces has also seen the model gaining rapid acceptance by large corporations (internal markets) and in developing countries.

Peter's goal is to establish and popularize the community-based business model into the mainstream markets for e-business. In his view, the iQLinux B2B e-commerce engine and community model represents the next wave, or third generation, of e-service business models that provides structured processes for virtual team building, contract negotiation/fulfillment, dispute resolution, and mediation by peers. Besides enabling safe e-commerce transactions, it creates a structured community marketplace where clients, consultants, vendors, and community members become active participants in shaping and governing their own business practices. It also provides an avenue for the product innovations and knowledge/skills of independent free agents and smaller companies to compete in the global marketplace without the fear of unfair business practices.

The core technology of the iQLinux engine comprises four key modules:

1. *Virtual Team Builder.* This module enables consultants and vendors to build virtual contracting teams composed of members with complementary skills or diverse geographical locations. Team members can collaborate securely, build business relationships, and grow their business collectively. The Virtual Team Builder module goes beyond simply growing a virtual team on demand; it also establishes a virtual distribution and reseller model for components and services as well. It enables each team member to focus on his or her strengths and competencies, and leverage collective client relationships and channels. The module also provides tools for project management, task assignment, and accounting.
2. *Contract Negotiation and Fulfillment.* This module enables contracts to be defined and refined through a structured online negotiation process. When the terms of the

engagement are finalized a contract detailing the responsibilities of the consultant provider and customer-client is formalized. The client places funds for the immediate deliverables in an escrow account managed by iQLinux. The consultant is also able to extend credit to the client using the site. The funds are released to the provider and subcontractors when the client is satisfied that the product or service has been delivered and after a seven-day grace period. A complete contract management system for handling each level of contract deliverables and fulfillment is provided.

3. *Dispute Resolution.* In cases where the client is not satisfied with a component of the work undertaken, a level-one dispute resolution mechanism enables the client and consultant to resolve the dispute together. This efficient and structured process enables adjustment of expectations and preserves the ongoing business relationship, because, as in other types of projects, perceptual differences and other external factors can sometimes contribute to contact disputes. This efficient and litigation-free process is advantageous to both parties, simply because it facilitates the communication of perspectives and enables the resolution toward a fair settlement of the dispute. The vast majority of professionals and businesses take the protection of their business reputations very seriously and like to be treated fairly in all business dealings.
4. *Mediation by Peers.* In cases where both the client and the consultant are unable to resolve their dispute independently, peer volunteers from within the larger community can help to mediate the case. This "jury of peers" process involves prominent and creditable community members who volunteer to mediate and contribute toward ensuring equitable business practices and high-quality work standards for their community. This is a level-two resolution process and is an efficient mechanism to curb escalating litigation cost and facilitates participation in a self-governing global community. As an alternative, for reasons of confidentiality the parties can choose to have their dispute arbitrated by professional mediation agencies as well, such as those provided by the Singapore's Judiciary or the World Intellectual Property Organization. The client generally bears the cost for this service. Case and contractual information is forwarded automatically by the engine.

This procedural B2B engine is well suited to the professional expertise and technical support industries where close to 60% of the service is already being provided by telephone. iQLinux has tested this model with different Linux user groups, vendors and consultants and it has been very well received. As Internet-based commerce is making business practices more transparent, there is a greater motivation for clients, consultants, and vendors to act as good community and business citizens. The iQLinux engine and business model recognize that the community instead of corporate/market power or domination is what regulates and controls the marketplaces of tomorrow.

MARKET SIZE AND COMPETITION

iQLinux.com's business plan highlights the growth of business-to-business e-commerce as summarized in the following assessment:

> B2B Internet-based commerce will reach $5.7 trillion by 2004. Industry leaders aim to move 60% to 100% of their transactions to the Internet over the next two years.
>
> —*The Report on E-Commerce Applications*,
> AMR Research, Inc., April 2000

The *Report* notes that although the Internet was gaining popularity quickly, it was in many ways still regarded as the "Wild-Wild-Web." The Internet lacked the formal business structure required to ensure safe e-commerce transactions for customers and providers, especially in the service sector. The business plan also notes that service transactions over the Internet are projected to grow at a compound annual growth rate of 120% reaching US$640B by the year 2004.

In addition to capitalizing on the high growth rate of the business-to-business services sector, the business model of iQLinux also exploits the high growth in its open source Linux target market. Linux is the world's fastest-growing computer operating system, with a user base that is now estimated at over 20 million users. AllNetResearch reports that the Linux market is expected to grow to 100 million users by the year 2003. Sales of Linux-based servers also now leads in the growing server market especially for Internet-based applications. As the associated demand for Linux open source solutions and support services increases in tandem, iQLinux.com and its community stand to gain collectively by providing best-of-breed components and technical support solutions that are globally supported in a truly open market environment.

The rapid introduction of Linux into the market spawned a flurry of competitive activity in late 1999 and early 2000. Many consulting and other companies vied for the dominant position as the pivotal source for Linux technical support and consulting. Many of these companies have tried to bring their services online with Web sites offering varying levels of support services. These include both Linux-specific and generalized support sites and they complement the existing non-organized support services found in the form of Linux user groups, Internet news groups, and traditional consulting services.

An example of competition provided by an online, Linux-specific Web site is Linux Start. It provides Linux-related news stories, discussion groups, links, and references to consultants and users who are interested in Linux development issues. However, such sites do not offer the structured business orientation nor the comprehensive and sophisticated contract negotiation or dispute resolution features present in iQLinux.com. The Question Exchange and Hot Dispatch are examples of generalized technical support sites that can also be viewed as offering some competition to the iQLinux business model. They offer access to experts who can answer questions on any subject including Linux. Such sites are becoming increasingly prolific as the general public continues to embrace the Internet. However, given that Linux is a highly technical and specialized subject even within the confines of the IT world, it is unlikely that such generalized sites will evolve to become the primary point for business access to Linux technical support services. They also lack the community-based quality control aspects of a dedicated and focused marketplace such as iQLinux. Linux User Groups (often termed LUGs) which have been organized in many large urban centres generally tend to serve the "techie" (technical development) market rather than business interests. The people who participate in this market generally tended to be technical programming types who are familiar with navigating Internet-based user groups, newsgroups, chat rooms, and other open source community resources. While these groups do to an extent represent the supply side of the value chain that iQLinux seeks to facilitate, mainstream business users of Linux do not participate in these LUG gatherings. From a business perspective, the fact that the support services received or given at the LUGs is on an irregular, voluntary, or no-charge basis means that it will probably lack the timeliness and reliability required by commercial users of Linux. Often only a few people will expend the time and effort necessary to deliver a high-quality response to a request for technical support made to the LUGs. iQLinux will build upon the free community model and enable paid options for those requiring guaranteed, high-quality, and rapid responses.

Linux consultants are companies or individuals who are hired to assist or manage the implementation or operation of Linux-based systems. The major consulting firms in this market include: Linuxcare, LinuxForce, Mission Critical Linux, VA Linux, IBM, and Hewlett-Packard. Some of these high-profile consulting firms have been known to charge up to $300 per hour for the Linux services that they provide. It is expected that the majority of open source consultants on iQLinux.com will be positioned below this high-end market and that iQLinux will not directly compete with this segment of the industry. Some Linux distribution companies sell their own variations or distributions of Linux and typically support only those customers who have purchased "their" Linux variations. The most well-known members of this category of competitors are: Redhat, TurboLinux (which is currently in the process of acquiring Linuxcare), SuSE, Mandrake, Storm, and Yellow Dog. These companies will also not view iQLinux as a direct competitor given its different portal-type business model. However, it is reasonable to expect that some of the smaller and medium-sized clients of these companies may try to develop alternative and more reasonably priced channels for technical support using the iQLinux portal.

From a competitive perspective, iQLinux, with its business-Web empowerment model, stands alone, because it is focused on providing the Linux community with a structured, self-governing marketplace that will facilitate working together in self-organizing teams, and provide best-of-breed solutions, products, and services to customers. Ultimate business success will be dependent on team commitment, service level, value, and customer satisfaction.

OPERATIONAL DEVELOPMENT OF IQLINUX: EVENT TIMELINE

Exhibit 1 provides a timeline of the major events that were part of the ongoing development of the iQLinux e-business portal. A unique characteristic of the development has been its global orientation. iQLinux originated out of western Canada, has an office in the Silicon Valley, recently located a key part of its operations to Asia, and is currently represented in northern Europe as well (where the Linux operating system was born). This is critical because of the unique nature of the global growth and distribution of the demand for and supply of Linux technical support services and components. Demand is currently concentrated largely in North America and Europe. However, there is a large shortage of supply in these markets. Asia's growth potential is significant from both demand and supply perspectives. Given that Linux technical support services can be provided to customers remotely through the telephone and over the Internet, iQLinux will try to exploit the large and growing pool of Linux expertise in Asia for servicing the demand in North America and Europe. On the demand side, many governments in the fast-developing countries of Asia, including China, have expressed strong interest in supporting Linux because of its open source flavour and the fact that it represents a viable alternative to the use of costly proprietary software. They are keen to avoid past intergovernmental trade tensions that focus on software piracy arising out of intellectual property disputes. Asia therefore represents a large market for both the supply and the demand side of the Linux technical

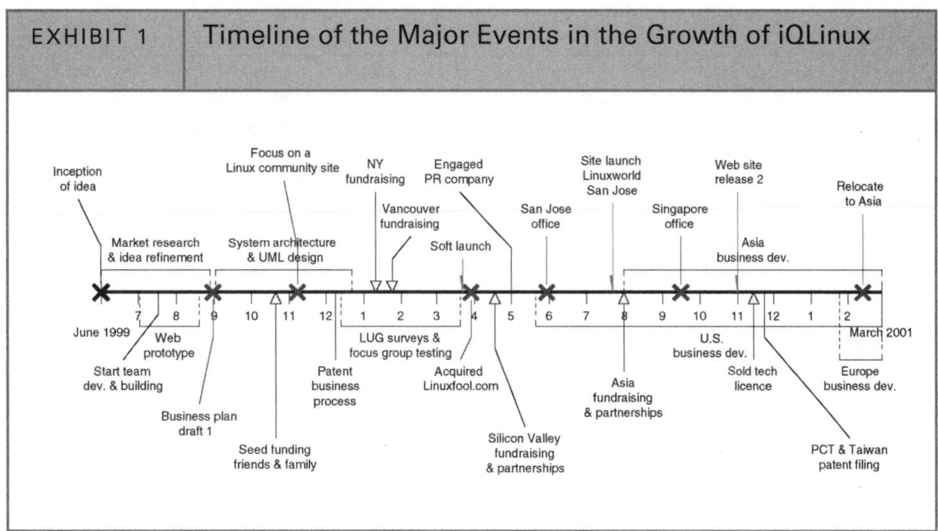

EXHIBIT 1 Timeline of the Major Events in the Growth of iQLinux

support supply chain. The global orientation has proved to be both a significant operational challenge and an asset in iQLinux' international expansion.

In the view of Peter So and his management team, it is imperative for them to maintain a global outlook given that the supply chain is inherently global. The real value of their portal exploits geographical differences in the distribution of Linux demand and supply to smoothen out the supply chain through market-making. There is also the possibility that iQLinux may work with partners with strengths in setting up global call centres that integrate telephone and the Internet technologies to provide a supply chain channel for Linux technical support as a value-added feature to complement the market-making aspects of their portal. The global orientation also helps the company exploit the talents, skills, capital markets, and legal support structures in growing its business. According to Peter, "unlike the likes of e-Bay and Onvia that concentrated on the North American market initially, we made a deliberate decision to go global during the early stages because this also assists us in ramping up to a breakeven critical mass of customers and consultants much quickly. This will help make us a profitable venture right from the start and this is critical in the e-business capital markets of today." On the other hand, however, going global at the start poses a string of implementation challenges that include higher initial capital requirements, Web localization factors such as cultural and language customizations, and the time and space challenges of international business management.

Table 1 provides a more detailed narrative of the actual business activities that were undertaken in the roll-out of the iQLinux business.

OPERATIONAL CHALLENGES AND CONCLUSION

Peter looks back on the past two years with much satisfaction at the rapid pace at which his venture has progressed from the idea stage to become a growing global facilitator of the Linux technical support supply chain. In his words, "Entrepreneurship is a love, a

TABLE 1 Operational Details of iQLinux' Development

Business Activities	Dates	Details
Inception of the idea Market research Idea refinement	*June 1999*	After the original idea was conceived, much effort was expended in carrying out market research, market segmentation, community evaluation, concept refinement, and initial site construction. The venture was self-funded initially.
Design of Web prototype Team development Building management team	*July–August 1999*	A semi-functional Web site was prototyped using ASP and a MS Access database. The initial management team came together. Team development and task ownership were initiated, and the writing of the formal business plan began. Various communities, strategies, and targeted market segments were mapped out.
Completion of business plan Start of system architecture and design	*September 1999*	First draft of the business plan was completed. Initial prototype development was done in ZOPE, but stability and scalability considerations forced evaluation of other commercial application servers as well. Finally settled on Coldfusion, which also released a version of Linux.
Secured seed funding from friends and family Release of UML design to development team	*October 1999*	System architecture and design went ahead using the Unified Modeling Language methodology.
Filed U.S. patent for the business processes Linux Users Group survey and focus group discussions support the notion that market would pay for Linux support services and that interest level was high	*December 1999*	Completed initial focus group review with the Seattle Linux Users Group. Site concept and business model were well received. Conducted two regional market surveys with the Vancouver Linux Users' Group with the following highlights: • 92% felt Linux is the future of the IT industry.

TABLE 1	Operational Details of iQLinux' Development (continued)	
Business Activities	**Dates**	**Details**
		• 70% would pay for technical support services. • 92% would pay between $20 and $100 for Linux technical support. • 76% would consult 4 to 16 hours per week on projects as independent service providers.
Fundraising in New York and Vancouver	*January 2000*	Initiated external fundraising process in New York at Venture Navigator's event, followed by local fundraising in Vancouver. Immediately noticed a distinct cultural difference between Canadian and U.S. VCs.
Soft launch of site Focus group testing Acquired Linuxfool.com that had approximately 400 000 page views per month and over 1000 members Additional funds injection by existing shareholders	*February–March 2000*	Soft launch carried out in March and Web site went into focus group testing for the LUGs community. Coldfusion running on Linux proved to be somewhat unstable, and a decision was made to do the soft launch on Solaris. Moved to acquire Linuxfool.com as part of ramp-up strategy to build critical mass. Linuxfool.com is a free community support site with strong community participation. Later determined that only a small percentage of the members were active contributors. Linux frenzy in the capital markets at this time.
Engaged public relations firm, USA Inc. Fundraising and business development in Silicon Valley Strengthened management team	*April–June 2000*	Business development and funding activity began in Silicon Valley. Established first partnership with a San Jose vendor. Established a marketing and business development office in San Jose. The talent pool in San Francisco was very tight and staffing was a challenge.

TABLE 1 Operational Details of iQLinux' Development (continued)		
Business Activities	**Dates**	**Details**
Efforts at growing site membership Executed official site launch at Linuxworld in San Jose Plan for Asian regional expansion developed Continued fundraising	*July–August 2000*	With Coldfusion becoming more stable on Linux, the site is officially launched. Site memberships grow to about 1300 members and 30 consulting teams. Linux sentiment began to wane in the capital markets. Explored Linux in the Asia market in terms of both funding and joint ventures partners. Three more partnerships were secured from Asia trip.
Established Singapore office Asia business development Web Site Release 2 with full functionality Extended patent protection to PCT and Taiwan Sold technology licence to Wizcontent.com Inc.	*September–November 2000*	Asia business development moved into full swing. Web site features were completed by the development team with the addition of the reseller model. The patent protection was extended for other developing countries, via the Patent Co-operation Treaty and Taiwan. Moved to explore the licensing of technology engine ahead of original plan partly because of further decline in market sentiment.
Delivered Wizcontent.com site in 14 days Reduced operations to slow down burn rate Relocated HQ to Asia	*December 2000—March 2001*	A licence was sold to a Hong Kong–based publishing company. Customization took 14 days to complete. Funding efforts continued although prospects became harder as the stock market was going through its adjustment.
Establishing European operations and partnerships Increasing company capitalization to bring it into full operational mode	*Ongoing 2001 plans*	Currently, the Cybercash filing for Chapter 11 restructuring affects our business operations. Continuing to look into the European Linux market. Continuing fundraising efforts and/or joint venture development to bring innovative business model to global market.

learning process, and a journey that never ends. Money can get you started, but people (and the markets) help get you there in terms of success in innovation and making a difference." He has learned a lot from the day-to-day operational struggles that are involved in executing his vision. Some of his realizations include the following:

- Outsourcing of systems development can be a harder and more risky proposition than internal development.
- While finding talent in e-business is challenging, developing and growing it is even more challenging, especially in an economic downturn.
- Building a winning management team is the most challenging task for an entrepreneur, but, once built, it represents the largest asset of the venture.
- In e-business, getting staff to perform at their peak is easy for a short while but keeping them going at the required pace for a startup requires much planning and a strong people orientation. He also feels that as CEO it is critical for him to lead in "eradicating the burnout virus before it starts" in managing a startup technology venture.
- Instilling ownership is a universal solution to most problems and leads to the creation of an invincible startup corporate culture. It is therefore imperative that his staff and business partners believe in and subscribe to the open source community philosophy that is at the heart of his venture.

The iQLinux marketplace and business model is unique given its community orientation to e-business and the focus on facilitating the supply chain of a virtual service rather than a physical product. It also capitalizes on the global trends toward entrepreneurship and the free agent work culture wherein the true economic value of the free agent is determined by the open market, rather than within the confines of a hierarchical organization. With the Internet bringing together global demand and supply, an open exchange model for human capital and skills will ensure that people are much more likely to deliver more to get what they are worth in a fair way. As well, both small and large organizations can engage the skills and services of the best, most talented technical experts at the best value. All that is required is a fair and structured collaborative environment such as iQLinux for them to prosper.

EPILOGUE

A May 7, 2001 news report by Reuters stated: "Microsoft has declared war on the Linux operating system and other rival software that share their basic instruction codes with the public, saying the open software movement poses a fundamental threat to commercial intellectual property rights." According to the report, Mr. Craig Mundie, senior vice-president of the world's largest software company, blasted the open source movement and described the open software movement as "flimsy and flawed and said open source software creates a greater danger of security risks, software instability and incompatibility."

case two

FishMarket International: Reengineering the Supply Chain for Fish

Jasbir Dhaliwal, Norwegian School of Management

Ajax Persaud, School of Management, University of Ottawa

While driving back to his office in the Sagveien district of Oslo, Are Herrem, the managing director of FishMarket International AS, pondered his latest success in the continuing development of his e-business venture. He was returning from a local hotel after the signing ceremony of an agreement that saw the largest bank in Norway investing NOK 9 million in his company. The agreement also meant that the two parties would collaborate on the development of financial services and products to be offered electronically to the fisheries industry over the Internet through the FishMarket e-business marketplace. The services would include safe user identification, international payment transfers, trade financing, and currency sales. In Are Herrem's opinion, this collaboration would go a long way toward enhancing the service his company could offer the users of its marketplace, besides providing much-needed industry endorsement.

He had long understood that success in supply chain management encompassed the coordination of three distinct but related types of flows: physical flows, information flows, and financial flows. With the agreement in place, he knew that his FishMarket marketplace could now provide integrated solutions to the coordination of all these three flows to its customers. The traditional supply chain for fish had been disjointed and based on an uncoordinated, ad hoc approach to the synchronization of these flows. He felt confident that it was now just a matter of time before he succeeded on his long entrepreneurial journey aimed at transforming the European supply chain for fish.

ORGANIZATIONAL DETAILS AND BACKGROUND

FishMarket (**www.FishMarket.no**) is a leading e-business marketplace for the sale of fish. The marketplace has been developed in collaboration with the fisheries industry and is designed to facilitate electronic fish trading between companies. Several large fisheries companies and other strategic partners with interest in the fisheries industry have financed FishMarket, and its aim is to become one of the primary marketplaces for fish trading in the world. It is a specialized marketplace for the trading of fish between enterprises and offers various informational and market-making tools for fish trading. Through its ownership and through collaboration with major players in the industry, FishMarket is ensured of a considerable turnover in the marketplace. Currently, it collaborates with leading European buyers and sellers of fish whose total turnover was more than three billion euros.

The company has innovated in terms of developing a technical solution for selling fish over the Internet that is based on existing fish trading processes and practices, and this has been well received by both buyers and sellers. FishMarket is a full-service market and covers all forms of fish sales between companies and the various categories of fish products. The company collaborates with suppliers of additional services, including transport, quality, credit insurance, and news, to provide an integrated service to its customers. Its plans are to generate revenues through a charge on sales in the marketplace. These charges would be considerably lower than the benefits derived from using the marketplace.

The market excitement about the potential of e-business in 1999 and 2000 led to the birth of between eight and ten startup Norwegian companies whose business models hoped to cash in on Norway's dominant role in the world seafood market. Norway was the leading exporter of seafood in the world with sales of close to US$3.3 billion in 1997 and had a 53% share of the world salmon farming market. The shakeout in the financial and risk capital markets in 2000 resulted in only two of these new ventures, Seafood-x.com and FishMarket.com, surviving, both of whom had recruited a varied mix of seafood suppliers and customers as strategic and investment partners. These two companies then proceeded to merge their operations in the summer of 2000 to form the current FishMarket enterprise. Seafood-x had been founded by Are Herrem, Jan Henry Olsen, and Terje Andreassen, who now respectively served as the CEO, VP–Sales and Marketing, and CFO of the company. Bjørn Staalesen, who now served as the Chief Operating Officer of FishMarket had founded the other together with some partners. Appendix 1 presents more details of the background of the company's management team.

FishMarket's board of directors and management had strong ties with the fisheries industry in Norway. The chairman of the board was Helge Møgster of Austevoll Havfiske AS, and was also the founder of American Seafoods. Other directors represented some of the largest European seafood companies including Skagerak Fiskeksport AS, Grieg Seafood AS, Domstein ASA, and Terra Seafood AS.

VALUE PROPOSITION AND A REENGINEERED SUPPLY CHAIN FOR FISH

Exhibit 1 shows how FishMarket's management envisaged the future structure of the fish trading industry. Their e-business model is to make FishMarket the central coordinating mechanism for the entire value chain of the industry from the fisher and fish farm suppliers to the ultimate customers. This means that they have to build the necessary functionality and mechanisms to ensure that the marketplace is able to service and add value to all the various intermediaries who made up the industry's supply chain. Currently, FishMarket has already established functional linkages with customers and suppliers. Its objective is to expand the set of linkages to include other intermediaries as well as other exchanges and consortiums such as GNX, Transora, WWRE, and others. Linkages to the sites of transportation providers and financial intermediaries, and vertical manufacturers of fish products and third-party business-to-consumer sites, are also being developed. The company plans to integrate all relevant technologies necessary for ensuring that the marketplace remains at the forefront of technological innovation. This includes interfaces to the ERP back ends of its customers, wireless access to the marketplace, extranet func-

EXHIBIT 1 Future Industry Structure as Envisaged by FishMarket

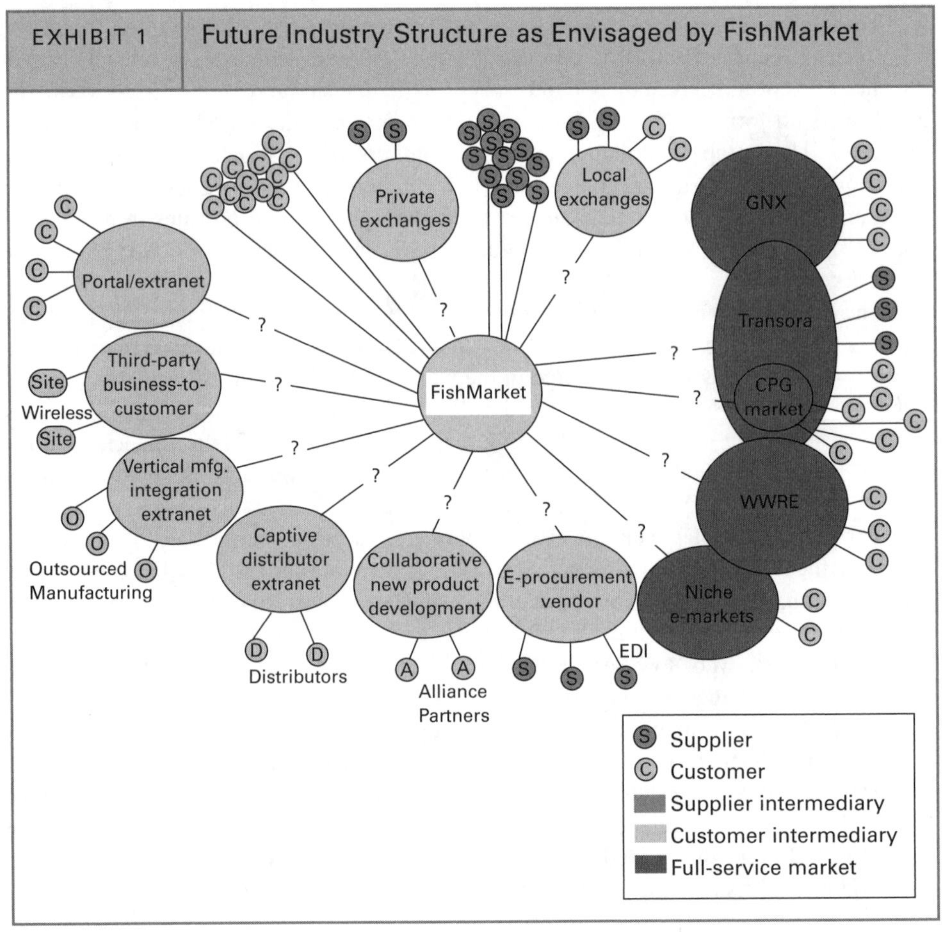

tionality, and connections to both buyer- and supplier-controlled e-procurement networks. In Are Herrem's view, while staying at the technological forefront is a necessary condition for success, technology development costs have to be balanced out with market development costs, given the inherent challenges of transforming the industry's traditional supply chain.

While a few local fish exchanges existed (with average transaction values of about 400 euro) FishMarket International is the leading fish trading e-marketplace in Europe. The average value of the typical FishMarket transaction is about 15 000 euro. In this category, it had two potential competitors, both based in other geographical parts of the world. Boston-based Gofish.com used to be the most significant competitor. It was positioned as a business-to-business marketplace with trading, credit information, news, and other services. GoFish was financed by GE and CMGI and in March 2000 had completed a third round of financing that raised US$45 million. While the bulk of the trade at the GoFish.com marketplace was mainly Asian and American frozen products, GoFish.com had intentions of expanding internationally. Largely because trade on the marketplace had not reached acceptable liquidity levels, GoFish had recently decided to collaborate with Seafood Alliance. This represents an alliance of nine large seafood companies and focuses on procurement solutions for the member companies. A second potential competitor is Asia-based FishRound, an industry consortium led by the Korean (Samsung) and Japanese (Nissho) seafood companies. Merrill Lynch is the financial partner in the consortium and three Asian transport companies are the logistics partners. It was known that FishRound was in the process of beta-testing its trading platform and would start operations in the near future. Japan was the largest importer of seafood in the world accounting for close to 35% of world seafood imports. Other, smaller participants in the marketplace included PEFA.com, WorldCatch.com, FIS.com, and Seafood.com. Given the geographical segmentation of the global market, FishMarket management considers all these potential competitors to be potential partners and participants in its marketplace.

Appendix 2 gives a before-and-after depiction of the impact of FishMarket on the European fish trading marketplace. Industry projections show that Norwegian fish exports are expected to register a fourfold increase in size by the year 2020. This makes Norway an ideal starting point for the development and launch of FishMarket. The FishMarket business model is naturally attractive for the seafood industry due to some of its fundamental dynamics:

- It is a large and fragmented market with many individual buyers and sellers.
- There is no existing common market exchange and there is significant geographical dispersion of producers and consumers.
- An expensive and complex distribution system spanning national boundaries is required for trade fulfillment purposes.
- Seafood is a perishable item that requires high-speed logistics.
- There is high growth and potential in the industry (in value-added products on the demand side and in fish farming on the supply side) because of trends away from meat and toward healthy meals.
- There are strong international efforts to deregulate trade barriers for seafood and seafood products.

- There is excess demand for fish because wild stocks cannot give increased yields and are being depleted globally.

The traditional process of fish trading that predominated was largely based on fax and phone communications and on the manual processing of sales and international trade documentation. Generally each producer marketed seafood independently and each buyer searched independently for supplies from the different sources. For example, in the fresh seafood market, sellers (fishers or selling intermediaries) would typically fax out their product information (size, location, species, etc.) on a weekly basis to between 20 and 200 potential buyers. On the other side, buyers generally consolidated the faxed sales offers that they received (averaging about 60) on Monday mornings for evaluation. This process typically involved sorting the faxed offers on large tables and then selecting a subset of them for further consideration and evaluation. Spreadsheet-based analysis of all the available options was seldom utilized, and optimization was not a major concern because gut-feel was largely involved in this selection process. The buyers usually struck deals on Wednesday or Thursday for meeting the consumer demand for the following week. Details of the deal were usually faxed back and forth between the two parties and preparation of the financial, shipping, and other trading documentation was then initiated. Payment was a key issue in deal completion, and because of historically high rates of default in unsecured deals about 80% of transactions were secured by credit insurance, which added to the cost. Some parties also preferred to deal on a relationship basis with a small set of other known parties to minimize their risk even though this made for a costly and imperfect market.

Given this scenario, the value proposition of FishMarket is significant to all the various parties. FishMarket offers value to its users: time and cost savings, and supply chain optimization benefits—as discussed in the sections following.

Time and Cost Savings

The use of FishMarket could result in cost reductions for both sellers and buyers. For sellers, cost reductions would mainly be realized through (i) electronic transactions and document handling between businesses and (ii) reductions in marketing and sales through less travel, advertising, phone, and fax costs. The marketplace would also allow them to optimize the selling opportunities they had. For buyers, FishMarket lowered transaction costs by reducing the time and effort required for making purchases. FishMarket provided a better overview of potential suppliers and this probably reduced costs associated with the search for reliable suppliers and supplies of high quality. Use of digitized documents would also reduce administrative work significantly. Electronic identifications, quality certificates, and the use of legally valid electronic signatures on trade documents would also bring about efficiencies and reliability. Industry analysts had estimated that use of Internet-based trading place could reduce transaction costs from between 150 and 175 to between 10 and 20 euro per transaction. Additionally, FishMarket's common trading platform would also enable its members to save costs on the development of their own Web solutions. A common platform based on industry-wide XML standards would be less expensive than inconsistent separate development of individual or localized trading systems.

Improved Marketing and a Transparent Seafood Market

The use of FishMarket enabled both buyers and sellers to reach a broader base of trading partners and make the market more transparent. FishMarket would provide sellers with access to customers all over the world and allow them to partition and allocate their produce (sales) to those willing to pay the best price, thereby maximizing revenues. Buyers too would benefit by getting a better picture of the overall supply availability and will now have the flexibility of being able to choose between different suppliers based on price and quality. The creation of one consolidated transparent market would facilitate efficient trading based on real-time and accurate market information and fair trading practices. The expansion of market reach would also increase direct sales by reducing the need for non-value-adding intermediaries and increasing selling prices while reducing buyer costs. The marketplace would also assist buyer and seller organizations to reduce their dependence on a scarce set of key employees who functioned as "expert" buyers and sellers based on personal networks in the industry. Recognizing that such relationship-based trading may be the preference of many parties for some time to come, FishMarket also facilitated such privileged trading relationships with pertinent features. For example, it offered the opportunity to keep preferred customer relationships confidential. Sellers or buyers could choose to make transactions "behind closed doors" on the Internet by creating an intranet for a limited set of preselected seller and buyer partners.

Supply Chain Optimization Benefits

The use of FishMarket would also provide major benefits arising from better coordination of both the physical logistical flow of fish and the financial flow of payments and credit. The availability of online quotations for freight movement and logistics handling services and FishMarket's tracking of product deliveries would also improve service, reduce costs, and save time. Prior credit approval validated by FishMarket membership and due diligence as well as its tracking of payment history also ensures the financial reliability and creditworthiness of approved buyers. The initial pioneering users of FishMarket had found that the use of FishMarket could cut the cost of an international payment transaction by approximately 80% from its current range of anywhere between 20 and 100 euro. As well, the time taken to complete such a payment (currently between four and eleven days) could also be reduced by about half. FishMarket was also currently working with the SWIFT international payment system to bring about instantaneous payment functionality to the marketplace in the future. On the physical flow side, FishMarket users were currently experiencing approximately 40% improvement in process handling through the use of electronic documents, load planning based on the early receipt of order information, and load planning and optimization methods. Several larger players in the fish transportation sector were currently working with FishMarket to optimize the supply chain especially for the land-based transport of fish and fish products from Norway to Europe. The EU countries accounted for 61% of total Norwegian exports of fish products. The major land-based fish logistics companies such as NSB Gods, Nor-Cargo, Linjegods, Danzas (ASG-Norway), and Tollpost were keen to see a transformation of current fish trading practices so that they could improve on their capacity utilization which was currently in the range of between 55 and 75%. FishMarket would also facilitate the contextual provision of online access to vital seafood industry information such as business news, weather reports, market prices, and analysis. This could also assist buyers, sellers and supply chain partners in more realistically planning their trading and service activities to improve the overall efficiency and cost structure of the industry.

FishMarket is focusing particularly on the special needs of the large companies in the industry in its value proposition. It is constantly enhancing its value proposition by increasing the scope of its complete integrated solution to their needs. It has designed its trading methods to consider all the variations including handling spot sales and long contracts with existing customers. Beyond trading through the use of electronic documents, standardized sales procedures, contracts management, improved quality control and documentation, optimized logistics, and efficient billing and payment, FishMarket is continuing to innovate in terms of its total value package. For example, it is developing internally a fish futures hedging solution that would assist the large fish-selling companies in counteracting the risk inherent in volatile prices. It is also working closely with these large fish companies on technology-based pilot projects pertinent to their specific needs for fish trading. Plans are also in place to offer branded Web-based storefronts to members of the marketplace.

THE BUSINESS PROCESSES AND TRADING MODELS OF FISHMARKET

The FishMarket site provides a structured set of business processes for fish trading to a closed group of members. Any party wishing to participate in the trading first has to register with FishMarket as a member. This can be done on the Web site. FishMarket conducts a basic level of due diligence on new members to ensure that only reliable parties engage in the fish trading. No subscription fee is charged to new members.

The trading process begins through the completion and posting of a "Specification of Product" document by either a seller or a buyer of fish who was registered as a member on the site. This document specified the product for available for sale or purchase in detail. Product description attributes include price, quality, quantity, payment and delivery terms, packing style, and any other characteristic of the products that the member wishes to sell or purchase. Trading on FishMarket is open both for branded and non-branded fish products.

Members can then select from among a set of trade or market-making alternatives that were offered by the marketplace. On the basis of traditional trading practices in the fish trading industry, the FishMarket marketplace offered four trading options: catalogue sales, sellers auction, buyers auction, and long-term contract sales.

1. *Catalogue sales.* Using this model, sellers posted one or more products for sale on the FishMarket catalogue by specifying the products. These product postings remained intact on the catalogue until a sale was completed, or if the seller made changes to or withdrew the offer for sale. Sellers could change or withdraw an item at any time before a sale was completed. Buyers, on the other hand, could review all the postings and accept any catalogue-listing offer of sale that was posted at the prescribed price. Buyers wishing to make a purchase could also give the seller a counteroffer to purchase some or all of the fish products at either a higher or a lower price than that which the seller had specified. They could also offer to purchase all the quantity/products at a lower price than the seller's listing price by proposing an alternative set of conditions

of trade. Acceptance by the seller of a counteroffer made by a prospective buyer led to the creation of an agreement between the buyer and the seller. From a legal contractual perspective, there were two methods of contract creation:

(a) In instances where a buyer accepted the catalogue posting at the prescribed price (or higher) and with all the product and quantity specifications intact as listed by seller, FishMarket would automatically create an agreement.

(b) In instances where a buyer made a counteroffer to purchase some or all of the products/quantities at a lower price or offered to buy only some of the products/quantities offered for sale, the agreement was created only after final agreement between the buyer and seller was reached. Thus the interaction process could proceed with the seller declining or countering buyers' counteroffers.

2. *Sellers auction.* Using this trading model, sellers could post a product for sale by an auction that was to be determined at a defined deadline. The auction would be open for buyer responses until the prescribed deadline and buyers could only bid for the entire quanta offered for sale. Buyer bids were binding until 15 minutes after the closing to enable sellers to check the credit limit of best bidders before accepting a bid. FishMarket would then proceed to draw up the contract.
3. *Buyers auction (reverse auction).* In this trading model, buyers developed a product specification and initiated the auction by requesting quotations from sellers before a set deadline. The auction was open for seller responses until the defined deadline. Seller offers were binding until 15 minutes after the deadline to enable the buyer to decide which of the offers to accept. If a seller's quotation had not been accepted 15 minutes after the deadline, the bidders were free from their bids.
4. *Long-term contract sales.* Long-term contracts could also be executed in the FishMarket trading system under the terms of an existing framework agreement between two parties. The terms of individual orders were made subject to the terms of the preexisting agreement between the two parties. Sellers and buyers could enter key elements of their agreed-upon framework agreement into the FishMarket trading system and make fulfillment of the calls and deliveries electronically on the system. This trading model assisted members in migrating all their trading activity to the integrated marketplace to provide them with control and continuity.

Sellers and buyers on FishMarket are able to select their trade partners within the marketplace. FishMarket kept personalized and updated member lists for each member and allowed them to select and specify their trading partners of choice. Each time a new member was registered, all preexisting FishMarket members could receive information about the new member on the site and had the choice of adding the new member to their list of preferred trading partners. This helped members develop confidence, trust, and longer-term partnerships over the system.

In addition to the preselection of trading partners, members could also select the target individual partner or groups of sellers or buyers for a particular offer for sale or request for quotations. For each trade, members had a choice of:

- Targeting individual customers or suppliers by name for closed one-to-one trading
- Targeting a select group of defined customers or suppliers as potential trading partners

- Targeting all members of FishMarket as potential trading partners
- Excluding one or several members from the targeted potential trading partners

FishMarket had carefully considered the legal aspects of fish trading on an international basis in the design of its business processes and user interfaces. For example, by bidding on an item on FishMarket, the buyer or seller certified that it had the legal right to sell or purchase the listed items. The CEO of the firm, who had prior experience as a Supreme Court attorney in Norway, often joked that a legal mind should be a critical knowledge requirement for running a business-to-business organization. In his opinion, the current lack of a defined legal framework for international e-business transactions was not a barrier to e-business success if one relied upon bricks-and-mortar legal arrangements in designing trading processes and user interfaces. In his opinion, trading on the FishMarket marketplace was as legally secure as taking a lawyer alongside for each trading activity in the bricks-and-mortar world.

Anonymity was a critical aspect considered in the design of the marketplace's business processes. However, buyers and sellers could not trade anonymously for purposes of quality assurance. In addition the name of a bidder and bid details remained unknown to other bidders. Binding agreements were also subject to satisfactory guarantee of payment or available coverage by credit insurance. FishMarket also logged all discussions between buyers and sellers in FishMarket's conference application, and members were informed that these were available as evidence of agreement between contracting parties. Members were also responsible for the content and information contained in all their communications through FishMarket, including its lawfulness, truthfulness, and accuracy. Members also agree not to disclose other members' and FishMarket's confidential information to third parties. The design of the business processes also precluded buyers and sellers from colluding in any way or otherwise manipulating the price of an item. Members were also prevented from interfering with the listings or auctions of other members. Are and his management team understood that building confidence and trust were critical elements in ensuring that all the various actors in the global fish supply chain had motivation to join their marketplace. They made every effort to ensure that there was a zero non-conformance level associated with their carefully designed e-business operational processes.

To make the user interface and jargon accessible and the trading processes easy to use, all prices quoted on the marketplace, and all orders accepted and billings rendered, were made inclusive of any relevant taxes, fees, or charges imposed by governmental authorities. This was of course subject to a different set of terms and conditions that two parties could agree to for particular trades, for example, DDP (dutied, delivered, and paid), FOB (free on board), or CIF (carriage in freight). Given that fish products were perishable and often in non-standardized format in terms of quantity, the definition of fulfillment quantity had to be carefully specified on the marketplace. Unless otherwise expressly agreed to by a seller and buyer, a seller could fulfill a contract by delivering the agreed-upon quantity plus or minus a variance of 5%. If the variance in quantity exceeded the 5% allowable limit, the seller had to contact the buyer for acceptance. Buyers had the option to maintain the contract as amended or decline the amendment to the fulfillment quantity.

The revenue model of FishMarket is based on charging a small transaction fee that is a percentage of the trade value. For all the four trading options (catalogue sales, sellers auction, buyers auction, and long-term contract sales), transaction fees would be split 50-50 between the buyer and the seller. It was also intended that this transaction fee would be differentiated on the basis of the value added by FishMarket's market-making and other services. During the ongoing testing period that lasts until June 30, 2001, all trading on FishMarket is free of charge for pioneering members. It is FishMarket's intention to finalize the rates on the basis of discussions with users to make sure that the fee is lower than the benefits accruing to users of its services.

FishMarket has a defined set of trade terms for members to follow to ensure consistency and reliability in the marketplace. Members undertake to follow the terms and procedures in these trade terms for all trading on FishMarket. Contracts between buyers and sellers were governed by these trade terms that conformed to generally accepted trade practices in fish trading. Members could choose alternative terms and conditions for trading if these alternative terms and conditions were expressly displayed in the offers for sale or requests for quotation. FishMarket facilitated the resolution of disputes between parties by negotiations in good faith and helped ensure that the choice of law and venue for dispute resolution followed established industry practice.

TECHNICAL ARCHITECTURE AND DEVELOPMENT

The current FishMarket solution is developed on a Microsoft platform in close cooperation with its technological partners, some of whom hold equity in the company. Exhibit 2 shows the various activities in the supply chain of fish as it moves from the sea to consumers. The first-generation technical architecture of FishMarket focused on automating the three market-making operations of the supply chain which primarily service the marketing, negotiation, and deal-closing functions associated with auction- and catalogue-based fish trading. The first-generation solution's user interface and trading functionality has been beta-tested and has been well received by both the buyer and seller communities.

As shown in Exhibit 2, the company is now moving to fulfill its vision of becoming a full-service collaboration hub for the whole industry by completing the development of the second generation of the FishMarket solution. It recognizes the need to develop close enterprise resource planning (ERP)–type integration with its supply chain partners besides offering comprehensive contract management functionality. This involves tightly integrating the ERP systems of buyers and sellers into the FishMarket system. Are Herrem and his technical team realize that standardization is a key issue for interorganizational connectivity in the supply chain and have developed an XML standard for fish trading for this purpose.

EXHIBIT 2 Supply Chain Operations

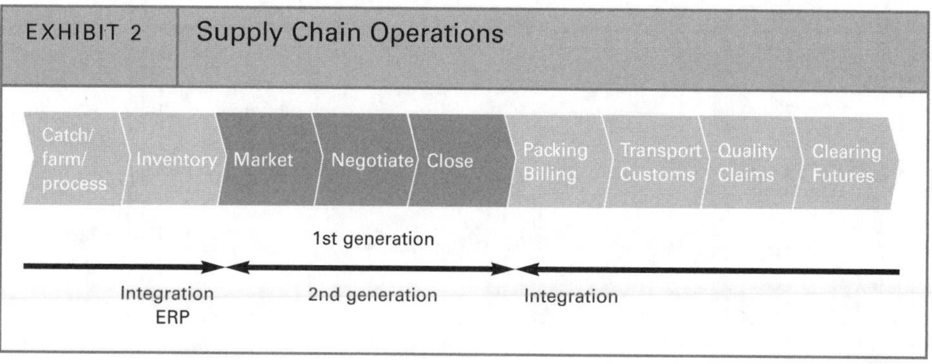

The application architecture of FishMarket is depicted in Exhibit 3 and consists of the following major components:

- *Core application components.* These are the transactional, settlement, back-end processing, procurement, and relationship applications that are the heart of the FishMarket trading engine.
- *Infrastructure components.* These provide the key connectivity, workflow, and e-process management functionality required to integrate all the activities and communications within the FishMarket collaborative business network.
- *Interface components.* These represent the key interfaces required by FishMarket to integrate with its external partners. They also include interfaces to participant ERP systems, external markets, application service providers (ASP), and the billing and cash management interfaces of financial partners.

EXHIBIT 3 Application and Service Components

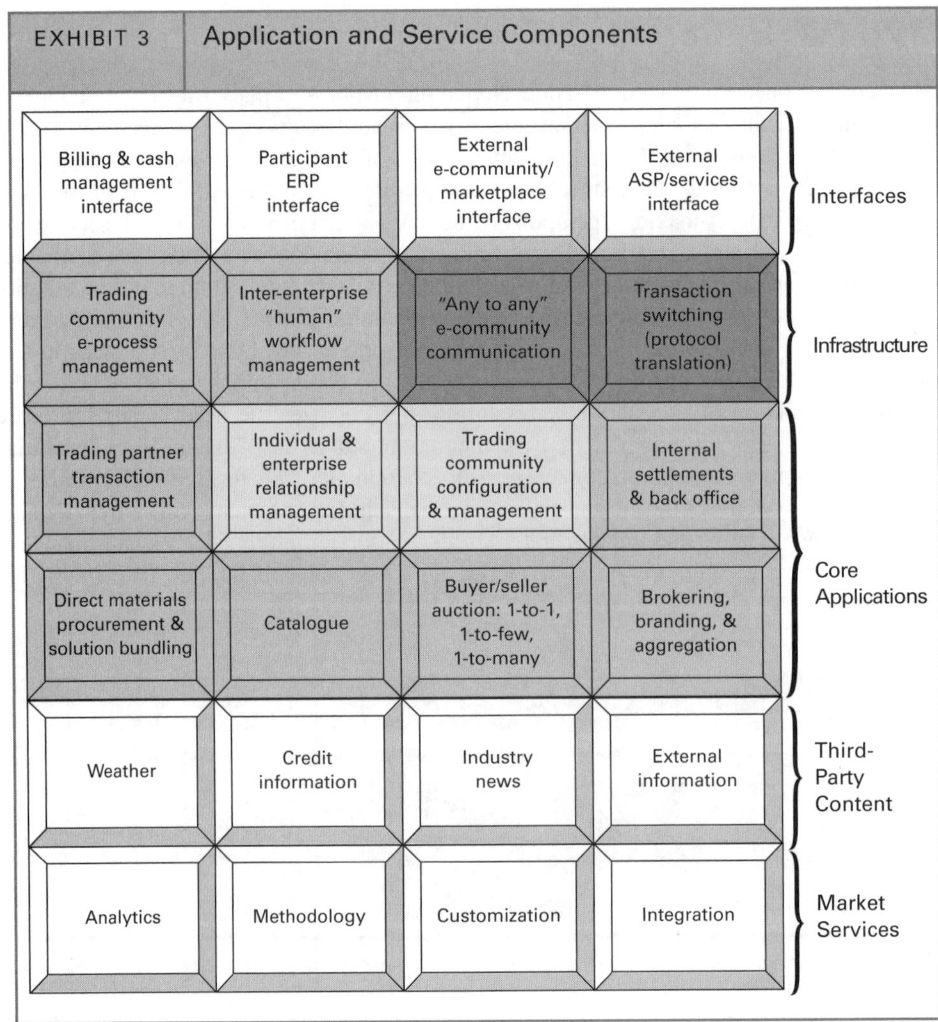

- *Third-party content components.* FishMarket's objective of becoming a full-service marketplace means that it has to provide value-added content to the industry as a part of its core offerings. Such content increases the "stickiness" of the Web site and helps to increase buyer and supplier dependence on it. Much of the content is to be provided by associated partners from the industry such as Intrafish. Some of them have equity interest in the venture.
- *Market service components.* These are value-added services offered by FishMarket to the marketplace participants. These include information services, process consulting, statistical analysis of trading trends, customization services for meeting other, related needs of customers, and integration of external participant applications into the collaborative business network.

The technology architecture of FishMarket is object- and message-based and business functionality can be implemented in a standardized manner, independently of the technical details embedded within the infrastructure layer and without dictating the nature of the external and internal applications being integrated. Additional business applications can therefore be developed independently of the architecture and can be plugged into the overall architecture with a minimal set of interface requirements. As well, the infrastructure is designed to support the scalability and reliability required for large business networks and communities.

THE ROAD AHEAD

Are Herrem and his team recognize that there are risks involved in any innovative venture, especially one that is attempting to modernize the total supply chain of an industry. They constantly evaluate the risk factors that could impact their organization and its plans. Table 1 presents an evaluation of the risk factors of the continuing development of the FishMarket marketplace.

FishMarket's management team realizes that the primary key to success lies in maximizing liquidity in the market quickly. The continuing challenge now is to accelerate the recruitment of new buyers and sellers and to increase the rate of use of the marketplace by existing partners. Given the recent shakeout in the e-business industry, they realize that customer acquisition costs would be prohibitive if they relied mainly on advertising and generic marketing strategies. They had to capitalize on the strategic ownership and partnership structures they had built with fish producers and customers and help both these groups migrate their trading habits over to the marketplace. Despite having spent more than half of their total expenditure to date on market and relationship development activities (including more than 150 visits with both the front-line employees and top management of buyers and producers), Are Herrem and his team need a coherent and comprehensive action plan for this immediately.

TABLE 1	Risk Factors Impacting FishMarket International		
Risk Area	**Typical Vulnerability**	**Risk Implication**	**Mitigating Action**
Market potential	• Market forecast volumes overly optimistic.	Reduced income	Estimate income-conservatively.
	• Customer take-up slower than projected.	Longer time to liquidity	Follow up on large customers. Support creation of market makers.
Financial	• Competition pressures pricing model.	Reduced revenues	Not likely in the shorter term. In the longer term establishment of financial market will compensate for low fee.
	• Start-up and operational costs higher than estimated.	Increased costs	Control spending and build organization in proportion to growth.
Technology	• Cost overrun on technology development.	Increased costs	Control development spending and time through fixed contracts and closely manage the development efforts.
	• Delayed rollout of operations.	Delay in development of technical solution	
Service estimation and delivery	• Difficulty in changing existing habits of traders.	Slow adoption	Revisit incentive system for use of system.
	• Inability to establish adequate operational environment.	Continuation existing behaviour	Educate and train users.
	• Reliability problems.	Claims and lack of trust.	Build trust through quality assurance partnerships: SGS/external auditors.
Competitive position	• Global consolidation encourages a single dominant player.	Lack of critical mass	Keep channels open for collaboration with other leading global initiatives.
	• Competition matches our functionality and value services.	Competitive edge blunted	Stay in close partnership with leading service partners.
	• Competition modifies competitive pricing model	Threat to existing revenue model	Continuously improve services and flexible pricing models.

Appendix 1

Backgrounds of the FishMarket Team

Terje Andreassen, Founder and CFO

Master of Business and Administration qualifications; senior business consulting experience at Fokus Bank; and broad fish farming experience from Biomar and Ernst & Young.

Ximena Arias, Sales Manager Chile

Ten years' sales experience in the fishing industry (canned fish, fish meal, and fish oil) of Chile with Pesquera San Pedro, Pesquera Pacific Protein; two years' trading experience at Tradco Private Ltd. in Sri Lanka.

Hege Charlotte Bakken, Sales Manager Europe

Master in Food Science qualifications and Project Leadership qualifications from the Norwegian School of Management; experience in product development and product leadership from Melbu Fiskeindustri, Norway Seafoods ASA, and Frionor AS.

Anita Engelsen, Site Manager

Information Technology qualifications from Polytechnical University and the University of Sør-Trøndelag; 13 years' sales, marketing, logistics, and technical experience from Austevoll Fiskeindustri AS and Sea Star International AS.

Are Herrem, Founder and CEO

Legal qualifications from Norway and Masters degree from Columbia University, New York; Supreme Court Attorney; management consultant at McKinsey & Company and attorney at Thommessen Krefting Greve Lund.

Roy Lavik, Senior Sales Manager, Salmon/Trout

Eighteen years' industry and trading experience at Rolf Olsen, Seanor, and Marstein Seafood.

Jan Henry T. Olsen, Founder and Marketing & Sales Director

Educated in economics and social science; 16 years' varied experience in the Norwegian fishing industry; served as Cabinet Minister of Fisheries; founder of fish export company and processing plants.

Geir Spiten, Chief Technical Officer

Eight years' technical programming experience; eight years at PricewaterhouseCoopers building five e-marketplaces for electricity and emission.

Bjørn Staalesen, Founder and COO

Candidate in Science in Fisheries; broad experience in fisheries with NORAD (in Namibia), Hydro Seafoods, and Stjernelaks.

Ove Thu, Senior Sales Manager

College candidate in Fish Marketing at Aalesund College; experience in production and sales of whitefish with companies such as Aalesundfisk AS, Longvafisk AS, and Normarine AS.

Appendix 2

Before-and-After Scenarios for the European Seafood Market

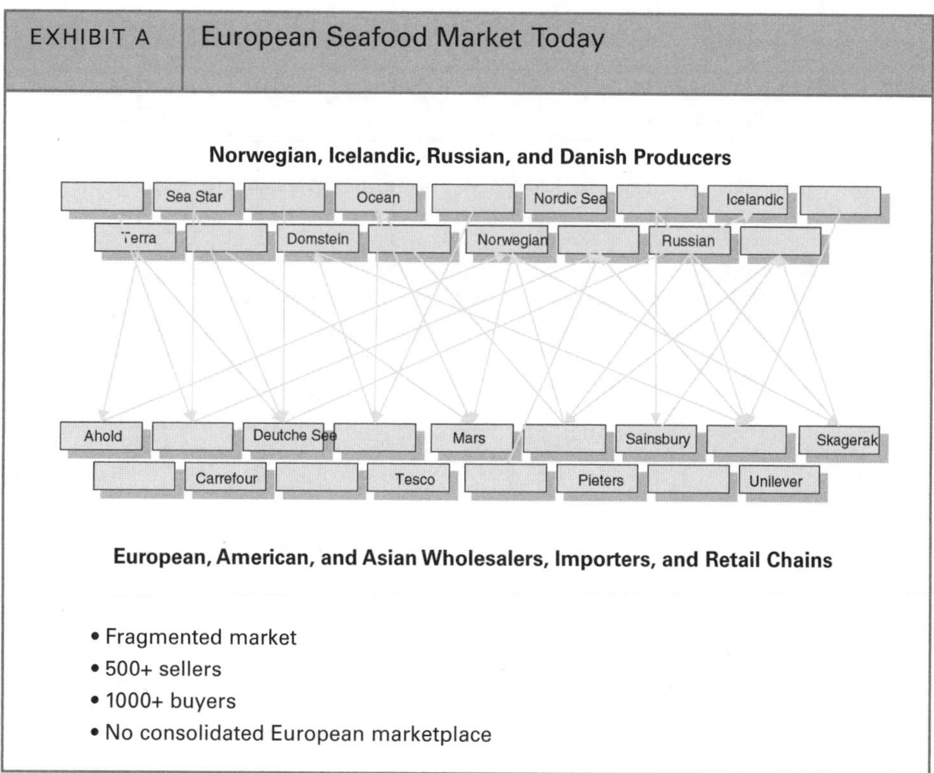

EXHIBIT B Future European Seafood E-Marketplace

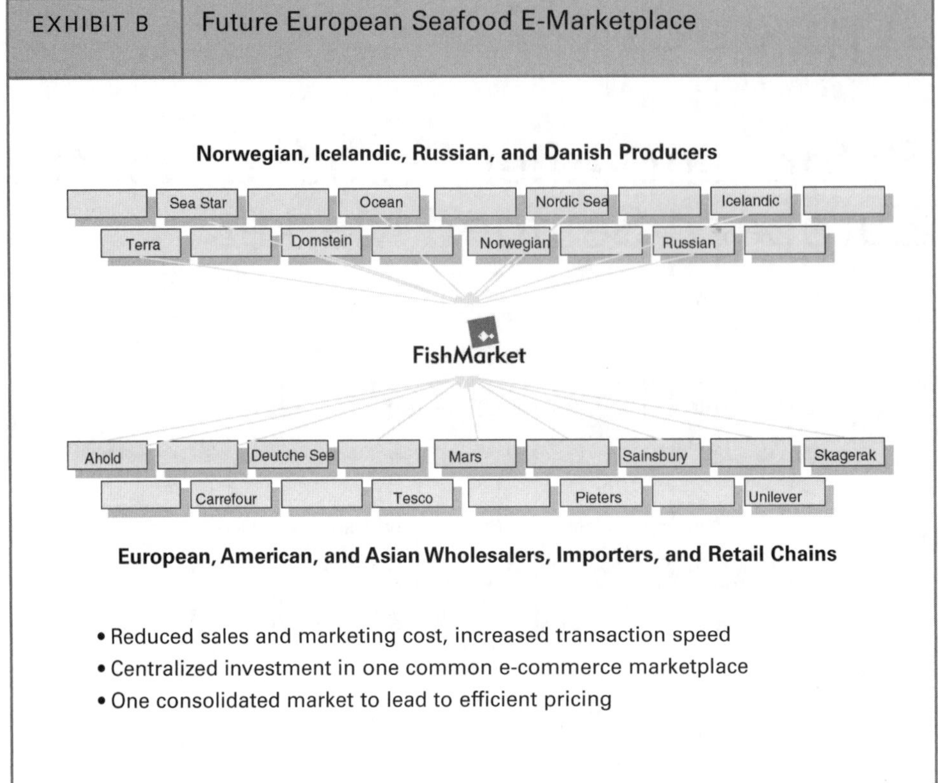

- Reduced sales and marketing cost, increased transaction speed
- Centralized investment in one common e-commerce marketplace
- One consolidated market to lead to efficient pricing

theme four overview

Localization and E-Business Implementation

By early 2002, more than 50% of the world's Internet users will live outside the United States.[1] Increasingly, managers of all forms of content on the Web will need to consider how best to reach clients in a format that is culturally appropriate. *Localization* is defined as the "process of adapting a product or service to a particular language, culture, and desired local 'look and feel.'" Localization requires conversion of media products developed in one culture into a format culturally and linguistically acceptable outside the original target market.

To truly globalize business on the Web, there is growing acceptance that adaptations go beyond simple language translation. When localizing a product or service, in addition to idiomatic language translation, such details as symbols, colour preferences, product or service names, cultural gender roles, or geographic examples must all be considered. A successfully localized service or product is one that appears to have been developed within the local culture.

Companies that ignore cultural sensitivities, or make mistakes related to culture, lose business as a result. For example, Hewlett-Packard was bruised in their early days of international e-business by posting non-localized instructions for use with its printers on their Asian Web site. HP used the image of a human hand with the palm facing forward as part of the instructions. Unfortunately this image is an extremely threatening gesture to Asians. In another example, a jewellery manufacturer that displays colours on a white background may find that the choice of colours offends customers. Also important is sensitivity to cultural differences in the development of e-loyalty.[2] Despite the embeddedness of culture with trust, to date little attention has been paid to how culture could influence relationship building in a Web-based environment.

Beyond cultural issues, companies must successfully take their e-business strategies through the implementation stage. Web-based technology is creating opportunities to reevaluate business models (as outlined in Theme 1 of this book). Traditional domains such as operations, marketing, or customer service can be enabled by technology to expand both in the speed and in formats for delivering services and products to customers.

Understanding strategies for success and learning from failures such as the dot-com "bombs" are important. Having a good product or service, a solid plan, and a management team with the ability to follow through on implementing goals are imperative. Both technology and people are central to this process.

NOTES

1. L. Yorgey, "Remember: you're open 24-7 worldwide," *Target Marketing*, 23(2000)(2): 46–48.
2. Dianne Cyr and Haizley Trevor-Smith, "Building e-loyalty across cultures and organizational boundaries in e-business," paper presented at the EGOS International Conference in Lyon, France, July 2001.

part one overview

Localization

The readings and cases in this part offer quite different perspectives on the topic of localization. The first case profiles CreoScitex, a world-leading supplier of computer-to-plate systems and solutions to the graphic arts and printing industries. In January 2000, Canadian Creo merged with an Israeli company Scitex, and together they plan to be leaders in their industry sector in Europe. Some of the challenges of the merger, and the concerns the company has as they expand into new cultures, are elaborated.

The second case profiles DNA Media, which until recently was Canada's largest localization company. Caught in the flood of recent consolidations in the localization industry, DNA's strategy and history are outlined. The case profiles the challenges faced by smaller localization companies, and the decisions required if they are to be effective service providers to globally focused client firms. In addition, the case is a valuable source of information about the evolution of the localization industry and its key players.

The readings in this Part consider the concept of *localization*, that is, of how culture must be taken into account in creating a positive and appropriate customer experience. An elaboration is provided of what localization is, along with hints from managers about how to do it well.

case one

CreoScitex: The Next Step

Dianne Cyr, Technical
University of British Columbia

INTRODUCTION

Mark Dance, president and CEO of CreoScitex, leaned against the desk and thought about the remarkable growth of the company over the past year. He wondered where the company would be in the future. And in the realm of CRM in particular, how would CreoScitex effectively internationalize its operations and expand into different cultures? Dance knew it would be an interesting challenge to adapt current product content to be relevant to various local environments.

Cultural considerations are nothing new for the company. CreoScitex is the merger of two companies and two cultures—Canadian Creo Products and Israeli Scitex. The company, formed in 2000, is a world leader in the creation of solutions for the graphic arts industry. The graphic arts industry encompasses not just printing, but all the steps needed to get to the printing press including creative design, document production, and preparation for printing. CreoScitex is in the business of creating the tools, systems, and processes to streamline the stages prior to reaching the press. The rise of the Internet and alternatives to print media are pressuring the printing world to become increasingly

The author sincerely appreciates the participation of Mark Dance, Michael Rolant, and Justin Malcolm of CreoScitex. Thomas Lee provided research assistance for this project. Financial support was provided by the Technical University of British Columbia.

efficient. To respond to these challenges, CreoScitex is systematically building all the components to enable completely digital print production.

The company is growing rapidly and expanding into new geographical locations. As Dance explains,

> CreoScitex is an operating division of Creo Products that has approximately 4,200 employees worldwide. Our goal is to lead the complete digitization of the printing industry and develop the necessary technologies, services and partnerships to [effect] this transition. We are a direct presence nearly everywhere in the world with significant regional operations in Canada, Israel, the United States, Belgium and Hong Kong, and corporate headquarters in Vancouver, Canada.[1]

Looking forward, Dance states, "In any high-technology market, competition and new technologies can threaten to make your products obsolete; therefore, CreoScitex will continue to have significant R&D investments in order to drive innovation. Printers are very pragmatic in their adoption of technology and they must see a ROI or they will not buy the products."[2] In this light, CreoScitex is aimed to be "a high-tech centre of excellence in Vancouver" according to Dance, with first-rate products and distribution channels. Dance further outlines the company's consolidation strategy as "to make each distribution unit number one or become number one. Each product line has to be number one. If it can't be number one, then the company has to partner with companies [that will allow achievement of this goal]."

The quest for excellence is reinforced at all levels in the company. In a conference call in February 2001, it was noted:

> CreoScitex claims a fifty percent share of the CTP [computer-to-plate] market and healthy twenty percent plus shares of imagesetting, proofing, and workflow sectors. CreoScitex can set the pace. To build on this critical mass and become, as the phrase runs, "the supplier of choice," there has been a focus on setting the company culture, adopting the open Creo approach to speed decision-making and feedback from customers. It is, the company says, "a key differentiator" setting it apart from the competition.[3]

HISTORICAL ROOTS IN CREO

The culture and philosophy of CreoScitex is firmly embedded in its past, growing from the parent company Creo Products. Examining Creo's roots, the company was formed in 1984 by two partners, Dan Gelbart and Ken Spencer, who wanted to start a technology company. The company name came from the Latin *creo*, "I create." Later, the partners discovered that *creo* means "I believe" in Spanish. Hence Creo's slogan, "Imagine, create, believe."

Ken Spencer, the CEO, was the businessperson and entrepreneur who knew how to grow and expand companies. Dan Gelbart, the president, was a brilliant engineer who knew the technical side of the business. He had an amazing grasp of technology and was involved in the development of leading technological products. At that time, Creo was very much an engineering-centric company focused on development of products with leading state-of-the-art technology. Many of the company's first employees were engineers with a focus on technology development.

In the early days at Creo, a number of advanced products were produced with technology far ahead of its time—so much so that the market failed to catch on to exactly what Creo was doing. Among these products were the Drexler machine which produced smart cards and the Optical tape recorder, an optically based device that could store a terabyte of information on a 12-inch reel. The optical tape recorder won numerous awards, and was heralded as a technological marvel that could also be utilized as an imaging device. The company also manufactured spinoff products based on imaging technology they were able to develop with previous products. However, one problem emerged in that while these products were successes technologically, they often lacked commercial viability.

It was in 1993 that Amos Michelson first became aware of Creo's products and strong technological offerings. He was impressed with Creo's in-house talent and product line that offered advanced technology at prices lower to the competition. Michelson convinced Gelbart and Spencer to formulate a revised market focus for the company. In 1994 Michelson joined the company as vice-president of strategy, and was instrumental in the development of a computer-to-plate device. Once developed, the device would take computer files and produce an image on a piece of metal called a printing plate, which was then mounted on a printing press to produce images. Specifications for the device were provided by a company called R. R. Donnelly which was looking for the particular technology, and was also willing to help fund its development. The product was successful, and was sold to other companies and demonstrated at trade shows such as GraphExpo.

EVOLVING STRATEGY AND FOCUS

The success of the computer-to-plate device led Creo to adopt the plate-setting business as its main line of business. Anything unrelated to printing or prepress was cast aside and sold, including the rights to the optical tape recorder. The importance of Michelson's role cannot be overestimated. As e-business product manager Justin Malcolm comments, "Amos was the guy that brought vision to the company."

At this time, Creo was mostly an engineering company, with little staff in marketing and sales, no support organization, and no communications group. The plate-setter device demonstrated Creo's engineering technological prowess, but at the same time revealed deficiencies in the company. Malcolm notes that at this point in the company's life cycle, "a number of pieces were still missing from the puzzle. Michelson convinced upper management to build a suite of products around the plate-setter device to become a supplier of solutions to the printing industry." Hence, a software division was created to develop solutions that would manage computer files and handle tasks previously performed by printing organizations non-digitally. Equally significant is the transition of Creo from a company that could create leading technology into a company that now provided solutions for customers.

Malcolm relates this to the core of the CreoScitex business: "Our whole business now is based on the premise of digitizing the printing industry and taking the older way of doing things, which was largely analogue, and digitizing the whole process into the next generation. In the process, we're also transforming the industry away from being a craft-based, very people-skills-centric industry into more of a manufacturing industry, making it more scalable, consistent, and predictable. That's having quite a lot of impact. This is our vision and what we're bringing to the world. It's been pretty successful."

The results have borne this out: in 1994 Creo started off with 100 employees, generating revenues in the neighborhood of US$10 million; six years later, in 2000, the company employs 4200 people worldwide with annual revenues hovering around US$700 million.

The combined companies will have production plants in 17 countries, and sales and distribution facilities on five continents.

INTERNATIONAL GROWTH THROUGH PARTNERSHIPS

Despite Creo's growth and success, the company tended to view itself as the underdog. According to Malcolm, the company was always looking for "the next Goliath to topple." Gerber, CPP, and Scitex were notable examples of larger companies perceived as possible competitors.

As Creo was growing and scaling up its computer-to-plate operations, it partnered with a number of significant companies. One joint venture began in 1997 with Heidelberg Press, a German press manufacturer. As partners, Creo would provide the technology and the engineering; Heidelberg Press would provide sales and service around the world. This immediately allowed Creo to "scale up" to a global presence—something that would have been far more difficult for Creo to achieve as a small company. The nature of the agreement permitted Creo to keep and maintain the sales and service functions it had already established. Further, the joint venture arrangement stipulated costs in the development of new products were to be shared equally, as were profits.

Creo was a company thinking strategically, determined to find the "missing pieces" that, according to Malcolm, would help the company succeed in the marketplace. Looking at the competition and on the basis of the financial resources available to the company (the money raised from going public and the share price of the company), Creo was looking for another strategic partnership that would give it the edge in the marketplace. That partner was Scitex, which offered product depth, a global sales and support presence, and an extensive network of dealers that was well established throughout the world. As a result of the partnership with Scitex, Creo no longer viewed the global sales and support staff of Heidelberg as vital to its operations. Further, the arrangement with Heidelberg Press was now viewed as inequitable because Creo was now bringing more to the table.

Given these parameters, Creo attempted to renegotiate the original joint venture agreement with Heidelberg Press, although the German company wished to maintain the existing arrangement without modifications. As it stood, the agreement stipulated the purchase of a company by Creo would be included in the joint venture. With the pending merger with Scitex, Creo decided the stakes were too high and decided to end the joint venture with Heidelberg Press in May 2000 to avoid sharing of assets. Nevertheless, Creo did maintain a relationship with Heidelberg under an OEM agreement where products sold previously in the joint venture agreement would continue to be supported by both parties. Despite this, Creo and Heidelberg soon became competitors selling similar products and services in the marketplace.

AMALGAMATING CREO AND SCITEX

Merging Creo and Scitex in 2000 was an opportunity, as well as a challenge. Mark Dance, the president and CEO of CreoScitex, notes two major impacts of the merger are increased number of customers and an increase in market share. When the merger took place, Creo (now CreoScitex) went from 1800 to 18 000 customers "all in one day"—a tenfold increase. Market size increased dramatically as well for CreoScitex, making the newly formed company the major prepress manufacturer in the world, and the principal division of Creo. CreoScitex was now engaged in the half-a-trillion-dollar printing industry.

Dance notes that with the merger the company "experienced tremendous interconnectivity between its products", especially in the computer-to-plate systems. The impact on its share price was huge: a 50% increase in its earnings per share, and resources now available to the company expanded between 20 and 30%. CreoScitex now had access to an increased number of direct sales channels. Dance comments that customers responded favourably to the merger as they now could obtain "best of breed connectivity of systems." He further notes the "sales force loved [the merger] because they now had more products to sell."

VP of business operations Michael Rolant adds the two companies had "a very similar infrastructure." However, Rolant continues,

> Creo believed in open, free communication. ... Scitex was much more mature, not expecting huge growth. ... We tried to do this merger on a consensus basis, but in some cases it didn't always work. But we are very positive. The merger was the right thing to do, and it was with the right company. From the customer point of view we will see a lot of benefits because we combined technologies together. We combined product lines together.

Despite the benefits of the merger, the size difference between the two companies proved a major obstacle. Scitex was much larger, with 2600 employees to Creo's 1600. It was Creo that acquired Scitex, and the business world as well as former customers were initially surprised by the smaller upstart taking over the larger, more established company. As Malcolm describes, "it was like Wendy's taking over McDonald's. ... What we've really tried to do is merge the two organizations under one cohesive whole."

In addition to size, the merger caused a number of issues to surface. Each company came to the partnership with different cultures and histories. Creo was the "up-and comer" and a rising star in the industry. The company was young, had grown quickly, with a "hip" set of young employees who enjoyed many remarkable successes. Creo was always trying to excel, and even build infrastructure faster than actually needed. There was a relatively flat hierarchical structure, and Creo gave employees autonomy, responsibility, and the necessary tools and support to do their jobs. Creo jobs and tasks were organized in a manner which enables employees to be accountable for their work. The Creo culture was embedded in the daily work of employees through six simple principles:

> Open communication with all employees
>
> Striving to be the best in the world in all that we do
>
> Caring about each other, our customers, our suppliers, and our shareholders
>
> Doing our absolute best to honour our commitments
>
> Believing that people are most effective when self-managed
>
> Striving to act with integrity and fairness[4]

On the other hand, Scitex was larger, was more established, and had experienced more ups and downs of the business cycle. Scitex was methodical in its business approach, constantly weighing the risks of any potential venture, and trying to mitigate possible disasters. The company had a more traditional structure and a greater degree of executive authority.

Such differences resulted in a fair amount of disagreement as to how to get things done, including the decision-making process. Creo perceived Scitex as being too conservative and unable to think strategically. Scitex viewed Creo initially as being "wide-eyed and naïve." Interestingly, both companies have strong Israeli roots, and some of the senior managers at Creo such as Amos Michelson, Michael Rolant, and Dan Gelbart, all have Israeli heritage. Over a short period of time it was discovered many employees shared similar ways of doing things. This allowed for quick success in bringing together teams for various projects.

In the afterlight, and according to Dance, there were two risks involved with the merger. In his words, CreoScitex could have been "clobbered" if it paid too much attention internally therefore losing sight of external contingences. Dance elaborates,

> Risk in any merger of this magnitude is twofold. One, when a small company takes over a large company, you have a huge issue with culture and management. Management people are overloaded just trying to deal with internal issues. The second risk on any merger of a similar scale is that you tend to lose sight of the market and customers, so you become internally focused for a period of time. ... So we knew it was going to be a very tough year, and from an operations point if view it has been.

In alignment with these sentiments, VP of business operations Rolant adds, "This year we focused on the internal organization—restructuring, making sure that we started operating as one company."

Despite some initial difficulties in the merger, the strategy seems to be working. According to Amos Michelson, CEO of Creo,

> We have made great progress during the quarter...Shortly after the merger, we renewed our product development focus on the rapidly growing print on-demand systems business, and we are pleased to say that we saw significantly increased revenue in this quarter as new products reached the market. As well, our European organization has made tremendous gains in the last six months and showed excellent results this quarter. We believe that we are still on target to finish most of the outstanding integration issues by April [2001] this year.[5]

Continuing goals for CreoScitex are to maintain its customer focus, use scale to optimal advantage, and expand into adjacent markets. These are necessary goals in Dance's eyes, as the printing industry "is a mature one growing at a rate of 3 to 4% a year." Certain countries and regions have been targeted as key elements of the CreoScitex strategy. Germany is a major target in Europe, as is Australia. The strongest market exists in the United States.

CUSTOMER RELATIONSHIP MANAGEMENT

Effective customer relationship management (CRM) is crucial at CreoScitex, with a goal of providing consistent and uniform service to customers. Customer perception is important, and leads to longer-term trust development between the supplier and the customer. As Rolant outlines, "From the CreoScitex side we are very, very customer-focused, and we pay a lot of attention to pre-sales activity and to the sales activity itself. We also take after sales seriously." Both cost and service optimization is key. Using the Internet as an important tool, Roland adds, "We want to channel to the virtual store."

In order to build trust, CreoScitex has several ways of interacting with its customers that are dependent on both the infrastructure available and the location. Over the years there has been a shift from a company-driven to a more customer-driven sales culture. Customer support often involves placing the necessary people on-site. Dance says, "Service is one-third of our organization." This has typically been an expensive proposition, as the costs involved in building a local sales force are high. A less expensive solution is to implement a call centre for clients.

To build effective customer relationships, CreoScitex places great importance on being informed about customer activities and the systems they use. ERP systems, or back-end systems, are used to track this information at CreoScitex. Business intelligence and the management of information are key activities driving how product and other decisions related to customers are made. To enable this process, the company empowers employees with the tools and decision-making authority to best serve customers. Empowerment entails "having the right information to drive decisions," according to Malcolm. The structure of the company further supports this goal.

LOCALIZATION ISSUES

In order to attract and retain customers, localization is of increasing importance at CreoScitex. Localization refers to creating content and communication that is culturally appropriate to a given audience. This includes language translation, but also cultural content and Web design features that are acceptable to customers. Dance notes, "Support definitely has to be in their own language." Further, CreoScitex is "trying to come up with a translation and documentation strategy." The VP of marketing speaks Dutch, German, Spanish, and Italian and represents the internationalized flavour of where the company is heading.

CreoScitex has a fully functional Web site only in North America. A Web site in Europe has yet to be launched; one deterrent is a requirement for multiple languages. For instance, according to Malcolm, in Sweden there is greater use of English as a language of business, but in Germany there is the expectation that business be carried out in German. In the future, CreoScitex is planning to establish Web sites to deal with the language and cultural specificities of every country in Europe.

Where content is published and how it is translated are issues with which CreoScitex is currently grappling. In some countries, content is centrally coordinated while in others it is managed locally. To capture e-loyalty, customers will ideally be able to customize their interaction with the service company. Dance elaborates:

> We're looking for tools and mechanisms whereby the data can exist across media, and across languages, so to control one core set of data. And then either through process or through technology, when a content change is made it will appear different on the Web page [to diverse client groups].

At present, there is an established customer support organization, or "focal point," in each country, where local representatives deal with issues of language, culture, perceptions of time, and priority of problems. Product mixes are different in different countries, and Dance notes, "The German team drives the business issues in Germany … using local resources." Overseeing these local areas is an after-sales response centre in Brussels with 30 people that provides tactical and marketing support. Additional marketing coordination is provided by people in corporate locations including Israel and Boston. The IS group is in Vancouver.

As the company continues to move into international markets, it is acknowledged that certain modifications in content and services are required. As Rolant says, "We are open to changes. We already know the European market, but Asian markets may not use the tools the same way." He elaborated that, concerning CRM, in North America orders come in through channels for buying online. In other markets this may not necessarily be the case, and CreoScitex "tries to enhance relationships with customers, to make them feel more comfortable."

CULTURE AS CONTEXT

According to Malcolm, North America companies are more self-reliant, and are satisfied with less infrastructure support than their counterparts in other parts of the world. Instead, North American clients seek access to tools necessary for them to use products and services efficiently. They want information and expertise. Related to support, CreoScitex performs "joint maintenance" with North American clients, which is more cost-effective. Clients are willing to obtain information they require directly from the CreoScitex Web site.

Alternatively, in Europe there is a higher expectation that the CreoScitex sales organization will understand a client's business. Building personal relationships in all facets of business is valued and nurtured. As such, European customers are not as comfortable with obtaining information they need over the Internet, nor are they readily receptive to online customer service. They prefer a salesperson who takes the initiative to understand their needs and requirements.

Another issue that arises with respect to conducting business cross-culturally is the notion of power distance.[6] Malcolm comments that in Germany it is extremely important to grant proper deference to senior management. "Services are much more culturally attuned to upper management than to middle or lower management" in European countries than in North America. Understanding this nuance will be important in the development of good customer relations to grow the client base. Dance comments, "Germany is the area in which we can grow the most. Germany is a major target for us."

Asia presents a different set of challenges and expectations, with many cultures and languages represented and a less developed Internet infrastructure. As a result, CreoScitex chose Asia-Pacific as the final locale in its global strategy, with an initially low investment of infrastructure and support. This was based on an assumption that there would be minimal interest in customer service on the Web, versus a desire for more face-to-face relationship development. In fact, according to Malcolm, the opposite proved true. Distribution units wanted the option of on-line sales, especially in the area of consumable products. Customers wanted direct access to core services, and to develop relationships with the company directly, rather than with individual sales or service people. However, as Malcolm further suggests, it is significant to note the importance of early relationship development between CreoScitex and Asian customers made the possibility of Internet connections a more viable option in the first place. To facilitate the process with a minimal investment at present, CreoScitex formed a joint venture with a Japanese firm to provide distribution of products and services. Dance observes that this arrangement "provides credibility and depth in the Japanese market."

Malcolm notes the level of information desired and shared also differs across cultures. In North America, substantial amounts of information are given to customers while in other cultures providing the same amount of information would be insulting. For example, "On the support side, there's a lot of pride in some European countries. In France they have a long history of what they're doing, and status comes from the knowledge and expertise acquired. So it's very important to only tell customers information about products which they assume it's reasonable not to have … otherwise, it's like trying to tell them how to do their job."

Cultural expectations also differ in the area of appropriate form and volume of communications. Malcolm describes that North Americans prefer "ease of use" Web site information that is relatively simple and digestible. Europeans prefer more structured information, while Asians want large volumes of information in order to effectively make comparisons between products and services. Malcolm also notes there is a need to be aware of the different methods of interacting with customers and transacting business around the world—including different levels of formality and timeliness of information. In North America and Southeast Asia after-sales followup is important. In Europe, a similar approach would be seen as "pestering."

FUTURE CHALLENGES

When looking at the future of the printing industry, there will be further innovation of products and services. Future success will likely depend on how well CreoScitex and similar companies integrate their knowledge of customers with databases and information systems. Customer service management will be a major differentiator in the printing industry. One-to-one marketing will become ubiquitous over the Internet, and will reach a larger range of clients around the globe. Customers will desire localization of content and services, and this presents an opportunity for the development of e-loyalty—if done well.

There are also technological issues to consider. CreoScitex is in need of a more comprehensive Web site platform and a global Web site capable of hosting multiple languages. Michael Rolant, vice-president of business operations at CreoScitex, observes, "there will be a need to think economically, and become more proactive and dynamic" especially in the area of customizing Web sites. Customers will "want to know there's human intervention."

At the start of the new millennium, several key questions prick at the imagination of the CreoScitex management team. They wonder the best strategy to pursue in order to remain a leader in the prepress industry. In particular, in the area of CRM and the establishment of e-loyalty, how can client relationships best be established and maintained? The issue of localizing content and services seems to be increasingly important if CreoScitex intends to pursue a significant presence in Europe and Asia. Is it worth the trouble? If so, how might they proceed?

NOTES

1. Anonymous, "Creo Products EVP Mark Dance talks to the Wall Street Transcript," *PR Newswire Association*, April 25, 2000.
2. See note 1.

3. Anonymous, "CreoScitex can set the pace," *Canada NewsWire*, February 7, 2001.
4. Anonymous, "Creo named one of best ethical stocks," *Canada NewsWire*, February 8, 2001.
5. Anonymous, "Creo Products Inc. announces first quarter fiscal 2001 results," *Canada NewsWire*, February 7, 2001.
6. "Power distance" refers to the degree to which power differences are accepted and sanctioned by society.

case two

DNA Media: Prospects for the Software Localization Industry

Dianne Cyr, Technical University of British Columbia

Richard Lew

It is another rainy day in Vancouver. Looking out his window toward the mountains on the North Shore, Steven Forth, CEO of DNA Media, reflects on some of the decisions his management team has made over the past few years. Was the organizational restructuring in 2000 the right move, and are the recent expenditures on technology and people really going to pay off by 2003? This afternoon he will meet with his senior management team to discuss the projected Q1 2001 business performance and plans to meet their 2003 business targets.

Steven is preoccupied with this year's turmoil in the stock market for high-technology companies. The NASDAQ index has peaked during the first quarter of 2000, prompting Alan Greenspan, Chairman of the Federal Reserve Board in the United States, to warn investors of "market over-exuberance" and rising interest rates. The high-technology sector crashed suddenly in April and continued its downward spiral for the remainder of the year. It seems the "get rich quick" bubble for Internet companies with stratospheric P/E ratios is coming to an end. Raising equity financing from venture capitalists to grow his company will be difficult, with increased investor scrutiny on the business model and corporate performance.

The authors sincerely appreciate the participation of Steven Forth, Jim Eagles, Mick McCallister, and Andrew Wilson at DNA Media for their insights and the time they contributed to this project. Financial support for this project was provided by the Technical University of British Columbia.

Nonetheless, the downturn in the high-technology industry will have direct implications for DNA Media. Businesses involved in the software localization industry[1] are strongly affected because many of their valued clients are high-technology companies, and no one knows how long this downturn will last. This set of events was not surprising to Steven, since his sales staff and many of his competitors were scrambling to find and retain clients over the last few months.

The year 2000 has just closed, marking the real beginning of the new millennium. "What a way to start the year and the new century," thinks Steven. How should DNA Media respond in the light of these recent developments, and will it change his company's four-year strategic plan that started in 1999? Small companies like DNA Media, with their limited financial resources, are under increasing price and service pressures from larger competitors. What strategy must DNA Media adopt to grow the company? He closes his eyes, rubs his temples, and begins thinking and smiling, "Life would have been easier if I listened to my mother and had become a professor."

DNA BACKGROUND AND BEGINNINGS

DNA Media is a small-to-medium-sized software localization firm employing approximately 60 people (45 in Vancouver and 15 in Japan). Andrew Wilson, the VP of business development, described the company as a "professional localization services company specializing in a smaller number of languages, internationalization, and engineering. We are not the lowest-priced firm, but we are price-competitive."

The company is headquartered in Vancouver and was founded by Steven and two partners in 1989. Within a decade, Steven grew the business from a home-based operation into one of the leading and most respected localization companies in Canada. The company specializes in Asian languages and computer/multimedia applications, which play to the strengths of DNA Media's location, the background of its founders and the skills of its employees. Steven attributes the early success of the company to the early adoption of advanced computer and telecommunications equipment like faxes to manage projects and to coordinate workflow with his clients. All the executives are fully bilingual, and English only became the official language at work after the company had grown to over ten employees. The unique multicultural environment makes the company distinct from most North American companies. There have also been significant challenges, and even with the company's growth, market pressures have forced the company to reinvent itself on a number of occasions. For a full chronology of the development of the company refer to Appendixes 1 and 2.

The company has come a long way. When Steven first started the company, he did not have a business plan. Now DNA Media has a mission to be one of the world leaders in providing multilingual production and content management. Senior management have targeted revenues to increase from $1.7 million (1998) to $10.4 million (2003), and net profit to increase from a modest loss (1998) to 10% (2001). DNA Media is halfway through the revenue growth plan, but, with the recent meltdown in the Internet industry, revenues are falling behind the plans. A major constraint for the company is the lack of financial resources, which affects the number and quality of workers needed for the business.

Historically DNA has either been debt-financed or financed out of the owners' pockets. There are advantages to this latter strategy. As Jim Eagles at DNA explains, "equity capital, as opposed to debt financing, allows companies to operate with losses with the promise of future growth and profits." In effect, debt financing requires interest payments, thereby reducing cash flow that might otherwise be used to grow the company.

However, choosing to avoid equity financing during 1996 to 1999 hurt the company's growth. Spreading its resources too thin and providing too many types of services has also worked against the company in attracting equity financing. Since the early years, DNA Media has tried to improve its attractiveness to local venture capitalists by restructuring the company, by being very focused on its most profitable core businesses, and by closing its unprofitable multimedia (CD-ROM) productions division in 2000.

Growing the company has been an expensive proposition. Money was invested into upgrading software tools, and internal accounting and project management systems. Effective marketing is a critical factor, and historically has been done by Steven attracting business through word of mouth, cold-calling, and networking—rather than by advertising. Locating in Vancouver and Japan limited the company's access to most of its larger clients in eastern Canada and in the United States, often requiring expensive and time-consuming flights across the country to meet with clients face to face. To balance these costs, a modestly valued Canadian dollar has made services more economical to American firms. Additionally, by paying employees in Canadian funds, DNA Media has an advantage over American-based operations offering comparable services.

Steven firmly believes DNA Media's business strength relates to five key factors, and he does not think this will change in the foreseeable future. These factors are: capabilities such as expertise and resources to localize in the desired culture and language; quality of interaction and relationship between developer and vendor and ability to facilitate partnerships; vendor reputation; project management expertise; and rapid turnaround time, which is especially important for software services.

LOCALIZATION MARKET OPPORTUNITIES

Despite all the negative news about the high-technology industry, DNA Media seems to be in the right spot at the right time. Localization services are growing all over the world at a very fast pace. Demographics and business globalization has forced the rest of world to adopt new technologies like the Internet, wireless networks, and computers. According to *eMarketer*,[2] even though over 61% of world users of the Internet are from the United States in 1998, this will decline to 37% by 2002. Demand for globalization and localization services will increase. How localization will be performed and in which language will be another issue. According to *Sapient Globalization Report* there are over 6700 living languages in the world; the 15 most popular are spoken by 49.5% of the world's population, while the other 51.5% speak 6600 languages.[3] Yet only about 6% of the world's population speak English.[4]

As reliance on communications increases as part of the information lifestyle via the Internet (including wireless devices and pagers), localization needs and service demand will increase. The adoption by the general population of increasingly higher levels of communication and database technology means that the user interfaces must become easier to use and more highly adapted to local conditions. This is an important market and recently completed work by DNA Media with Nikon on user interfaces for consumer devices confirms this.

Media versioning (i.e., dubbing) is also an important market for localization services. The explosive growth of DVD and interactive media like the Internet and Web TV all require some level of localization for global markets. For many years DNA Media has been involved in media versioning of movie productions and the Internet, and has the expertise to grow in this market.

As the world increases its use of computers for consumer and business, the demand for industry-specific productivity software for particular industries (e.g., medical, training, etc.) will also increase. Augmented software product complexity means localization becomes increasingly complicated; forms higher barriers to entry; and increases demand on localization firms. Further, the ability to attract and retain talented people is becoming more competitive. Not only is it becoming more difficult to attract talent, but also more talented people will be needed to perform increasingly complicated localization projects. Consequently, the growth of the localization industry will be limited by the supply of skilled people. Andrew Wilson at DNA Media notes that, "unlike computer programmers that can be mass-produced in schools, skilled localization people are very difficult to find and the necessary quality and range of skills needed by companies in the industry takes years to develop."

Five large companies that arose primarily from consolidation in the mid-1990s dominate the industry. Appendix 3 summarizes the general profile for the software localization industry, and Appendix 4 profiles the key players. Companies such as Bowne Global Service, Alpnet, and Lionbridge offer a wider range of languages and technology services, and are better able to invest in new technologies, than smaller companies.

In 1996 Steven felt his company was uniquely positioned in the market and was growing quite well on its own, and that not much would be gained from consolidation. In hindsight, Steven wondered whether he might have at least tried to raise equity capital to finance his company's growth when the market was hot, instead of relying on debt financing. As a result, DNA is a much smaller player than companies that decided to consolidate. Table 1 compares the major consolidated companies with DNA Media.

TABLE 1 Comparison of Large Consolidators and DNA Media in 1997

Company	No. of Countries	Staff Level	Languages Offered	1997 Revenues (US$) Attributed to Software Localization	1997 Market Capitalization
Alpnet	14	475	40	$40 800 000	$95 M
Berlitz	35	N/A	200	$80 500 000	$265 M
BGS	>7	>700	N/A	$71 000 000	$768 M
L&H Mendez	25	N/A	>20	$31 600 000	$2629 M
Lionbridge	7	350	N/A	N/A	N/A
DNA	2	50	8	$1 700 000 (C$)	N/A

Source: E. Person, "A strategic analysis of a software localization company," unpublished MBA thesis (Burnaby, B.C.: Simon Fraser University, 1998).

The actual size of the localization market is debatable, and, at times, quotes from industry leaders are contradictory. The CEO of Bowne Global Services recently stated that the market is "growing at approximately 30 percent annually."[5] Mark Homnack, the CEO of SimulTrans, does not believe the market is as big as many reports suggest, and that growth projections are being promoted to hike up stock prices.[6] Table 2 illustrates the generally held market sales expectation.

TABLE 2 Revenues from Localization Services (US$)

	1995	1997	2000 (projected)
Globalization	$1 700 000 000	$2 800 000 000	$6 260 000 000
Software localization	$561 000	$1 100 000 000	$2 380 000 000
Japanese localization	$101 000	$322 000	$737 000

Source: E. Person, "A strategic analysis of a software localization company," unpublished MBA thesis (Burnaby, B.C.: Simon Fraser University, 1998)

To date competitive rivalry between industry players is only moderate, and has facilitated the general expansion of the industry since there is currently enough work for everyone. However, if consolidation increases or when the industry matures further, competition will increase. This will put pressure on smaller companies such as DNA Media that have limited resources and a narrower range of services. Again, talented personnel are one of those scarce resources. Mick McCallister at DNA Media, a localization practitioner for almost 20 years, adds, "Localization assets are highly intangible; they are people expertise. People are not assets that can be bought and sold. Clients don't have to do business with you just because you bought the company. After a merger, you can't buy people or the clients, and hardware is a depreciating asset. The localization industry sells potential; revenues are not a promise that can be reached every year."

Smaller companies may be unable to compete with larger players on the basis of price and range of services. Jim Eagles, the COO of DNA Media, observes that a unique characteristic about this industry is that "it acts like a mature industry yet has no economies of scale." Appendix 5 profiles the evolution and challenges of the localization industry.

Andrew Wilson further observes consolidation was in principle a "good idea" for the industry. "It allowed companies to gain skilled assets that otherwise will take years to develop in-house. This was one way for companies to consolidate a fragmented industry and to gain resources to scale-up and grow." In general this strategy has worked for numerous capital-intensive industries, but the localization industry is a knowledge-based service that depends heavily on its human capital. Refer to Appendix 6 for an overview of medium-sized companies as they compare with DNA Media.

DNA MEDIA'S MARKETS AND PRODUCTS

In 1999, DNA Media provided localization services to five major market segments: (1) software application developers, (2) government and general, (3) multimedia publishers and developers (CD-ROM, DVD), (4) versioning for broadcasters and recording studios, and (5) firms requiring software design and engineering services. The most profitable services are software design and engineering and video versioning; the least profitable are general work and multimedia localization. However, software application localization and government and general localization contracts are the largest contributors to total revenues. A breakdown of the five market segments in which DNA Media participates appears in Table 3.

TABLE 3 DNA Media Market Breakdown

	Software Application Developers	Multimedia Publishers and Developers	Broadcasters and Recording Studios (Versioning)	Software Design and Engineering Services	Government and General
Projected revenue for 1999 (C$)	$750 000	$400 000	$300 000	$300 000	$600 000
Percentage contribution	32%	17%	13%	13%	25%
Number of key customers	10–12	5–6	4–5	10	20
Sample customers	Cognos Seagate Red Brick	Dorling-Kindersley Radical	NHK	Nikon cameras	
Sector attractiveness	Key to future growth	Important for future growth	Considerable potential in DVD segment	Area of high untapped potential	Government cutbacks will negatively affect growth; limited profitability
Price-sensitivity	Moderate	Least sensitive to price; may be due to complexity of projects	Moderate		Very sensitive to price; highly competitive segment

In 1998, the majority of DNA Media's customers were located in Canada (50%), particularly in eastern Canada. The market share is further broken down to Japan (25%), the United States (15%), and Europe (10%). Given the strong Asian-language expertise and history of the company, it is not surprising that Japan was the second-largest contributor to the company's revenues.

Asian languages are DNA Media's area of expertise and contributed to over 60% (50–60% Japanese and 10% Chinese) of the company's revenues in 1998. Additionally, Asian languages like Japanese and Chinese require "double-byte encoding," which is technically more complicated than the systems used for European languages. Although European languages contributed 30–40% of revenues (1998), it is not a high-margin service due to the high availability of expertise and conventional level of computer programming difficulty.

Although the "core" localization business has a lot of potential growth with the expansion of the Internet, communications, and global trade, profits are very narrow. Every job is customized, consuming the time of skilled personnel and thereby constraining the ability to increase both profits and revenues. The challenge facing DNA Media will be to find ways to squeeze profits from business operations, and to accommodate development of new products and services.

Andrew and Mick at DNA Media both agree with Jim's points and add, "the language translation component is the least profitable part of the localization business. It is also most subject to error, most subjective to evaluate, is normally outsourced at commodity prices, and is the 'least-liked' part of the business. A client may read the result and not like it because it does not 'feel' right. According to Jim, translation gross margins are typically 25 to 35%, but the net margin can quickly disappear with unexpected revisions. The best margins are in consulting, engineering, testing, content management, and design of systems for managing content."

KEY OPTIONS AND CHALLENGES FOR DNA MEDIA

The main goals of the business plan are to achieve (1) long-term competitive advantage, (2) improved profitability, (3) strong revenue growth, and (4) control of the company while seeking new financial backing. Steven Forth sees three key areas of focus for DNA Media in the short-to-medium term:

1. *Ensuring profitability.* Limited growth rates are likely due to cash flow restrictions, even though DNA Media is ideally positioned for the convergence of digital media. The company has relied on debt financing to grow the company. Corporate revenues have risen from $1.7 million (1997) to $2.3 million (1998), but the profit margin has declined during this period. Steps were taken in 1998 to implement a comprehensive project management system to control costs, improve use of resources, and match capacity with growth. But there is significant competition from consolidation in the industry, and competition from aggressive companies that are expanding both geographic reach and market share. DNA Media must be concerned about retaining its customers and winning clients away from other companies.
2. *Growth strategies.* DNA has a variety of choices in order to expand the company. First, there is growth by acquisition. This may be the quickest way to expand DNA Media to $10 million by 2003. However, the company does not have the resources for acquisitions and for integrating the organizations. Second, strategic partnering may be the answer. DNA Media can partner with vendors, customers, and suppliers. This will involve financial transaction for services, and possible exchange of some ownership equity. Alliances may be formed with other mid-sized companies. This allows smaller players the opportunity to compete with bigger players for high-profile projects. Third, there can be growth by geographic expansion. DNA Media lacks location diversity, and it has hurt the company's growth internationally. DNA Media's management had discussed opening satellite (one-person) offices in Eastern Canada, Southeast Asia, and the United States to establish a presence and test the market.
3. *Development of new products and services.* DNA Media could introduce new, high-value added services or business models like content management, development, and

distribution. As one solution, DNA Media can market itself as a full-service localization company, and move away from only language translation. Alternatively, DNA Media can aim to differentiate from competitors, and concentrate on a focused market niche. On the basis of DNA Media's strengths (available technology resources, skilled staff, Vancouver's high-technology environment), a likely target market would be multimedia software applications. DNA has experience and skilled resources with technology, visual materials, and new-media content. In this vein, Steven has considered the development of a new product in e-training and e-learning. The business model is based on application service provider (ASP) technology that allows centralized control and content management. The object-based data architecture DNA Media plans to use will make the system extremely customizable and allows it to track learning progress and users' competencies. Steven agrees with his management team that the eTraining/eLearning "transformation strategy" is a high-risk plan, but there is tremendous upside considering the recent strides in the development of ASP technology. This can enable the company to move from a professional services firm to a technology platform vendor with a professional service component. Core assets for this new service will be knowledge management, client relationship management, and the multilingual platform technology that DNA Media will maintain and support. Niche markets will initially consist of the company's existing client base and channel partners and end-users over the Internet in multiple languages in Internet time. Target customers are large technology companies looking for customizable solutions, ongoing training for customer support, and an international market presence. The ASP platform is ideal for employee training and will generate revenues from hosting, managing content, and attracting third-party content providers and partners. DNA Media can be clearly positioned as a solution facilitating collaboration between clients and contractors.

Steven has scheduled a meeting to discuss the above options with his management team. Jim Eagles has expressed his view that DNA Media must make a paradigm shift in its thinking if the company is to grow. He uses the "razor blade" analogy to explain this shift in strategy and business model. According to Jim, "there is a need for DNA Media to break the mindset that the company is just selling razor blades. The company is really selling value-added services and products that make the person look better … like a shave, a hair cut, or a facial." The question is, how can DNA Media best make this happen?

DNA Media is behind in its four-year plan. The investment in management tools has helped control costs, but the company will not meet this quarter's profit targets due to a small overinvestment in new technology and staff. New growth strategies and value-added services could well be ideal ways for DNA Media to distinguish itself from its competitors.

So, in the area of profitability, can DNA continue to rely on debt financing? Or what other ways might there be to control costs while increasing revenues? How might various growth strategies figure into this option? Could alliances or acquisitions work, and how could this contribute to the revenue stream or to global expansion as a result?

And what exactly should be the new products and services? Steven has thought about this new ASP-based service again and again, and is a little concerned. DNA Media's core competencies are in localization, Southeast-Asian language translation, consulting, testing, application software, and Web-based technologies for B2B and B2C. However, DNA

Media's perceived core competency is culture and language. Clients may not consider them to be a technology company.

Steven recalled a memo he received last month from Mick McCallister, his VP of Technology. Mick brought to his attention the November 11, 2000 Lernout & Hauspie Mendez (L&H) Speech Products press release stating that the company had just filed a Chapter 11 petition for reorganization protection under the U.S. bankruptcy code, and would file a request for a concordant reorganization under Belgian law. L&H was one of the leaders in the speech and translation technology niche in the industry. It now appears that high-technology translation software solutions may not be the "silver-bullet, killer application" for the software localization industry. To add to this negative momentum, a recent issue of the *Localization Industry Standards Association (LISA) Newsletter* featured an interview with the CEO of SimulTrans, Mark Homnack, who predicted that the localization industry would be littered with bankrupted globalization technology companies by the end of 2001.[7] Would it be right to take a more conservative approach under this pessimistic economic outlook, or should one go for an innovative expansion or transformation in the product and service area?

It is now time for Steven to meet with his management team. What must Steven do to put the company back on track for its revenue and profit targets for 2003? Can the expansion strategies be viable given consolidation in the industry? Are there legitimate concerns about the ASP business model, or is this just another case of cold feet?

EPILOGUE

Shortly after this case study was originally written, DNA Media closed its doors in April 2001. It was a very difficult decision for CEO, Steven Forth, who founded the company and who had to break the bad news to his 60 employees. Despite credible strategic and marketing plans to diversify into higher-value services with newly developed eLearning and eTraining products, the timing couldn't have been worse. The floodgates opened on the bursting telecom and dot.com bubble, and many companies who geared for growth had to cut back their operations to survive the slowdown.

Steven's reasons for shutting down the operation are given below, but these problems affected the entire industry.

- It was bad timing for any new IPO offerings or for obtaining new equity financing. The dramatic drop in the stock price over the past year in high technology and telecommunication companies made any new IPO offering unwise. Steven felt the stock market was unjustifiably punishing the localization business for problems arising from eService companies like Sapient and Scient.
- The localization industry was struggling during this economic downturn, and there were no signs of recovery in the foreseeable future. The larger localization firms had seen their stock prices drop precipitously, and even major players like Lionbridge were facing a cash crunch due largely to the industry-wide decrease in demand.
- The business environment for the technology sector has become even tougher with the downturn in the economy. Smaller players like DNA Media were forced into the role of second-tier translation services providers. Margins on just translation services are

low, only about 10%, and without design and engineering the localization business was not a very profitable business in the long run.

Business failures often reveal lessons. In hindsight, Steven felt he learned some harsh lessons, but is now ready to start a new business with his new company, Recombo. He attributed specific failings of DNA Media to the factors below, and will not likely repeat these mistakes in the future:

- DNA Media invested too much on R&D in an attempt to diversify the business. Despite some successes with the spinning off of ThoughtShare, and now Recombo, not enough sales revenue was generated to save the company from its cash flow crunch. A large cash reserve would have helped to sustain the company during this economic downturn.
- With 22 and 28 percent annualized increases in sale revenue over the two years since 1998, the company increased its management costs by acquiring additional management talent to specifically help direct and sustain the growth. Based on sales projections using information from September and October of 2000, the business plan looked to be on track. When demand for localization services started to collapse in November 2000, the company could not respond quickly enough to the downturn.
- Management misjudged the dramatic collapse in demand for localization services. A short-term plan was adopted which included a 50% cut back on operating costs for marketing, management, office and R&D, and an equal proportion in sales and production costs. Despite these cuts, the targeted sale revenues fell short of meeting the breakeven cash flow requirements. Monthly sales fell from $420,000 in November 2000 to $180,000 in March 2001 (a drop of over 57%), reflecting the overall slowdown in the technology sector. When it became apparent that the downturn was going to be prolonged this plan was no longer viable.
- Lastly, Steven's earlier reluctance to obtain equity financing haunted him again. Using cash flow and debt financing to fund the company's expansion was a major tactical error. He felt if the company were equity financed, it could have survived this downturn. Again, without the benefit of hindsight, no one really knows how long the recent economic downturn would last.

TABLE 4 The Sale Revenues for the Final Months of DNA Media

	Monthly Sales	**Comments**
October 2000	$420 000	Company was performing well
November 2000	$280 000	Examined internal cost savings in sales and production processes
December 2000	$120 000	
January 2001	$170 000	Established three month plan targeting break even sales of $200 000 per month
February 2001	$180 000	
March 2001	$180 000	
April 2001	$120 000	Closed the company at the end of April

Appendix 1

Chronology of DNA Media

1989

- Steven Forth returns to Canada after ten years in Japan as an analyst and computer consultant to raise his family.

1990

- Steven Forth and two partners found Fact Media International (FMI). The business offers Japanese translation services for clients in North America and Japan.

1992

- FMI expands its service range by becoming the first company in Vancouver to offer Japanese desktop publishing services.

1993

- FMI expands into video versioning (i.e., dubbing) services for corporate and production companies.
- FMI also expands into software localization by initially focusing on modifying existing English graphics applications for use in Japanese.

1994

- FMI invests in DATT North America Multimedia Inc, a joint Canadian-Japanese venture in multimedia production. FMI creates Japanese versions of all DATT's productions including the acclaimed CD-ROM version of *The Silk Road*.

1995

- Milestone year.
- FMI undergoes corporate reengineering from a bicultural (Japanese and English) to a multicultural organization (expanding into Chinese and European languages).

- FMI reaches ten employees in size.
- First bank financing received; prior to that the company was financed out of pocket.
- FMI expands into multiple languages, multimedia development, and television product work (versioning). The company's growth is driven by demand for localization services in international markets, affordability of computer technology, and growth of the company's internal resources.

1996

- FMI does not participate in industry consolidation that led to the emergence of powerful companies like Alpnet, BGS, L&H, and Lionbridge.

1997

- Milestone year.
- In hindsight, a major mistake is seen to have been made in not seeking equity financing as an alternative to bank financing, which stifled the growth of the company. Steven feels the company is uniquely "packaged" (multilingual development package is more valuable than a straight localization package), has a distinct market position, and can grow independently.
- FMI has a 20 to 30% revenue growth rate. With equity financing, Steven feels, in hindsight, that they could have grown the business almost ten times faster.
- The Japanese market collapses, but it does not affect service contracts at the time.
- FMI makes significant progress in localizing software, Web site development, computer user interface designs, acquisitions, and promotions. Contracts are landed with major players like Cognos, InMedia, Dorling Kindersley, Nikon, and Intel.
- FMI invests in IT infrastructure hardware: microwave link to the Internet and servers for Web testing and hosting.
- FMI reorganizes its corporate structure (refer to Exhibit 1 below and to Appendix 2) and the holding company is called DNA Media Group.
- May 1997, DNA Media Group launches an Internet Division that assists companies in developing a multilingual online presence (Japanese, Chinese, Korean, and English). Projects result with BC Tel, Ropak Inc., and Tumlare Corporation.
- Short-lived investment in L.A.-based new media publishing startup, Masterworks Media Corp.
- Spring 1997: DNA Media Group acquires the production division of DATT North America Multimedia Inc. from DATT Japan and renames it DNA Productions (DNA-P).
- The CD-ROM market collapses. Without a viable revenue model, this market segment for DNA Media Group is not sustainable without equity financing where several years of financial losses can be tolerated until the company establishes itself in the market.

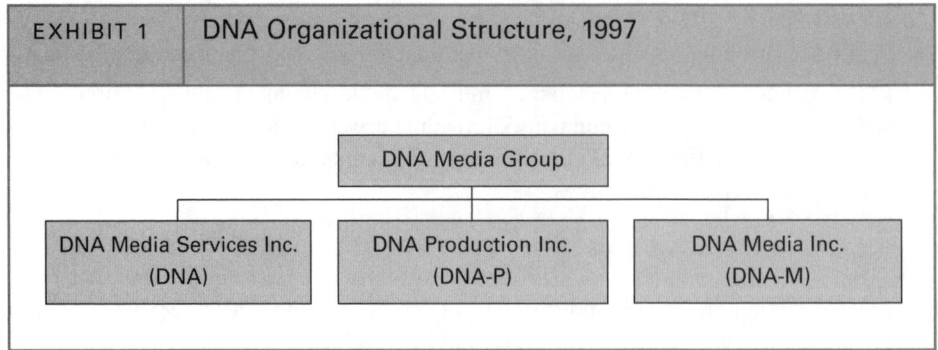

1999

- Milestone year.
- DNA Media Group tries to get equity financing from venture capitalists but they want a "pure play." As a result, DNA Media Group reorganizes and spins off ThoughtShare as a separate company. This group contributed to about 10% of DNA Media's revenues. Equity financing is received for ThoughtShare.
- The need for global networking to penetrate the global market is realized.

2000

- A new operating company is established in January 2000 called DNA Media Inc. All assets and people from DNA Media Services are transferred to DNA Media Inc.
- DNA Productions (DNA-P) is put into hibernation. CD-ROM products are unsuccessful in the market.
- DNA Media Inc. initiates a "transformation" from a "service provider" to a "technology vendor plus professional services provider." This includes higher-value services in client relationship building; technology platform in the general area of multilingual learning over the Internet (ASP model); training applications for channel partners; and content management. The reasons for these changes are to concentrate on core competency, established relationships, and in-house expertise.
- DNA Media Inc. invests heavily in technology and management, but this results in a small loss for the company in fourth quarter of 2000.

Appendix 2

Detailed DNA Organizational Structure, 1997

	DNA Media Group (DMG)	DNA Media Services Inc. (DNA)	DNA Productions Inc. (DNA-P)	DNA Media Inc. (DNA-M)
Main corporate function	Holding company owns all assets (intellectual property, financial assets, physical assets) and is responsible for financing, governance, and overall group strategy	Provides design, engineering, production, and localization services (the "core" capabilities of FMI)	Responsible for the development of products across key media	Creates intellectual property and maximizes the long-term value and revenue generation
Products	N/A	Media versioning and software localization; experts in interface design, translation, graphic design, programming, and cross-platform development	CD-ROM, Internet-based projects, in addition to books and short TV programs	Publishing packaged media materials in North America; developing international content packaging and sale of rights
Market focus	Manages sales to corporate and institutional sector; relies on word of mouth, cold-calling, and direct sales techniques; does not advertise; has a Web site	Main focus on East Asian languages; market driven by outsourcing of localization functions by large corporations; increased market growth in international version of software, satellite TV (versioning services), and DVD	Sells its services to DNA-M and DNA; DNA-M handles sales of products and broadcast media while DNA handles sales to the corporate and institutional sector	Education market; progressive parents and empty-nesters with disposable income for travel; secondary market is elementary, high school, and post-secondary institutions

	DNA Media Group (DMG)	DNA Media Services Inc. (DNA)	DNA Productions Inc. (DNA-P)	DNA Media Inc. (DNA-M)
Long-term strategy	DMG to eventually move to an Asset Management Model	Expected growth in 1998: multimedia localization, 35% per year; DVD- and video-related localization, 45% per year; general translation, 11% per year	DNA-P will eventually develop its own content and sources of external revenue	Develop inventory of content that can be reused; driving force behind development of new concepts and IP

Source: E. Person, "A strategic analysis of a software localization company," unpublished MBA thesis (Burnaby, B.C.: Simon Fraser University, 1998).

Appendix 3

Industry Profile for the Software Localization Industry

	General Comments
Barrier to entry/exit	• High barrier to entry due to expertise needed in language, engineering, and design. Capital costs moderate. • Shortage of specialized talent in localization. • Steep learning curve for new entrants. • Requires network of clients, and reputation to survive in service industry, and this will take time to develop. • As industry consolidates, barriers will increase with time as global networks strengthen.
Dominant players	• Consolidators: Alpnet, BGS, L&H Mendez, Lionbridge, Berlitz.
Breadth of languages	• SLV (single-language vendors); small size, sharp focus, small players. • MLV; large companies, especially consolidators.
Capital costs	• Moderate but climbing due to evolving hardware and software requirements and tools.
Pace of technology change	• Very high. Hardware and software tools are constantly changing. Software being localized has short life cycle. • Distribution channels expanding; DVD, Web TV, Internet.
Economies of scale	• Low scalability. Each project is a customized product requiring significant input from skilled workers, and the product is not scalable as volume of work increases. • Modest scalability with marketing, advertising, infrastructure, and management expenditures.
Learning curve	• Very steep. Costs decline once expertise is gained, but it takes time to gain experience and competency. • Translation management tools like Trados and source code management tools like Corel Catalyst enable improvement in efficiencies for repetitive jobs and content. Does not replace skilled personnel.
Vendor-client loyalty	• Generally, vendors who do initial localization jobs will do projects for the life of the software package. There are significant pressures to win the first contract with vendors.
Industry profitability	• Low to moderate.

	General Comments
Industry driving forces	• Competitive rivalry is moderate due to 30% annualized industry growth rate. However, consolidators will be more competitive and dominating as the industry matures. • Power of suppliers; shortage of skilled personnel—growth in demand outstrips supply of people available to do projects. • Power of buyers; top ten industry leaders like IBM, Microsoft, and Oracle dominate 50% of the market.

Source: E. Person, "A strategic analysis of a software localization company," unpublished MBA thesis (Burnaby, B.C.: Simon Fraser University, 1998).

Appendix 4

Top-Tiered Consolidated Companies

Top-Tiered Company	Characteristics
Berlitz	• Worldwide market leader in language instruction and translation services. Only "brand name" in the industry. • 1997 total revenues of $366M, and software localization contributing 22% or $80.5M to total. • Three divisions: Language Instruction, Translation Services (software localization, interactive media, translation, general interpretation), and Publishing. • Translation Services is focused on IT, automotive, medical technology, and telecommunications market segments. • Strong in international scope of operations (325 training centres, 200 languages, brand name). • Weak in not foreseeing market growth for software localization, and has fallen behind competitors in this area.
BGS (Bowne Global Services)	• Became a major localization player in less than two years due to consolidation. Refocused business on "Empowering Information"; distributing client's information to any audience, in any language, anywhere in the world. • View service as a standardized end product. Believes clients like consistent content across all locations. • Basis of competition is quality of service, project management skills, and breadth of languages offered. • In 1998, purchased Linguistix, a multi-language machine translation tool. • Strong: it is the premier player in software localization. Provides quality and breadth of services. • No significant weaknesses.
Alpnet	• Views service as a standardized end product. Believes clients like consistent content across all locations. • Basis of competition is quality of service, project management skills, and breadth of languages offered. • Founded in 1980 in Salt Lake City, Utah. • Three product lines: localization (45% revenues), documentation (40% revenues), and translation (15% revenues). • Alpnet targets market niches in ERP, computer-based training, and the global automotive sector.

Top-Tiered Company	Characteristics
	• Strong in its size and global network which includes partnerships with Compaq, Intel, Dell, Baan Computer, Oracle, Lotus, and Chrysler. • Weak in offering consistent quality and reliance on aging translation technology that was developed in-house and has not kept up with current technology offerings.
Lernout & Hauspie Mendez	• L&H parent company is technology leader in advanced speech technology and translation services. • Founded in 1987 in Belgium. • Four divisions: Core Speech Technologies/Dictation/Translation and Localization/Language Technologies. • The T&L group, known as L&H, is among the top-tier localization vendors. • Customers include Microsoft, IBM, SAP, Exxon, Lucent, and Medtronic. • L&H Mendez contributed 32% or $31.6M (1997) to parent company's revenues. • Strong presence in Latin America, part ownership by Microsoft, L&H translation technologies. • Weak: historical reliance on European languages, and lack of exposure to Southeast Asia.
Lionbridge	• Founded in the 1980s in the Netherlands. • Focused on providing the technology and linguistic skills necessary for localization services. • Customers include Microsoft, Lotus, Baan, Sun, Parametric Technologies, and Trados. • Lionbridge targets financial applications, operating systems, and Web technologies. • Strong: management team with experience in Fortune 500 technology companies; employee ownership; value-added relationship with Trados. • About 50% of revenues come from Web-based activities and products, while the other 50% come from operating systems and desktop applications. • Weak: poor integration of recently acquired Japanese Language Services in 1997 resulted in inefficient operations and poor customer satisfaction.

Source: E. Person, "A strategic analysis of a software localization company," unpublished MBA thesis (Burnaby, B.C.: Simon Fraser University, 1998).

Appendix 5

Evolution of the Localization Industry

PRE-1996

Prior to 1996, localization was essentially a cottage industry. The largest companies earned $US1 000 000 to $US2 000 000 per year. Key success factors for business in this industry mainly revolved around language expertise, project management, and resource management. The business model was based on charging rates for "dollars per word" translated.

1996 TO 1999

The industry structure and climate changed significantly during the consolidation period that began in 1996. Consolidation resulted in the emergence of very large, well-capitalized players like Berlitz, Lionbridge, L&H, Alpnet, and Bowes Global Services (BGS) in a traditionally fragmented marketplace. Some drivers for consolidation were the growing equity financing market, the rise of the Internet, the low cost of computer technology, the trend toward outsourcing, and the growing use of non-English languages on the Internet. Subsequently, the nature of the industry changed. Some of the consolidators tried to commoditize the business by reducing the business model to "pennies per word" through the use of translation software. At the same time some companies began marketing a one-stop high-value-added service.

1999 TO PRESENT

In 1999, the big players in the industry drove the next evolution of localization services by moving toward "global solutions." The large consolidated companies moved localization beyond the IT industry, and began focusing on content flows, hosted applications, databases, and knowledge bases. Extensive use of tools like XML, content management, and testing tools grew, allowing enterprises to leverage their translation investment by allowing content to be "reused." Localization services grew to include translation management (e.g., Internet portals, workflow, and connectivity), multiple-language real-time content on the Web, global rendering, and global testing. Globalization is expected to evolve toward an integrated value chain model from the fragmented piecemeal approach to services currently being used. The business model has shifted toward an added-value service model emphasizing time, quality, cost, availability, subscription, platform, and retainer, all in an effort to increase profit margins. The days of large software projects with large companies will slow down due to the move toward an ASP model, and open up business opportunities with small-to-medium-sized enterprises (SMEs).

Appendix 6

Medium-Tiered Competitors

Medium-Tiered Company (Less Than 100 Employees)	Characteristics
DNA Media	• View service as customized. Consumers will demand software that is easy to use because it has been localized with sensitivity to local cultures. Requires localization service to account for cultural nuances. • Have always had a computer focus or component in the business. • Strong: wide range of services (traditional localization services/desktop publishing/software engineering/interface design) and flexibility; premier service in Asian languages. • Weak: financial backing and flexibility.
EnCompass Globalization	• Fifty-person company located in Seattle, Washington. • Specialized in Japanese, Chinese, Taiwanese, and Korean markets. • Strong: software engineering, translation, and testing services. • Formed EnCompass Ventures—responsible for providing turnkey services to software developers that includes localization, capital investment, distribution, and marketing support.
Rubric	• Located in London, England. • A software, documentation, and Web site localization company. • Offices in North America, Europe, and Asia, and offers localization services in 20 languages. • Focused on servicing the information technology industry, and not languages in particular.
Clockworks International	• Based in Dublin, Ireland. • Provides software localization services: project management, translation, desktop publishing, and Web site localization. • Founded by engineers, not linguists. • Has distinct technical edge over competitors; pursue technically challenging, leading-edge projects beyond scope of typical localization providers.
Arial Translations	• Located in Cody, Wyoming. • Provides Asian language translation and localization services including desktop publishing, double-byte output and Web site localization.

Medium-Tiered Company (Less Than 100 Employees)	Characteristics
	• Clients include Nike, Intel, Adobe, Hewlett-Packard and Polaroid. • Strong: heavy use of technology to improve efficiency of localization services like Internet servers, high-speed network connections, backup systems, and translation tools like Trados and S-Tagger.
Source: E. Person, "A strategic analysis of a software localization company," unpublished MBA thesis (Burnaby, B.C.: Simon Fraser University, 1998).	

NOTES

1. *Localization* refers to content adaptation to accommodate various cultures and cultural references. This includes language translation and adjusting content to capture the meaning of the message, as well as consideration of various Web design features such as the use of appropriate colours and navigation tool preferences.
2. "The 1998 eOverview report," *eMarketer* <www.emarketer.com>.
3. "The post-localization era: the best is yet to come!" [keynote speech by Roger Jeantry], *LISA Newsletter*, 9(2000)(4), available <www.lisa.org/newsletter/about.html>.
4. S. Richards De Wit, "Going global with your online presence requires more than just quick translation," *Business in Vancouver*, January 2001: 23–29.
5. C. A. Pinkus, speech at the Bowne Annual General Meeting, March 27, 1998.
6. "The future of globalization technology: is it the graveyard?" [interview with Mark Homnack], *LISA Newsletter*, 9(2000)(4), available <www.lisa.org/newsletter/about.html>.
7. See note 6.

part two overview

E-Business Implementation: Planning for Success and Learning from Failure

Venture capitalists who invest in the e-business sector consider "execution" a key investment criterion that they use in deal-making. They define execution as being the ability of an e-business management team to successfully implement their business model with efficiency and effectiveness. In the context of the recent shakeout in the dot-com sector of e-business, it is becoming critically important to differentiate between ventures that fail because of ineffective business models and those that fail because of poor implementation and suboptimal execution strategies. In determining an appropriate implementation strategy, managers of e-businesses have to make many critical decisions pertaining to how they wish to spend their scarce resources and the timing and nature of their execution activities.

The two cases of this Part provide a rich contextual backdrop to the analysis of such implementation decisions. The Priceline.com case presents the context of an e-business that is widely acknowledged as having an innovative and powerful business model that it tried to implement in various application contexts. The Boo.com case emphasizes the importance of carefully balancing and timing technical development and market development activities in e-business implementation.

The readings of this Part provide a conceptual model for understanding the critical implementation issues, especially in terms of lessons that are to be learned from failed attempts at implementing e-business models. They suggest that more attention needs to be paid to implementation issues early in the initial conceptualization and strategic planning of an e-business venture. Other implementation issues of importance include

J. Dhaliwal, A. Persaud, and A. Sorensen, "An exploratory study of decision making contingencies and alignment in electronic commerce venture deal making," *Proceedings of the Asia Pacific Decision Sciences Institute (DSI) Conference*, Singapore, July 18–21, 2001.

the role of top management in e-business implementation, project management considerations, and the relevance of market conditions and timing in e-business implementation.

As both the Priceline.com and the Boo.com case represent the context of e-business startup ventures, issues pertaining to e-business implementation in large corporate organizations can be explored using the Den norske Bank case study that is included in Theme 3 of this book.

case one

Priceline.com

Patrick Adams

Carol Cho

Colin Clark

Gloria Plottel

Beatrice Yu

Li Zhang

In the spring of 1999, Jay Walker, founder and vice-chairman of Priceline.com, could not have been in a better mood. Priceline.com had sold common stock in its initial public offering at a price of $16 per share. By the end of the first day of trading, the market valued each share of Priceline.com at $69, a whopping rise of 331%, giving the firm a market capitalization of $12 billion. In valuing the firm, investors concentrated on Priceline.com's patent for a demand collection service that enabled it to sell excess inventory in the four largest travel segments: airlines, hotels, rental cars, and cruises. Wall Street analysts touted the stock, with one analyst citing: "In our view, Priceline.com's business model lends itself to being one of the most successful we've ever seen."[1] Positive sentiment grew, and by late April 1999 the market capitalization was $28 billion. The company's founder and vice-chairman, Jay Walker, had a personal stake in Priceline.com worth over $11 billion. Investors raced to get shares of what many viewed as legal monopoly and in the process made Walker an extremely wealthy man … on paper.

MBA candidates Patrick Adams, Carol Cho, Colin Clark, Gloria Plottel, Beatrice Yu, and Li Zhang prepared this case under the supervision of Professor Christopher L. Tucci, for purposes of class discussion rather than to illustrate either effective or ineffective handling of an administrative situation.

In September 1999, Microsoft announced that its Expedia travel service would offer a competing "name your own price" service for hotel rooms, one of Priceline.com's core product offerings. In the subsequent months, Priceline.com's stock price fell to a post-IPO low of $45.50 per share, more than 70% off its high (see Exhibit 1). Walker's personal wealth diminished $8 billion—an amount rarely matched on CNBC's wealth meter. Did investors doubt Priceline.com's patent would endure a legal challenge? Or were investors losing confidence in the firm's ability to execute its business plan?

JAY WALKER AND PRICELINE.COM

Jay Walker was an originator, a developer, and an entrepreneur. In 1994, he founded an intellectual property R&D laboratory called Walker Digital. Walker poured his heart and soul into conceiving and developing innovative concepts that could be taken to market. His ingenuity and drive paid off big in 1997 when he conceived of a unique business model that would eventually thrust him into the forefront of the Internet world and rank him among the most influential business leaders in the digital age.

TRANSACTING ON THE INTERNET

The emergence of the Internet in the mid-1990s offered significant economic benefits to those transacting online. First, the Internet provided substantial economies of scale and scope. A single Web site was infinitely "scalable" and could cover the globe with a small increase in costs. Moreover, the Internet made it far easier to branch into new product lines once a firm had succeeded at one product.

EXHIBIT 1 Priceline (PCLN) Stock Price Chart

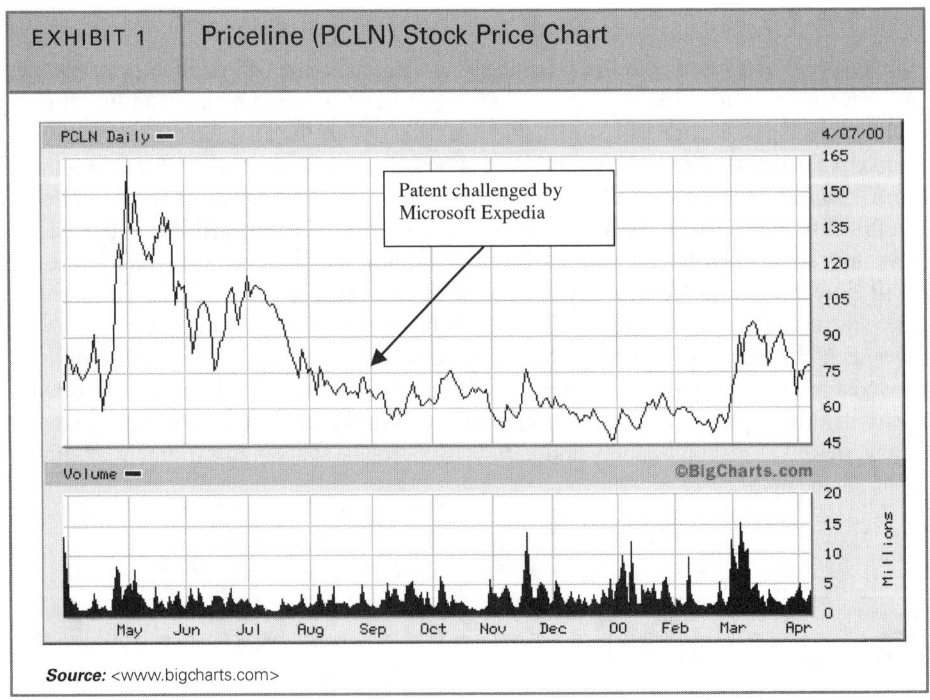

Source: <www.bigcharts.com>

Second, the Internet allowed firms to gain better familiarity with their customers and provide greater richness and customization of services. Customized features enhanced loyalty, resulting in less customer churn.

Third, e-commerce allowed firms to dispose of much of the traditional retail value chain. In the bricks-and-mortar world, sales were typically transacted through a chain of participants including manufacturers, wholesalers, retailers, and finally consumers. The Internet allowed sales to be conducted directly from manufacturers to consumers, which helped to eliminate middlemen and reduced transaction costs and time to market. Moreover, digital links with customers, distributors, and suppliers improved supply-chain management and reduced inventory costs.

Perhaps the most significant economic benefit was the Internet's effect on pricing. The Internet acted as an important price-deflation mechanism. Online auctions ushered in a new era of negotiated prices with better-informed consumers freely searching for the best price in electronic stores. A pricing revolution was occurring and the war cry was "Fixed pricing is dead!"

The Internet rekindled interest in the auction by efficiently bringing together buyers and sellers from all over the world through a frictionless electronic medium. Cyber start-ups entered the scene and dramatically affected the transaction process and product pricing. E-commerce models emerged and began to take on different forms. Internet-enabled business-to-business (B2B) exchanges emerged as large companies like Cisco and Oracle transferred their purchasing to the Web. Additionally, business-to-consumer (B2C) trade evolved as companies like Amazon and Charles Schwab transacted normal retail transactions on the Web. Moreover, consumer-to-consumer (C2C) auctions began to take shape, epitomized by eBay's business model (see Exhibit 2).

THE C2B NEW PRODUCT CONCEPT

Walker contemplated how he could capitalize on the e-commerce trend. Finally, he conceived of a unique and revolutionary model. In the typical online auction, the seller was in charge. The seller set the price and consumers were presented with prices on goods and services that may or may not be the best value. Under Walker's model, economic power would be transferred to the consumer using a "reverse auction technology." Consumers would submit offers for goods and services below prevailing prices in the marketplace

EXHIBIT 2 The E-Commerce Matrix

	Business	Consumer
Business	**B2B** Cisco/Oracle	**B2C** Amazon
Consumer	**C2B** Priceline	**C2C** eBay

Source: *The Economist,* February 26, 2000.

using a "name your own price" business model. Walker's demand collection system would stand in the middle as a low-cost provider linking consumers to suppliers.

Not only did Walker's consumer-to-business (C2B) model provide a novel way for budget-conscious consumers to buy products at a lower price, but also the system was advantageous to sellers. The C2B model allowed sellers to capture demand that otherwise might have been lost, thereby increasing the seller's revenues. Additionally, sellers could use the system to get rid of excess inventory for which they would normally have to reduce prices or create demand, which required additional expenditures. The primary advantage of the system, however, was that it allowed sellers to fill multiple orders at different prices at the same time without disrupting established retail prices or current distribution channels.[2]

INTELLECTUAL PROPERTY ADVANTAGE

Walker acquired a seasoned management team and in April 1998 the service was launched under the name "Priceline.com" (see Exhibit 3). Priceline.com's core asset and most obvious advantage was that it had a "business methods patent" on its reverse auction technology. Priceline.com's proprietary technology offered them the potential to be a dominant

EXHIBIT 3 The Priceline Management Team

Management	Age	Position	Years of Experience	Previous Experience
Richard Braddock	57	Chairman and CEO	35	Citicorp
Jay Walker	43	Vice-chairman & founder	23	Walker Digital
Dan Schulman	41	President & COO	18	AT&T
Heidi Miller	44	CFO	24	Citigroup
Michael McCadden		Chief marketing officer	19	The Gap Stores
Ron Rose	48	CIO	26	S&P
Jeffrey Boyd		Executive VP and general counsel	18	Oxford Health Plans
Tim Brier	50	President, travel	28	Continental Airlines
Christopher Soder		President, hotels	18	AT&T
Maryann Keller	55	President, auto services unit	28	ING Barings
Jeannie Wisniewski	40	EVP, human resources	19	Oxford Health Plans
Michael Diliberto	33	SVP, technology	11	News Corp.
Mitch Truit		SVP, corporate development	8	Oxford Health Plans
Andrew Abowitz		VP, operations and customer service		Oxford Health Plans
Tom D'Angelo	40	VP, finance and controller		Direct Travel Inc.
Gary Goldberg	30	VP, business-to-business	9	Deloitte & Touche

Source: Priceline.com, Janney Montgomery Scott, Goldman Sachs.

player in the C2B space and provided a competitive advantage that was difficult to reverse. This proprietary standard would allow Priceline.com to lock-in customers and suppliers for longer periods of time, reducing uncertainty.

> This patent is very general, it covers a method, not just a specific implementation. The patented method is the one by which (1) a buyer enters into a system a guaranteed offer, (2) the offer is made available for inspection by sellers, (3) sellers can accept the offer, and (4) one of the sellers receives payment. … The patent covers all sorts of variations on the buyer-driven purchase model including: (1) different ways and sequences for the transmission of the information, (2) establishment of mechanisms to select one seller from among those that accept the offer, (3) mechanisms to make offers irrevocable by a certain expiration date, (4) use of credit cards to guarantee offers, and (5) use of computer hardware, proprietary software, Web software, and even telephones as a processing infrastructure"[3]

With the patent in hand, the firm spent heavily on marketing in an effort to create awareness, build loyalty, and establish a brand name. Priceline wanted consumers to associate its name with great buys. As a first mover, with patent protection, Priceline felt it could afford to spend to attract customers.

EXECUTING THE CONCEPT: AIRLINE TICKETS

Priceline's first product offering was surplus airline tickets (see Exhibit 4). Walker felt that the C2B model was tailor-made for selling airline tickets online. The airline travel market was attractive because ticket buyers were willing to trade off brand and flexibility for price. Equally attractive was the industry size ($65 billion), availability of surplus inventory (35% unsold inventory), and estimated market opportunity ($29 billion) for the surplus.[4] On the basis of December 1999 figures, the top eight airlines were taking off with over 687 000 empty seats daily. Since it cost airlines only $5 for every incremental seat sold, Priceline thought it would be easy to convince the airlines to join in order to maximize their revenues. However, Priceline found reluctance on the part of major airlines because they felt that the excess inventory market was not worth going after and were afraid of downward price pressure from the sale of discounted tickets.

EXHIBIT 4	A Typical Priceline Airline Ticket Transaction

1. The consumer specified the cities, travel dates, airports, times (peak hours and/or red-eye), and maximum number of stops (the minimum was one). The more flexibility, the greater the chance the order would get filled. The consumer named the price and provided a credit card number to guarantee the offer.
2. Priceline's proprietary system looked for a match with its available inventory.
3. If the offer was filled, the customer's credit card was charged and a non-refundable ticket was issued.
4. An email confirmation was sent to the customer within 24 hours.

To get the airlines' cooperation, Priceline initially offered very generous terms in its agreements. In exchange for unspecified quantities of tickets, Priceline gave Delta, its first strategic partner, 18.6 million warrants, and also agreed to restrict competing airlines from accepting bids on flights to and from Atlanta, Delta's primary hub.[5] Priceline even conceded non-exclusive agreements and their termination on short notice. Despite these inducements, Priceline still experienced supply shortages during the first half of 1999, resulting in disappointed customers. This supply/demand imbalance underlined the importance of the supplier relationships.

Priceline therefore aggressively pursued additional partners to have access to more seats. This brought up the bind rate (the rate at which Priceline fills orders) from 42% (in the second quarter) to 50% (in the third quarter).[6] Still, many customers complained that their orders were going unfilled. Without support from the major airlines, it became clear that demand would remain well ahead of supply.

Priceline finally achieved critical mass on November 17, 1999, when the firm was able to obtain major inventory from every major U.S. airline (representing 90% of total U.S. market share), and was able to increase its inventory by 94% as a result of these deals.[7] This signalled a shift of power from the airlines to Priceline, since airlines had to participate or risk losing significant market share to competitors that were already selling through Priceline. In fact, once United was on board, American and US Air quickly came to an agreement with Priceline, as neither would likely have wanted to be last to cut a deal. In achieving critical mass, Priceline gained leverage to ask for more inventory at more favourable prices.

Currently, 28 airlines are participating (including 20 international partners).[8] "There's a calculation that we do that demonstrated that the airlines using Priceline were growing faster than those that weren't," Mr. Braddock, CEO of Priceline, said. "And the reason for that growth was basically Priceline. The airlines saw that, too. They decided we were grown up enough."[9]

PRODUCT EXPANSION

Through its success with the airlines, Priceline was able to convince other suppliers of perishable products or services that the company offered a compelling value proposition. Priceline had demonstrated its ability to offer suppliers incremental revenue from another distribution channel while maintaining the price integrity of their products in the traditional distribution outlets.

Braddock commented on the attributes of the new service:

> Priceline.com does something that no single company, no matter how large, can do—we collect demand and then let multiple sellers see and selectively fill that demand in ways that complement, but never harm their retail prices. Our success in the airline industry reveals the strength of the Priceline.com business model to incrementally grow sales and revenues for all of our partners simultaneously, including companies that are direct competitors. ... We expect that the airline business is only the first in a long line of industries to benefit from broad utilization of the Priceline.com system.[10]

In November 1999 Priceline expanded in scope and licensed its business model to the WebHouse Club, who in turned launched a reverse auction grocery selling platform in ten states offering savings averaging 35% on consumers' grocery purchases. Thirty major supermarket chains, including Grand Union, Stop & Shop, and Pathmark and two dozen manufacturers, jumped on board. As in the airline model, consumers gained access to WebHouse Club through Priceline's home page.

The WebHouse site currently hosts more than 500 brands and 140 products. Sales surpassed $100 million in the first 120 days, and, by March 2000, 250 000 people had used the service and 10 million items had been sold.[11] A nationwide rollout was planned for the third quarter of 2000.

From the WebHouse Club venture, Priceline gained not only licensing revenue but also thousands of new and repeat visits to its home page, which created numerous cross-selling opportunities (see Exhibit 5).

EXHIBIT 5 Priceline's Grocery Business

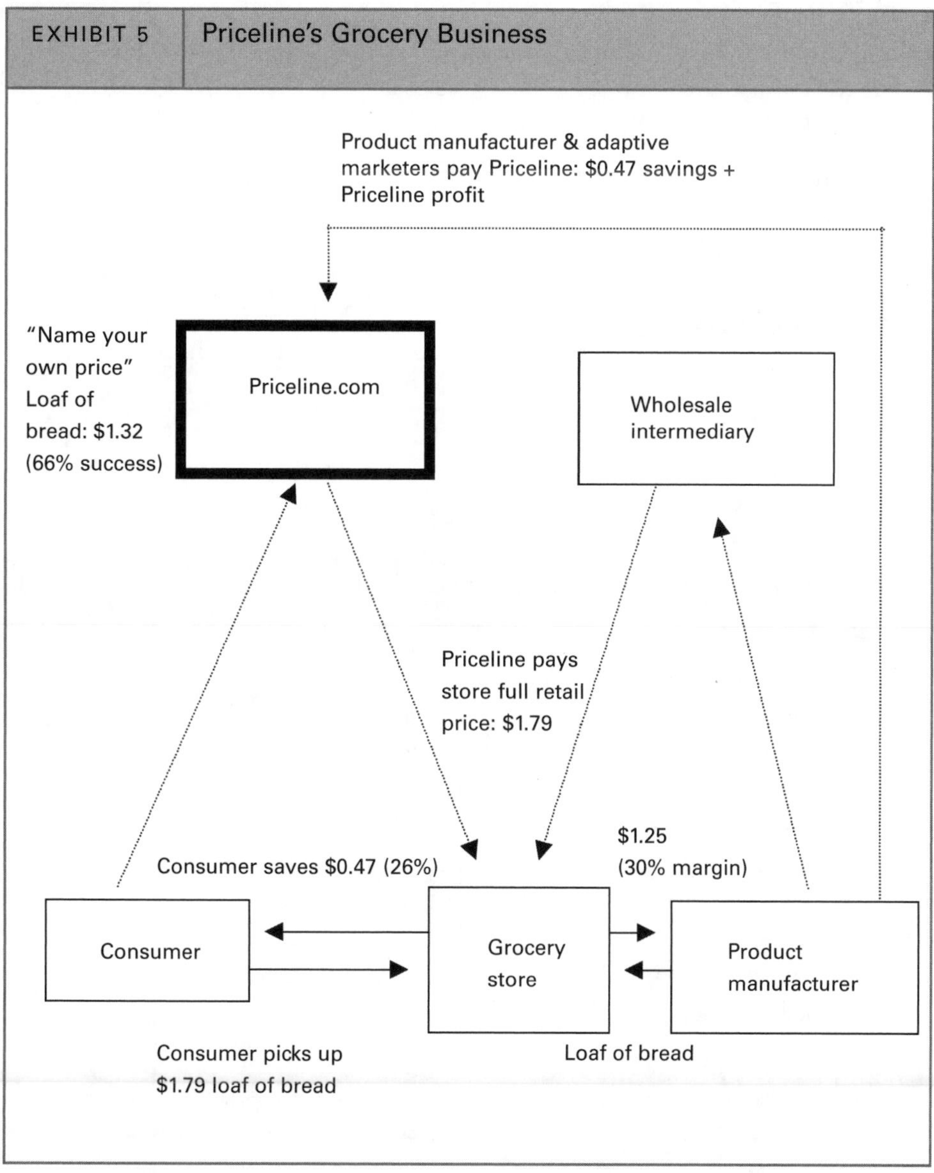

By year-end 1999, Priceline's sales had reached $482 million, a 1200%+ increase over 1998 sales (see Exhibit 6). In the year 2000, Priceline planned to apply its DCS platform to 18 new initiatives, including telecom, credit cards, gasoline, office supplies, media buying, and life insurance (see Exhibit 7 and Exhibit 8).[12] However, in order for Priceline to survive, supplier partnerships were paramount.

EXHIBIT 6 Priceline.com Financials

	December 1999	December 1998
Revenue ($ millions)	482.4	35.2
Percentage growth	1270%	—
Net income ($ millions)	–1,055.10	–112.2
Diluted EPS	–$7.90	–$1.41

Source: Company reports.

EXHIBIT 7 Timeline of Priceline's Product Offerings

April 6, 1998	Leisure airline tickets
July 6, 1998	New automobiles
October 28, 1998	Hotel room reservations
November 1, 1999	Groceries
January 19, 2000	Used merchandise (yard sale)
February 3, 2000	Rental car reservations
March 23, 2000	Mortgage services
May 2000	Long-distance telephone service
May 2000	Gasoline

Source: Press Releases, Investor Relations, Priceline Web site, accessed June 26, 2001 <www.priceline.com>.

EXHIBIT 8 Priceline.com Earns Multiple Revenue Streams

1. Transactions Revenues		2. License Revenues		3. Ancillary Revenues		
Spread-Based	*Fee-Based*	*Domestic and International*	*Partners*	*Slotting Fees*	*Market Data Research*	*Other*
• Airlines	• New cars	• WebHouse Club (groceries, gas)	• Alliance (mortgages)	• Net2Phone	• Ford	• Travelocity
• Hotels	• Mortgages	• Perfect Yardsale	• Budget (car rentals)	• Computer Reservation Systems		• Rental Car Bounceback
• Car rentals		• My Price (Australia, New Zealand)				• Travel Insurance
		• Hutchinson Whampoa				

4. Sponsorship Revenues from Adaptive Marketing Revenues

5. Advertising Revenues

6. Transaction Revenues

(A) *Spread:* The difference between what consumers are willing to pay and the price suppliers are willing to sell the product for. Priceline pockets the difference.

Example: Customer: "I'll pay $X for a ticket." Airline: "I'll sell a ticket for $Y."

(B) *Fees:* Priceline receives an established fee for matching up a willing buyer and a willing seller for an item that has been previously specified at an agreed-upon price.

Example: Customer: "I'll pay $A for this particular car." Dealer: "I'll sell you that car for $A and pay Priceline a fixed fee of $B."

7. Licensing Revenues

Priceline.com earns royalities from companies to which it licenses its business model. The licensing fees are in the low single digits as a percentage of sales. These licensees have the same customer management system as Priceline.com and service as a zero-cost customer-acquisition tool, as WebHouse Club and Perfect YardSale customers must access those areas via the Priceline.com home page. Priceline.com attracts these customers with low-value, high-frequency purchases such as groceries, and has the opportunity to convert them to higher-value, lower-frequency purchases, such as airline tickets or new cars.

Example: Licensee: "I'll pay Priceline $Z or Z% of every transaction so that I can use its 'name your own price' technology."

8. Ancillary Fees

If a customer chooses not to name his or her own price on a rental car and instead clicks through to the Budget site, Budget pays Priceline.com a lead-generation and click-through fee.

9. Adaptive Marketing

Priceline.com uses adaptive promotions to improve a customer's offer so that it has a higher likelihood of being accepted. For example, applying for a credit card gives a customer a $30 credit toward an offer for an airline ticket.

Sources: Goldman Sachs research, March 31, 2000; Paine Webber research, February 11, 2000.

SEVENTEEN YEARS OF PATENT PROTECTION?

Surprise, surprise. Microsoft, through its Expedia subsidiary, announced in September 1999 the introduction of its own reverse auction service allowing consumers to bid for hotel rooms. On October 13, 1999, Priceline.com filed suit in U.S. District Court against Microsoft/Expedia Inc., claiming that Expedia.com's recently introduced reverse auction service infringed upon Priceline.com's patent. But a positive outcome for Priceline was far from guaranteed. The suit drew massive attention from intellectual property experts, Internet entrepreneurs, and Priceline.com's potential competition, highlighting the uncertainty surrounding intellectual property rights on the Internet. The case would be a test of a company's right to patent not just a technology but also a business process.[13]

The Internet retail industry had very little history of legal battles to help define intellectual property protection. A similar patent-infringement lawsuit was filed in 1999 by Amazon against its rival BarnesandNoble.com and resulted in Amazon's winning a preliminary injunction barring BarnesandNoble.com from using a "one-click" ordering system. And in 1998, the U.S. Supreme Court, in *State Street v. Signature Financial Group*, declared "software-enabled business methods and process to be patentable as long as they were novel, nonobvious and produced tangible results."[14]

In addition to preparing to fight Microsoft in the courtroom, Jay Walker campaigned for Priceline.com in the public forum, attempting to gain support from the tens of thousands of entrepreneurs staking out their claim on the Internet. According to Walker,

> Patents are as important to the future of commerce on the Internet, we believe, as they are to pharmaceutical companies or to biotech companies. In the past, the information structure of your business didn't matter. ... What's different here is in the case of Priceline is we're protecting a method of doing business, which by the way, had never come before. What the patents matter to

EXHIBIT 9 Comparables

Company	Revenues ($ millions)*	Market Capitalization ($ millions)
Priceline.com	$ 482	$12 876
Expedia	58	1 023
Hotel Reservations	162	305
Travelocity.com**	91	2 000
Hilton Hotels	2 300	2 720
Marriot International	8 700	7 868
Starwood Hotel	3 700	4 730
AMR	19 000	4 526
Delta Air Lines	15 000	6 469
Northwest Airlines	10 000	1 437

*Latest 12 months.

**Includes Preview Travel.

Source: Barrons as of March 20, 2000.

> Priceline is they ultimately help us protect our profits margins long term, from very deep-pocketed powerful players who will, if we continue to succeed, compete with us! So ultimately, your patent helps define your profit and loss statement a little bit better.[15]

Walker's critics countered with claims that Priceline.com had little grounds for patenting its reverse auction business method:

> Look-and-feel property rights should not, of course, be upheld willy-nilly. There's no way courts should let Priceline patent entire business models, as it claims it can and courts aren't going to. Patent law is already well fortified against vague, overboard, unoriginal or simply obvious patents, patents that enable little more than predatory lawsuits.[16]

Clouding the issue further, the Patent and Trademark Office, responding to criticism that it hands out business method patents too easily, announced "it was changing its evaluation procedures to ensure that such patents cover true innovations."[17] But could and would the Patent and Trademark Office revoke Priceline's patent?

Skepticism mounted and competitors foamed at the mouth. James McQuivey, senior analyst at Forrester Research, put it simply: "It's only the patent that is holding the barbarians at the gate. If not for the patent, what would Priceline have to stand on?"[18]

NOTES

1. Keith Benjamin, "Priceline.com: initiating coverage of a powerful, new Internet business model," *BancBoston Robertson Stephens—Research Report*, April 26, 2000, p. 2.
2. Keith Benjamin, "Priceline.com: initiating coverage of a powerful, new Internet business model," *BancBoston Robertson Stephens—Research Report*, April 26, 2000, p. 4.
3. Tomas Isakowitz, "Priceline.com—initiate coverage with an accumulate," *Janney Montgomery Scott—Research Report*, September 8, 1999, p. 20.
4. Tomas Isakowitz, "Priceline.com—initiate coverage with an accumulate," *Janney Montgomery Scott—Research Report*, September 8, 1999, p. 12.
5. Tomas Isakowitz, "Priceline.com—initiate coverage with an accumulate," *Janney Montgomery Scott—Research Report*, September 8, 1999, p. 13.
6. Mary Meeker, "Priceline.com—momentum and leverage (part II)," *Morgan Stanley Dean Witter Research Report*, January 27, 2000, p. 3.
7. Sara J. Zeilstra, "The airline group—it's only the beginning," *Warburg Dillon Read Research Report (Consumer E-Commerce)*, December 7, 1999, p. 5.
8. Sara J. Zeilstra, "The airline group—it's only the beginning," *Warburg Dillon Read Research Report (Consumer E-Commerce)*, December 7, 1999, p. 3.
9. Amy Higgins, "More airlines board flight to Priceline.com," *The Cincinnati Enquirer*, November 18, 1999, p. B16.
10. Mary Meeker and Mark Mahaney, "Major expansion of airline partnerships," *Morgan Stanley Dean Witter Research Report*, November 17, 1999.
11. Eliot Walsh, "Priceline—the next Godzilla roars," *Individual Investor Online*, March 9, 2000.
12. Anthony Noto and Coralie Tournier Witter, "Priceline.com Incorporated," *Goldman Sachs Research Report*, March 31, 2000, p. 27.
13. Michael Learmonth, "Expedia.com files to dismiss Priceline suit," *Industry Standard*, December 21, 1999, p. 1.

14. Kevin Rivette and David Kline, "Surviving the Internet patent wars: the next online battle will not be fought over who has the best Web site but who owns and defends the best technologies and strategies," *Industry Standard*, December 6, 1999.

15. Transcript from "Entrepreneurs only: the patent café—founder, CNNfn," *Cable News Network Financial*, August 23, 1999.

16. Peter Huber, "The state of the art," *Forbes*, November 29, 1999, p. 164.

17. Sabra Chartrand, "Federal agency rethinks Internet patents," *New York Times*, March 30, 2000.

18. Mike France, Timothy J. Mullaney, and Diane Brady, "A Net monopoly no longer: Microsoft is challenging Priceline's patent on Web auctions," *Business Week*, September 27, 1999, p. 47.

case two

Boo.com (A)

Heidi Connal

Brigida Munoz

Ipek Ozilhan

Andrei Outkine

Edith Solovey

Ernst Malmsten, CEO of Boo.com, hung holiday decorations in his new Notting Hill apartment and pondered the upcoming 1999 Christmas retail season. The much-anticipated November launch of Boo.com, a cult-chic streetware e-tailing site, met with mixed reviews from customers and the industry. The site naturally didn't appeal to everyone, but there were also technical difficulties in the cutting-edge technology. Malmsten's investors were inquiring about future product plans and holiday revenues. Should the Boo team focus on the technical problems at hand, or should they redesign the product to appeal to a wider market?

RIDING THE INTERNET WAVE

In 1997, Swedes Ernst Malmsten and Kajsa Leander founded the Internet bookstore Bokus.com, which they sold a year later for a monstrous amount of money. By 1999, Bokus had become the third-biggest online bookstore in the world.[1] But the European entrepreneurs were far from finished with their online ingenuity. Malmsten, a "Six-

MBA candidates Heidi Connal, Brigida Munoz, Ipek Ozilhan, Andrei Outkine, and Edith Solovey prepared this case under the supervision of professor Christopher L. Tucci, for purposes of class discussion rather than to illustrate either effective of ineffective handling of an administrative situation.

foot-five version of Elvis Costello,"[2] and Leander, a former model for the Elite modelling agency, then went on to attack the online retail industry. Seeing a market for sporty streetware, Malmsten and Leander wanted to offer fashions in the United States and Europe from dozens of international companies that have cult followings but are hard to find in chain stores. In the summer of 1998, Boo.com was born (see Table 1 at the end of this case for a full timeline).

Boo.com would not be any ordinary Web site. The goal was to create a true shopping experience for hip young consumers looking for a one-stop shop for sporty fashion. Luke Alvarez, a former BCG Consultant and Boo's global business development director, stated that Boo was a "killer Web site" on top of a "global business model," which would lead to a "first-mover advantage."[3] While this may sound like the typical intro to any new startup company, Boo.com wanted to establish itself with a particular presence. Leander put it best by saying that "you can use the Internet to fulfill your fantasies,"[4] and Boo struck out to do just that. Global from day one, the founders believed that the world of electronic commerce was ready to move beyond the first-generation of discount Web retailing sites. Boo would offer full-price retail products in addition to a cutting-edge technological interface.

By 1999, Boo had significant financial backing from large investors within both the financial industry and a veritable who's who of European fashion. These investors included J. P. Morgan, Luciano Benetton, and Bernard Arnault, to name a few (see Table 2 for investor information). Boo was ready to begin creating a high-tech company for the sporty streetware shopper (see Table 3 for management team).

THE E-TAILING INDUSTRY IN 1999

The retail industry had definite growth potential. Forrester Research reported that 7% of the $20 billion apparel sales market would be online by 2003.[5] In addition, International Data Corp predicted that the demographics of Internet users were quickly shifting. IDC estimated that the majority of Internet users would live outside the United States by 2003.[6] John Jordan, director of e-commerce research at Ernst & Young, claimed, "the first one or two players can carve up a market." Boo.com was trying to do just that.

In 1999, most American department stores were slow to create significant Web presences. However, a few clothing manufacturers had developed their own online stores. Examples were Levi's custom-jeans fitter, Eddie Bauer's virtual dressing rooms, and Lands' End personalized virtual models. Much to the fashion world's chagrin, the online e-tailing market had done little to pay homage to the glitz and glamour of the fashion world. Those fashion Web sites that did exist were text-based, offering customers the ability to search by price and size, but not by picture—the images took too long to transmit over Internet lines. As the retail industry struggled to reinvent itself online, Boo.com was closely watched.[7]

As regards competition, existing fashion manufacturers could start their own Web operations, but Boo didn't consider that to be a problem. Charlotte Neser, manager of Boo's partnership relationships, explains with an example: " Ralph Lauren operates his own flagship stores, and he sells his clothes in other stores. There isn't a problem."[8] Boo believes that customers will blend clothing styles from a wide menu of selections, and that customers won't find this selection on the site of any single brand. With this idea in mind and a prototype of the site, Kasja Leander used her contacts in the fashion industry to win over suppliers. In no time at all, Boo.com had signed some of the most impressive names in the fashion world (see Table 4).

WHY BOO IS DA BOMB

The *pièce de résistance* of the Boo.com product was most definitely the online technology —the like of which had never been seen before on the Internet. The cutting-edge Web site included 3D technology, Virtual Dressing Rooms, a Virtual Shopping Assistant, and real-time inventory availability. With the exception of the 3D technology, the Boo.com technical team built these technological wonders from scratch, customized for the needs of the company and its customers.

3D IMAGING AND VIRTUAL DRESSING ROOMS

The 3D technology utilized an existing technology called Flash to let customers take each item "for a spin." In other words, customers could zoom in and/or rotate each product 360 degrees in any direction to get a closer look at the details—all the way down to the shoelace threads. The 3D imaging required taking 18 to 24 photographs of each item, then used special software to stitch them together.[9] The Virtual Dressing Rooms were another value-added technology for the customer's shopping experience. Given that the store was online and customers could not physically try on the items, Boo.com allowed customers to drag the clothes into a virtual dressing room and drop them on mannequins to see how they look together. For a second opinion, shoppers could email the dressed-up mannequins to their friends.[10] To accommodate the difference in manufacturer sizing, Boo provided detailed information on how sizes varied by brand, and eventually planned to record and scan body measurements to make size selection even more precise.[11]

MISS BOO

And if the 3D technology and virtual dressing rooms weren't enough, Boo.com created a shopping assistant, lovingly dubbed "Miss Boo" to assist the customer with their shopping needs. She could assist with everything from product questions to shopping ideas, and even flirted when the time is right. Her secret vocabulary included double-entendres such as "Feeling antisocial? I'll shut up. Just push my button and I'll zip my lips."[12] Miss Boo was a dearly loved personality within the Boo team. A style consultant had advised regarding Miss Boo's looks and colouring, and Leander joked about Miss Boo's life before being a Boo Shop bot: "She was in the Betty Ford clinic for a while, and she really likes guys."[13] To further expand on the creativity of Miss Boo in addition to accommodating the different tastes of the customers, the team had brainstormed "seven 'archetype' characters that would make up Miss Boo's posse of friends."[14]

GLOBAL DISTRIBUTION SYSTEM

Finally, the critical operational component of the Boo.com product was its Global Distribution System. Real-time inventory was a crucial feature—there was nothing available for purchase on Boo.com that did not physically exist in a warehouse somewhere. Boo had established a "flexible inventory model," which incorporated two inventory management approaches to maximize their cash flow.[15] First, the core inventory was held by product suppliers with whom Boo had no financial commitment. Warehouse and dispatch facilities were established in Louisville, Kentucky and Cologne, Germany with the aim of achieving overnight dispatch of ordered goods to customers.[16] To encourage customers to take a chance on the Web site and the clothes, Boo.com offered free shipping anywhere in North America and Europe,[17] accepting returns at no charge, and included return shipping labels with each package.[18]

Boo.com was truly a global business, providing services and delivery in seven languages and eighteen countries.[19] Every order placed on the Web site was automatically calculated in the appropriate currency and country tax.[20] Boo used a proprietary messaging system incorporating EDI and XML to tie in to warehouses operated by key logistics partners.

For example, a shopper from Spain could order the latest Puma gear. The order was dispatched to the German warehouse, where the system automatically recognized that the order came from a Catalan-speaking region of Spain. That led to the creation of invoices, receipts, and shipping forms in the proper language and in Spanish pesetas.

Jay Heratti, president of Boo.com North America, claimed, "We realized that in order to sell hip fashion, we had to serve global customers with a very customized experience. Our aim is to be a global style editor, and to do so, we have to remain on the cutting edge both with the clothes we sell and with the technology."[21]

THE LAUNCH OF BOO.COM

By the summer of 1999, the launch of Boo.com highly anticipated in both the United States and Europe. The company had already spent approximately $25 million[22] on a PR blitz and advertising campaign with London ad agency MBP DDB. Malmsten and Leander were featured on the cover of Fortune Magazine in July 1999 as part of a cover story aptly titled "Cool Companies."[23] The hype was huge, and it was fuelled even more when the company had to postpone its May launch to June because of technical problems. Despite the delay, the Web site was logging 60 000 hits a day.[24] Bain & Co named Boo.com "one of the U.K.'s top 25 e-commerce companies" before it had sold a stitch of clothing.[25] In June, Boo again postponed the launch to September, then to October, citing technical problems. Rumours swirled around the Internet world speculating on the exact date, and fans waited in anticipation. *The Standard* stated that Boo.com was "the most talked about e-commerce startup in the U.S. and Europe, especially as the weeks [drag] on with no definitive answer from Boo officials about when it [will] open for business."[26] Finally, on November 3, 1999, with 27 brands on board, Boo.com launched in 18 countries around the world—just in time for the all-important holiday season.

BOO GETS BOOED

The reviews of the Web site were not what Malmsten had anticipated. There were technical hiccups, bugs, speed problems, compatibility issues, and all-round criticism. The team had waited as long as they could before launching the site, and the overall technology was an amazing accomplishment. How could the reviews be so negative?

The hiccups were a minor problem that could be fixed, but they were extremely detrimental to retaining customers. Said one user, "Oh look, 'Page not available.' I'm trying to look at Converse One-stars as we speak but forget it, it's way too slow. Which is a shame, because I'd like that pair."[27] In addition to the hiccups, reviewers claimed that the site was difficult to use. One site review said, "Many of the steps open new browser windows and with as many as 10 Boo windows open at a time, opportunities for confusion abound. Close the wrong one and you've got to close them all, reopen your browser, and get back to the site's home page to start over."[28] Another reviewer stated, "Boo.com's merchandise is displayed on an animated banner that moves in different directions and speeds, depending on the placement of the mouse on the banner. With products zooming all around the page, customers practically have to play target practice to select the product they want."[29]

The largest complaint by far was the speed of the site. Because of the graphics, use of the site required a 56K modem or faster.[30] Every item had to reload if a user wanted to look at the different product aspects (zoom, colour, etc). This reload took time, and was even worse if the user was viewing the site from a modem connection. In addition to the slowness of the site, there were complaints that the site timed out after a few minutes of inactivity.[31] Boo's response to the speed problem was that they "are not a regressing site—we built a site that's optimum and perfect for new technologies."[32] Unfortunately, 99% of European and 98% of U.S. homes lacked the high-bandwidth access needed to run the site.[33]

Also, Boo.com was not compatible with Macintosh computers. This should not have come as a surprise to anyone, as Boo.com had a warning on the site notifying Mac users that they might have trouble accessing the site.[34] The Boo.com team had plans to make it compatible, but was not sure when this would come to pass. Along the same lines, PC users were critical of the Flash plug-in required to access the product pictures. Many in the industry said it was neither popular nor standard.[35] Robert Chapman, executive producer of Nickelodeon, pointed out that "almost all e-commerce sites do the hard stuff on the server. Here, Boo's use of Flash has made the hard work client-side rather than server-side—and that's not customer friendly."[36]

One reviewer noted about the Virtual Fitting Room, "Silly me. I pressed the 'try on' button and the dressing room window popped up, with a big gray cutout silhouette in the center and my chosen shirt in the upper left. Problem is, the silhouette doesn't resemble me *at all.* ... So I dragged the shirt over to the cutout and voila, it fit. Big surprise there—have you ever seen clothes that *don't* fit on a mannequin?"[37] Despite the horrible reviews, a site review by *Industry Apparel Magazine* stated, "With a greater breadth and depth of product selection, our users said they'd readily bookmark Boo.com."[38]

WHAT THE BOO TO DO?

Malmsten hung a wreath over his marble fireplace and looked out the window at his unobstructed view of London. He had spent most of his funding on employee hiring and a lavish marketing campaign. The company was looking at the bottom of the barrel of funds, and he needed to determine a sound product strategy—*fast.* The publicity surrounding the Web site didn't help to make the decision any easier. Expectations were high and most of the retailing industry was watching Boo.com very, very closely. Should they expand the site to appeal to more customers, or should they focus on fixing the technical problems? He needed to decide which choice would help the company survive this crucial holiday season.

NOTES

1. Kristina Grish, Kellee Harris, and Matt Powell, "Boo.com," *Sporting Goods Business* (San Francisco), July 6, 1999, p. 61.
2. Henry Goldblatt, Melanie Warner, Eryn Brown, and Erick Schonfeld, "Cool companies 1999," *Fortune*, July 5, 1999, p. 98.
3. James Ledbetter, "Boo.com's bold fashion statement," *The Standard*, May 10, 1999, accessed July 29, 2001 <www.thestandard.com/article/display/0,1151,4525,00.html>.
4. See note 3.
5. Leslie Walker, "An Internet dress address," *The Washington Post*, July 1, 1999, p. E1. Available online, accessed August 19, 2001 <www.washingtonpost.com>.
6. Matt Hicks and Anne Chen, "Dress for global success," *ZD Net eWeek*, April 3, 2000, accessed July 29, 2001 <www.zdnet.com/eweek/stories/general/0,11011,2478461,00.html>.
7. See note 5.
8. See note 3.
9. See note 5.
10. See note 5.
11. See note 5.
12. Mark Gimein, "Boo to boo," *RedHerring.com*, November 5, 1999, accessed July 29, 2001 <www.redherring.com/insider/1999/1105/news-salon-boo.html>.
13. See note 3.
14. See note 3.
15. Ken Cottrill, "Aiming for the gold," *Traffic World*, March 6, 2000, p. 17.
16. Michael Kavanagh, "Boo.com opens its virtual doors," *Marketing Week*, June 10, 1999, p. 43.
17. See note 3.
18. See note 5.
19. Liz Bailey, "Boo gets booed," *The Guardian*, November 11, 1999, p. 4.
20. See note 3.
21. Matt Hicks and Anne Chen, "Dress for global success," *ZD Net eWeek*, April 3, 2000, accessed July 29, 2001 <www.zdnet.com/eweek/stories/general/0,11011,2478461,00.html>.
22. Bernhard Warner and Polly Sprenger, "Surprise! Boo.com finally launches," *The Standard*, November 3, 1999, accessed July 29, 2001 <www.thestandard.com/article/display/0,1151,7389,00.html>.
23. See note 2.
24. See note 3.
25. See note 19.
26. See note 22.
27. Quote from Alice Taylor in Liz Bailey, "Boo gets booed," *The Guardian*, November 11, 1999, p. 4.
28. "Who will e-tail your products best?," *Apparel Industry Magazine*, February 2000, p. 40.
29. "Boo.com plays tricks on customers," *ZD Net eCommerce*, November 8, 1999, accessed July 29, 2001 <www.zdnet.com/ecommerce/stories/evaluations/0,10524,2399916,00.html>.
30. Justin Hunt, "E-commerce: where did Boo boob?," *The Guardian*, May 25, 2000, p. 14.

31. See note 22.
32. Quote from Boo's Paul Kanareck in Liz Bailey, "Boo gets booed," *The Guardian*, November 11, 1999, p. 4.
33. John Cassy and Mary O'Hara, "E-finance: it all ends in tears at Boo: founders 'take time to reflect,'" *The Guardian*, May 19, 2000, p. 28.
34. See note 22.
35. See note 19.
36. See note 19.
37. Mark Gimein, "Boo to boo," *RedHerring.com*, November 5, 1999, accessed July 29, 2001 <www.redherring.com/insider/1999/1105/news-salon-boo.html>.
38. See note 28.
39. Ben Roiser, "What went so horribly wrong with Boo.com?," *Marketing* (London), May 25, 2000, p. 9.
40. See note 2.
41. Polly Sprenger, "Where is Boo.com?," *The Standard*, September 17, 1999, accessed July 29, 2001 <www.thestandard.com/article/display/0,1151,6446,00.html>.
42. See note 22.
43. Christopher Cooper and Erik Portanger, "Spooked: money men liked Boo and Boo liked money, then it all went poof—flashy Web site for clothes had lots of cool ideas, few financial controls—'Miss Boo' and her makeovers," *Wall Street Journal*, June 27, 2000, p. A1.
44. See note 2.
45. Randall Rothenberg, "Still hooked on 'fast branding'? Ponder the lessons of Boo.com," *Advertising Age*, May 29, 2000, p. 52.
46. Alice Rawsthorn, "E-trepreneur," *Management Today* (London), June 2000, p. 90.
47. See note 43.

OTHER SOURCES

John Cassy, "Boo opens online," *The Guardian*, November 4, 1999, p. 29.

John Cassy, "E-finance: Boo sale risks sneers, designer sportwear outfit performs u-turn," *The Guardian Manchester*, January 26, 2000, p. 25.

Berhard Warner, "Boohoohoo.com," *The Standard*, January 28, 2000, accessed July 29, 2001 <www.thestandard.com/article/display/0,1151,9249,00.html>.

TABLE 1 Boo.com Timeline

Time	Event
Summer 1998	• Five-page business plan envisioned by Ernst Malmsten and Kajsa Leander. • Pitched in New York; J. P. Morgan interested to help find investors. • Luciano Benetton in for \$5 million; son Alessandro to sit on board. • Bernard Arnault in for \$12 million.
Winter 1999	• J. P. Morgan comes on board to raise \$12 million now, \$12 million in 6 weeks, and \$40 million midsummer. • Patrick Hedelin becomes CFO. • Hedelin asks \$390 million valuation.
Spring 1999	• Goldman Sachs invests \$3 million in Boo, much to the fury of J. P. Morgan. • Hariri family of Lebanon in for \$41 million.
May 1999	• Web site logs 50 000 hits a day, despite the fact that there is nothing on it; demonstrates the strength of the marketing push.[39] • Launch pushed to June due to technical problems. • Boo opens offices in Munich, Paris, London, Stockholm, New York, and Amsterdam.
June 1999	• Launch pushed to September due to technical problems.
July 1999[40]	• Boo.com employee count: 200.
September 1999	• Launch delayed to November due to technical problems. • Management has burned through nearly \$70 million; needs more money. • Boo.com employee count: 300.[41]
November 3, 1999[42]	• Boo.com launched to mixed reviews.

Source: Christopher Cooper and Erik Portanger, "Spooked: money men liked Boo and Boo liked money; then it all went poof—flashy Web site for clothes had lots of cool ideas, few financial controls—'Miss Boo' and her makeovers," *Wall Street Journal*, June 27, 2000, p. A1.

TABLE 2 Financers

Name	Business History
J. P. Morgan	Elite financial services company that rarely backed startup companies. (According to Malmsten, "J. P. Morgan doesn't do startups. The last startup they did was General Electric.") However, it was intrigued by the Boo.com idea.
Goldman Sachs	Financial services firm. Invested \$3 million.
Bernard Arnault	Chairman of luxury-goods empire LVMH Moët-Hennessy Louis Vuitton. Company also owns Christian Dior. Invested \$12 million.
Luciano Benetton	CEO of Benetton empire. Invested \$5 million, and offered his son, Alessandro, to take a seat on the board.[43]
Bain Capital	Elite strategy consulting firm and high-tech investor.[44]
Boston Consulting Group	Elite strategy consultant whose book *Blown to Bits* had become "a *Bhagavad-Gita* of e-business."[45]
Hariri family	A family in Lebanon who made their fortune in construction. Invested \$41 million.

Source: Christopher Cooper and Erik Portanger, "Spooked: money men liked Boo and Boo liked money; then it all went poof—flashy Web site for clothes had lots of cool ideas, few financial controls—'Miss Boo' and her makeovers," *Wall Street Journal*, June 27, 2000, p. A1.

TABLE 3	Management Team
Name	**Background**
Ernst Malmsten, CEO	Six-foot-five, 29-year-old Swede who co-founded Bokus.com, an Internet bookstore, with Kasja Leander. Malmsten sold Bokus for millions.
Kasja Leander, CMO	Swedish-born ex–elite model who co-founded Bokus.com with childhood friend Ernst Malmsten. Leander studied art history and modelling in Paris, London, and New York before reuniting with Malmsten, whom she assisted in organizing a Nordic poetry festival before founding Bokus.com.[46]
Patrik Hedelin, CFO	Thirty-one-year-old Swedish who met Kasja and Ernst while working as a junior investment banker at HSBC Holdings PLC.[47] Hedelin arranged the sale of Bokus.com and eventually assisted the dynamic duo in their quest to finance Boo.com.

TABLE 4	Suppliers
Adidas	Jil Sander
Cosmic Girl	New Balance
Converse	North Face
DKNY Active	Patagonia
Everlast	Paul Smith
Fila	Puma
Fred Perry	Reef Brazil
Fubu	Royal Elastics
Gotcha	Tretor
Helly Hansen	Vans

case two (continued)

Boo.com (B)

Heidi Connal
Brigida Munoz
Ipek Ozilhan
Andrei Outkine
Edith Solovey

On January 26, 2000 Boo.com announced that it would start discounting merchandise by up to 40%.[1] Company representatives assured the media that discounting was only a short-term plan to clear out goods for Spring 2000 clothing, but investors couldn't help being skeptical of the situation—especially when Boo refused to reveal any revenue figures or breakeven targets. In addition, rumours abounded that Boo's staff of 400+ were beginning to defect from the company. In fact, Malmsten later confirmed that Boo had cut the number of its employees from 430 to 342 and lost its third co-founder, Patrik Hedelin.[2]

Despite the skepticism permeating the media and investors, Boo announced plans to add 13 countries in South America and Asia to its market by the end of the quarter.[3] It attempted to assuage skepticism by revealing that its return rates were below benchmark mail-order guidelines and 500 000 unique visitors were logged in February.[4] To curb this low visitor rate, Boo offered a low-bandwidth version of its site and signed up with portals Yahoo and France's Wanadoo.[5]

Eventually, by late April, Boo was beginning to run short of cash. Boo's investors refused to provide an additional $32 million in the light of Boo's monthly sales report

MBA candidates Heidi Connal, Brigida Munoz, Ipek Ozilhan, Andrei Outkine, and Edith Solovey prepared this case under the supervision of professor Christopher L. Tucci, for purposes of class discussion rather than to illustrate either effective of ineffective handling of an administrative situation.

of just $1.1 million when expenses were ten times that amount.[6] Malmsten and Leander scrambled to get $50 million from Texas Pacific but ultimately had to call in the liquidators on May 17. Fashionmall.com acquired Boo's brand, Web address, advertising materials, and online content for approximately $400 000.[7] Bright Station PLC acquired Boo's back-end technology and intellectual rights for a mere $372 500—"a fraction of its development costs."[8] The ambitious global Web store failed. Nine months earlier when Bernard Arnault was asked about his investment in Boo.com he commented that the Web would never replace the sensory pleasure of shopping in one of his luxury boutiques, but he was covering his bets.[9] Was Boo's concept doomed from the beginning? Fashionmall.com doesn't think so.

Fashionmall.com is utilizing Boo's global concept to expand its retail portal model. On October 30, 2000 Fashionmall relaunched a lean version of Boo.com. Online shoppers could directly link to retail sites where products are sold and Fashionmall carries no inventory.[10] Much of Fashionmall's success has been its reliance on retail clients to fulfill back-end processes and its ability to provide quick and easy navigation for online shoppers to get what they want.

Perhaps Boo.com could have succeeded if it had paid closer attention to the needs of online shoppers. Fashionmall CEO Ben Nasarin believes that Boo got "married to [its] product because [of its investment]. We used to have a universal shopping basket of our own … and redesigned it. … [T]he day we rolled it out sales dropped 50%. We left it up for one week to make sure it wasn't an anomaly and then we threw it away and took our lessons from it."[11]

NOTES

1. John Cassy, "E-finance: Boo sale risks sneers, designer sportwear outfit performs U-turn," *The Guardian Manchester*, January 26, 2000, p. 25.
2. Ken Cottrill, "Aiming for the gold," *Traffic World*, March 6, 2000, p. 17.
3. Cate T. Corcoran, "More than style: fashion sites need to be exciting and stylish," *Wall Street Journal*, April 17, 2000, page 68.
4. Ben Roiser, "What went so horribly wrong with Boo.com?," *Marketing* (London), May 25, 2000, p. 9.
5. Kerry Capell, "Boo.com is getting downright scary," *Business Week* (New York), May 22, 2000, p. 22.
6. Christopher Cooper and Erik Portanger, "Spooked: money men liked Boo and Boo liked money, then it all went poof—flashy Web site for clothes had lots of cool ideas, few financial controls—'Miss Boo' and her makeovers," *Wall Street Journal*, June 27, 2000, p. A1.
7. See note 5.
8. Ann M. Mack, "Stayin' alive," *Brandweek* (New York), June 12, 2000, p. 84.
9. Carol Matlack, "Bernard Arnault," *Business Week*, September 27, 1999, p. E-40. Available online, accessed August 19, 2001 <www.businessweek.com/1999/99_39/b3648030.htm>.
10. Carol Sliwa, "Boo.com to rise again, run by Fashionmall," *Computerworld* (Framingham), August 21, 2000, p. 35.
11. See note 10.

theme five overview

Future Developments

The trend in e-business technologies generally heralds cost containment coupled with improvements in capabilities, ease of use, increased availability of software, ease of site development, and improved security and accessibility. PCs are continuing to be smaller and cheaper, providing increased technology access to a larger number of clients in a variety of cultures and locations. Clustering of servers can add processing power in ways that offer economies of scale, and networks are becoming more expansive as broadband technologies (such as XDSL) dramatically increase bandwidth. The future evolution and integration of the computer, the TV, and the telephone including cellular telephones will increase accessibility to the Internet, and therefore accessibility to e-business.

Improved technology will also contribute to advances in transactional and service efficiency. In one example, Cisco reported 70% of support calls were resolved by a visit to the Cisco site, US$86 million saved with electronic downloads, and US$107 million saved with online configuration and documentation, and customer satisfaction was 25% higher. Further on the e-business side, 90% of orders were placed online with a less than 1% error rate.[1]

Further, new developments and technology aspire to creating a more real and multi-dimensional experience for the customer. Lands' End and a growing number of businesses are experimenting with the rapidly emerging field of 3D Web technology. As David Holland of G. Wagen, a Web site development company providing services for Mercedes-Benz, comments, "Ultimately, we will have a virtual showroom that will allow people to view different colours and options, walk around, see what the vehicle's inside looks like—even test-drive an offroad course." Getting technology sufficiently advanced to support virtual reality is the continuing challenge.

With advancements in technology come requirements for new business strategies and models, coupled with new legislation and legalities. Caution in protecting intellectual property is critical. According to *Euromoney*,[2] dot-coms are notorious for not protecting their only source of value—intangible assets. In fact, in a survey of 400 managers in European dot-coms (split between the United Kingdom, France, Germany, and the Netherlands), there was little interest in the threat that legal risk poses to their survival—and a full 20% of dot-coms surveyed were not worried by any legal risk. Moreover, a large number of dot-coms fail to protect trademarks and patents. In an unforgiving marketplace, lack of attention to legal risk management can severely undermine the development of trust-based customer relationships, especially when security is of concern.

International legal risk is a continuing and serious challenge for both larger and smaller e-business companies. The Net has spawned a multijurisdictional legal minefield, with e-business regulation a priority around the world. With the advent of electronic agents and click/shrink/Web wrap contracts, basic legal principles on the formation of contracts and their enforceability are currently being reexamined in the EU, the United States, and other countries with significant e-business activity. Competition law or the abolition of barriers to trade between countries will also have an enormous impact on products such as sound recordings, movies, and software.[3]

One recent technology development with legal implications includes fingerprinting software. The latest version of Napster's file exchange software includes technology that can be used to identify characteristics of sound. According to Associated Press, in a posting on Napster's Web site, "the company said sound fingerprinting will be used to comply with a federal judge's order to block the free exchange of copyright songs. … As the technology available for the identification and tracking of music files has evolved extremely rapidly over the past few months, Napster has quickly embraced it in order to better protect copyright holders and improve our users' experience."[4] Presumably companies like Napster are pushing the envelope not only for new technologies, but also for new business models that respond to a world of music on the Web.

Technology is also leading the way for legally binding e-documents. However, it is expected to be a year or two before a digital signature in an electronic document replaces an ink signature on paper. The e-signature is turning out to be costly and difficult, with legal, technical, and psychological obstacles. According to Douglas Graham of KPMG, the biggest difficulty in adopting digitally signed e-documents is the confusing patchwork of laws and regulations and the absence of a global commercial code.[5]

NOTES

1. J. Hoffman, "E-doing it right," *Oil and Gas Investor*, 21(2001)(3): 85–87.
2. N. Page, "Dot coms don't appreciate legal risk," *Euromoney*, 383(2001)(24): 24–25.
3. The authors would like to thank Tony Fogarassy, legal counsel at TechBC, for his contributions about contracts and competition law.
4. "Napster has fingerprinting software," *Associated Press*, May 7, 2001.
5. C. Wilde, "Legally binding E-documents move closer to reality," *Informationweek*, 776(2001).

part one overview

Technology Issues

The Industrial Revolution of the middle nineteenth century represented the first major instance in which technology was applied intensively for business innovation and growth. Sixty to seventy years later the commercialization of the internal-combustion engine had a similar impact on business and societal growth. The next technological wave, the business computing revolution, came less than 30 years later in the 1970s and 1980s. This was followed by the technological transformation of industries, work, business models, and society by the Internet in the mid-1990s. Given that the time periods between these technological revolutions have been shortening rapidly, it is reasonable to expect that we are due for the next technological wave of change.

The readings in this Part address various trends related to technology in e-business. Topics included are the integration of software, infrastructure and service delivery requirements in e-business, and who controls the technology. Issues of interest are the rise of mobile computing devices and wireless networks; broadband access through fibre optic and newer technologies; smart appliances, with computing power embedded in everything from refrigerators to automobiles; and the convergence of computing technologies.

As e-business continues to grow, there will be increasing pressure to develop a fast and effective company infrastructure (including hardware, software, and services). According to *Informationweek*,[1] an e-business infrastructure should demonstrate scalability, availability, security, and manageability. To avoid problems in handling huge volumes of business, a reliable e-business infrastructure must be in place that is robust and has core business production and fulfillment functionality. The "New

Infrastructure" will apply to a wide range of developing areas, such as biotechnology or efforts to globalize/localize content and systems.

As part of the technological planning process, companies are seeking shortcuts to meet goals. To this end, application service providers (ASPs) can host a company's software application and databases on their server, saving the company costs and maintenance headaches. According to the ASP Industry Consortium, "An application service provider manages and delivers application capabilities to multiple entities from data centers across a wide area network, giving customers a viable alternative to procuring and implementing complex systems themselves."[2] As technology becomes more complex and transient, ASPs are one solution in the e-business realm.

The online articles on technology in this Part can be considered in the context of the other readings and cases in this book. For instance, how might technological improvements contribute to supply chain or operational issues, or to the enhancement of CRM, or for real-time business intelligence processing?

NOTES

1. A. Radding, "Pressure grows for e-business infrastructure," *Informationweek*, 805(2000): 118–126.
2. "Looking for an ASP," *Modern Materials Handling*, 56(2001)(1): 98.

part two overview

Legal Issues

Readings in this section address some of the requirements and challenges of legalizing e-business. Issues introduced include how to maintain confidentiality on the Web, the authenticity and acceptance of digital signatures, and the technology to support those systems. A pending question for consideration is: Where does "offer-acceptance" occur in legal contracts (i.e., how does it depend on where the buyer is, where the seller is, where the server resides, where the business is registered, and where the goods are received)? Further, suggestions are offered throughout the readings for how to reduce legal indemnity in a world where legal precedent is lacking for the resolution of technological issues.

Another important issue to consider is how culture impacts the legalities of e-business. What is acceptable in one country is a legal violation in another. For example, 411.com, an Internet telephone directory absorbed by Yahoo, places "cookies"—digital markers that can trace Internet usage—on the PCs of Web surfers who use their service. However, under French privacy laws cookies are illegal; further, the French are concerned about invasion of privacy. Therefore, when 411.com expanded into France, the company decided to eliminate the use of cookies on its French-language site. In the future, the legal development of e-business will need to be addressed at the international level, the degree to which international laws can be harmonized is unknown.

Index

Name and Organisation Index